JUST ONE QUESTION

JUST ONE QUESTION

A Road Trip Memoir

TY SASSAMAN

MCP Books
2301 Lucien Way #415
Maitland, FL 32751
407.339.4217
www.millcitypress.net

Printed in the United States of America

ISBN-13: 978-1-54560-137-2

This book is dedicated to my father

QUESTION JOURNEY ROUTE

Map illustration by Anton Benson

CAMBRIDGE, MA
ESOPUS, NY
KALAMAZOO, MI
LOUISVILLE, KY
HAZELHURST, MS
ELY, MN
DES MOINES, IA
FREDERICKSBURG, TX
CAR CATCHES FIRE HERE
REDFORD, TX
EL PASO, TX
BLACK ROCK CITY, NV
PRESCOTT, AZ
OAKLAND
SANTA BARBARA, CA

ACKNOWLEDGMENTS

This book was a long time coming and relied on the support of many incredible people. A very special thank you to those that donated to the crowdfunding campaign, my steadfast editors, and supportive friends:

Thomas Samuel Reed Murphy Bailey, Shira Richman, Sally Franson, Randy Hendee, Rachel Cohen, Elizabeth Dingmann Schneider, Kelly Henderson, John Huston, Matt Gross, Phil Barry, Todd Carter, Caitlin O'Sullivan, Jessie Kushner, Sara Bible, Tim Streeter, Dain Ingebretson, Dan Higgs and Emmy Matzner, Aramy Cho, Iggy, Bellamy Ford, Eric Guetschoff, Sarah Oppelt, Patrick Santelli, Amanda Lutz, Doug Sassaman, Denise and Ken Goldman, Patty Norgaard, Joe Kane, Eric Sassaman, Anthony Gaudio, Jill Pearson, Sohail Hines, Ann Wang Reed, Mark Higgins, Beth Anne Vernon, Katie Pratt, Emma Nadler, Yuko Saito, Abby Fenton, Sheppy Douma, Peter Thomas, Rob Mann, Joanne and Chuck Knox, Kevin Dooley, Mickey and Kristin Ott, Dan and Mary Grace Ott, Bill Rivers, Kellie Bohanon, Scotty Reynolds, Bonnie Dundee, Julianna Sassaman, Julie Gawendo, Kathryn Rummell, Joel Haskard, Carly Lichtenstein, Samuel del Favero and Georgia Welle, Janelle Werner, Brian Jost, Jon and Jane Streeter, Allison Rohner, Steven Grande, Dan Thiede, Nancy Rosenbaum, Debbie Dignan, Katie Fox, Kara Balcerzak, Diane Black, Thom Streeter, Kira Knox, Tony Miranda, Leslie Treece, Kara Ullestad, Kim Neuschel, Amy Shepard, Samantha Bernier, Christine and Billy Norton, Jodi Pinkham, Peter Ralph, Nadia Lubeznik, Josh Tolkan, Rodrigo Gutierrez, Pondie Taylor, Benjamin

Gaudio, Jess Ross, Karen VanLent, Phoebe and Dave Backler, Gary Swartz, Chris Newman, Josh Schobel, Susannah Carr, Sarah Loving, Anras Nave, Holly Jo Sparks, Craig Koltes, Stacie Fox, Katie O'Connor, Emily Torgrimson, Alison Ehlke, Chris Polking, Melissa Langlous, Mike and Junko Hartman, Elizabeth Liedel, Marcie Sassaman, Meg Sassaman, Marilyn Sassaman, Scott Harwin, Kit Filan, Andy Messerschmidt, Alan Zimmer, The Men of SHUVL, Josie and Dave Sassaman. My heart to Heather Greeley Benson for her support.

Finally, heartfelt thanks to all of you that that contributed questions for without you, there would be no book.

NOTE

Just One Question began as a road trip but over the years, the project has grown and I've written to famous and influential people to solicit their questions. Though they were not part of the journey, I've included some of those postcards at the beginnings of chapters and as section headings.

In the back of the book is an appendix with hundreds and hundreds of questions from the entire project to date. Enjoy these questions as a way to learn more about yourself, ask them to friends and family, or use one to start a conversation with a stranger. Now, more than ever, we need to make sincere connections, not assumptions about each other.

When I set off on this adventure, I did not know this project would become a book. Some of the interactions were very candid, therefore most names have been changed. This is a true story, as all the question-askers will attest, but some scenes and characters have been compressed to better fit the spirit of the journey.

As you read, you might come up with your own question. Please visit the website below to contribute your thoughts.

www.justonequestion.org

PROLOGUE

I n the distance a figure appeared. A red dot against the distant horizon became a shirt, then, as he neared, the blue of a denim jacket and well-worn jeans came into focus through wavy lines of heat. I squinted, shirtless, watching in disbelief as he approached. The bearded man, overdressed for the heat of the Black Rock City desert of Nevada in the dog days of summer, continued toward me.

Behind, the Burning Man festival was in full swing, an energized carnival of weird. It was a remarkable scene, a splash of bright colors on a flat desert palate, but I needed a break from the persistent pounding of techno music and the masses of revelers. I had stepped out to be alone, to just go for a walk, when I saw this man far off, following the same furrowed tracks made by cars driving across the desert crust. As he came into sharper view, I realized by his look that this was the wanderer, the Arctic Traveler. It was straight out of a Western, both of us ambling directly toward each other. I quickened my pace. I had a question to ask him.

News of the man who had driven all the way down from the Arctic Circle to attend Burning Man had achieved legendary status. People in my camp had talked about him all week.

"Yeah, a friend of mine saw him yesterday," said Sean, an IT guy from Silicon Valley, whose primary article of clothing was Day-Glo body paint. "He was dancing like a maniac at the tribal stage. Supposedly he wanted to check out the spectacle of Burning Man and he just up and left his log cabin and drove down to check the whole scene out." Here

Sean goofed, aping a lumberjack's wide-stanced walk and swinging an imaginary axe over his head. "Left his axe right in a chunk a *far*-wood." We all laughed at his forest simpleton, but the image floated through my thoughts. Someone who chopped their own firewood and lived in a small cabin in the Arctic Circle working with the native Inuit was purposeful, unlike the neon cowboy hats and glow stick necklaces currently on display. "I'm going to find that guy," I said, "and ask him my question."

The Burning Man festival was midway on my journey around the US, interviewing people with a single question. It was a project I had cooked up, at first to see what I would learn about Americans, but I was beginning to see that it wasn't just whimsy that had beckoned me out to the open road.

A couple months before, I had completed a master's degree in education focused on school leadership, a scholastic transition that was itself challenging; I uprooted my life, left my job as an elementary classroom teacher, moved from one coast to the other and entered the world of academia. Now having done the research and jumped all the hoops, I found myself on the other side with a degree, but no job, no partner, and, most uncomfortably, no clear direction. I wasn't trained to be a high-powered analyst or work in policy. I also wasn't ready to go back into overwhelming classroom-teaching world. I thought that by interviewing others, I'd come to a better understanding of my own singular question, and my identity in the world. On my first stops after leaving Boston, I interviewed with temerity. But by my arrival at Burning Man, I was no longer afraid.

"You must be the Arctic Traveler," I said, smiling.

"Yes, I drove here from the Arctic Circle," he said politely, a little quizzically.

I knew it! In this seething mass of 40,000 revelers on the ancient sea floor of a remote Nevada desert, I had come across someone people had been talking about and it felt like pure luck. A little interviewer *ka-ching*.

"Can I help you with something?" he asked. His soft voice reflected an unassuming character; I expected him to be gruff and manly. Turns out nothing about this adventure would be typical.

"Yes," I said. "I'm on a journey interviewing people, asking a particular question. Can I interview you?"

"Certainly," he nodded a single nod.

"Ok, here's what I'd like to ask: 'If you could ask everyone you met just one question, what would you ask them?'"

"Oh, now that's a big question," he said, rolling back on the heels of his well-worn hiking boots, pushing round, dusty glasses up on his nose, squinting in concentration. We were a fair distance from the crowds in the flat desert, but a car artistically designed to look like a butterfly floated slowly past. Little flakes of dust drifted in the air like snowflakes. I could see them landing on his beard. I wondered how this desert environment felt compared to his life so far north, so deep in the woods.

He and I stood together for a moment in complete silence. I waited, ok with silence. I too had driven my car for days to get to this spot, and I'd drive for many more days on my journey. An electronic beat kicked up in the distance, a dance party siren seeking lost souls.

"Alright man, I got it," the traveler said, interrupting my thoughts. *"What's the meaning of life?"*

Generally, my rule was to not respond to people's questions, to let them process their thoughts while I played the role of sponge. I didn't want to press any particular agenda, or influence the train of thought. I sought primarily to listen, to hear how our spinning solar system sounded from someone else's vantage point.

But this time I couldn't help it—the Arctic Traveler's question spoke to my core. Here I was, thirty-five, on the road, using a single question to try and get to the core of things. Hearing someone actually answer *What's the meaning of life?* seemed important.

"Yeah, wow," I said, "I would certainly like to hear someone answer to that one." I kicked at a chunk of desert crust.

"OK," he said, "I can tell you what creates meaning in my life: the sun comes up every day and the sun goes down every day. That's a truth that will never change. So, my challenge is living every day and making the best of it. Sleeping good at night with a clear conscience and no guilt. Watching that sun come up every day and living righteously. Doing the right thing and being with good people. That's what makes me tick." He paused, collecting his thoughts. "Every day that the sun comes up, I'm closer to finishing what I started. I'll be dying eventually, but for now, I'm on a mission of goodwill, enlightenment, and," he paused, smiling, "helping people. That's the meaning of my life." We stood in silence again for a brief moment.

"Hey, thank you," the Arctic Traveler said finally, setting his hand on my shoulder. "You've given me a lot to think about. No stranger has ever asked me a question like that out of the blue. I appreciate it."

I smiled back. "And thanks to you, for your thoughtfulness," I said. "You've given me a lot to think about, too."

He continued on his way, but I stayed still, looking out across the blue expanse of the wide-open sky at the jagged mountains that rimmed the far-off horizon. I felt empty after our exchange. He had done what I'd asked, engaging his deepest, most reflective self. It was pretty cool of him, after all. But an unease was growing; my project felt like it was unraveling. I started out just having fun, collecting interesting, light-hearted questions, but here in the desert, the true nature of my journey was beginning to reveal itself.

CHAPTER 1

CAMBRIDGE TO KALAMAZOO

```
The question I DO ask of everyone I
meet is, "What is your name?"

                    DEAR ABBY
```

The question I do ask everyone is: What's your name?
- Abigail Van Buren (best known as
"Dear Abby," advice columnist)

"Hello there," came the voice from behind the tinted window. It slid back to reveal a park ranger, hat tipped forward. She sat, unmoving, like a bust on Mount Rushmore. Her voice was stern, and certainly did not contain a smile.

My first day driving and I'd made it into Pennsylvania. Picking up a payment envelope at the state park entrance, I eased forward to the ranger station, a dark brown building with a single window and a green-trimmed door. Before responding, I realized that this was the first person I'd come across on my journey. My stomach jumped to my throat, instantly fluttering in butterflies. *Was I supposed to ask her The Question?* My mind reeled.

Earlier that day, I watched Boston in my rearview mirror until it disappeared. Strong feelings percolated in a mix of excitement and trepidation; I wasn't just leaving for the first destination; I was venturing off into the whole country. *America!* An excited charge ran through me, chased by the spark of fear. I had come up with a question, and plotted an itinerary circumnavigating the US, but I'd never done anything like this before.

A black X marked my departure date on the calendar, and here I was living it. There was no more making believe, no more whole days to pretend. I waited until that very morning to look over my belongings and decide what to take. I packed what gear I needed, confident in what would keep me warm and dry and alive, but not confident I wouldn't be right back home as the result of some car problem. Or some money problem. Long stretches on the open road have the potential for crushing sadness, but naively, I didn't consider that either. I just grabbed the gear I would need—a few pairs of pants, a handful of shirts, the guitar I had spray-painted pink, sandals (it was hot), bike on top, my camera, sleeping bag, and shorts.

Carting the last armload of goods out to my little red Honda Civic, I closed the trunk and climbed into the front seat. I turned the key in the ignition and shut my door. And because no one really kept tabs on me in my three-floor communal house, no one knew I had hatched a big travel plan, only that there would be a subletter in my place for the next six months. It was the same with my family; everyone in my life thought that everyone else knew my plans. Almost no one knew I was planning to drive around, asking people a single question. As though that were a plan.

Backing out of the driveway, I took a final look at the old house and waved to an empty porch. I drove slowly, turning one corner and then the next.

Before I knew it, I was passing Springfield, then Albany. As the miles rolled on, the heat of the black asphalt highway pulled the sun down into late afternoon. I'd made it to Pennsylvania, a little more than halfway to Kalamazoo. Evening would fall soon, and I needed to camp.

"Overnight, or day pass?" the ranger asked briskly. Her brown eyes were clear and she inquired in that way police have of asking questions, word choice spare, eyes subtly inspecting the interior of the car while conversing. On the passenger seat sat a mini recorder and a brand new navy blue loose-leaf notebook, ready to catalog every question I would hear on the journey.

You don't have to start interviewing right now on Day 1, the timid fifteen-year-old in me whispered. *Ease into it, there's no need to rush.* While in Cambridge, I decided what question I would ask on this journey, but I didn't have real confidence with it. On the road, suddenly it felt overwhelming, a project the size of America.

"I, uh–," words failed. I couldn't think how to begin. I should have practiced this part. "Camping," I finally said.

"I'm assuming you're planning to camp *overnight*, so that's thirteen dollars," she said, holding out her hand. I passed a twenty through the window and she rifled through a cash box for change.

Here were the facts: I was thirty-five, a successful teacher of five years, and I was rudderless. I didn't have much money for travel, but I had time. Having recently graduated, it was not strange to respond that I was "looking over my options," for what I planned to do next, and boy did I milk that one. I was lucky to have that time off, believe me. I knew that it was unique and that it might be the only time in my adult life I'd be able to hit the road on this scale. Substituting the cost of rent for the cost of gas, my final summer semester of student loans would be enough to live on for a while, so I decided to take advantage, to use the time to learn about myself, learn about my country and the people that populate it. I was also feeling the pressure of new expectation that came with my degree. I found myself reacting with visions of ripping off my sleeves, bleaching my hair, getting into my 1993 Honda, and driving myself into the middle of something interesting.

I was out on the road to immerse myself in the adventure that is America, but there were other, deeper reasons. I was searching for my own question, a question that would help me place my mish-mash of spiritual beliefs on a map. I pulled from many different traditions to answer the Big Questions in my life, but I subscribed wholeheartedly to none. I sought a question I could ask myself that drew together these disparate fragments of belief.

Like the Arctic Traveler, I wanted to land upon my One True Question, the one I could ask everyone, confident in my own answer. I was traveling and interviewing to find *me*, to find where I existed between school teacher and researcher, between adult and middle age.

When I spread out a map, a potential route became clear instantly; there was outdoor work as an instructor and guide for Outward Bound in the North Woods of Minnesota, the Burning Man festival in Nevada, and the possibility of presenting my first academic paper at an educational research conference in Texas. Throw in a visit to each parent on either side of the country and I faced six months of travel, easy. Enough time to stop and explore, to interview, to get into the fabric of America.

"So, I'm actually driving all over the country interviewing people," I began. The ranger paused her hunt for more ones, unfazed.

"I'm interviewing people with a single question. Well, I'm trying to, anyways. Can I ask it to you?"

"OK" she said, her face blank. "What's your question?"

It was happening! Even though I knew the question, I felt unprepared. My hand rested on the side-view mirror and I squinted off into the distance, thinking it might make me look like a real interviewer.

"OK, um, *If you could ask everyone you met just one question, what would you ask?*" I finished the question, but she waited like I wasn't done.

"That's the question?" she said. "Your question is '*What's your question?*'" She smiled for real, like maybe I was an idiot.

"That's the question," I said.

I *was* kind of an idiot. Passing farms and grazing cattle on Interstate 90 on my way to Pennsylvania, I gave myself a pep talk, listing interview guidelines in my mind. They were a bit different from the "Rules for Interviewing" I looked up on the Internet, because the rules I chose were the exact opposite:

1. Do not come prepared: Spontaneous interaction was the goal. I would engage without pretense.
2. Do not ask follow-up questions: It's just one question. What would happen next, I wanted the asker to decide. Only in cases of emergency could this be broken.
3. Finally, No Monkey Business: This is a big project and it is important to take this thing really, really seriously.

These rules seemed solid, though I did amend that last one. There would be Some Monkey Business. Who was I kidding? There would be a lot of Monkey Business.

Laughing helped me remain calm for a short time. But the farther I got from the east coast, the bigger it all appeared and the more weight it carried. What would I find out?

Winding along the Charles River, heading out of town, and for a good half hour outside of Boston, negative thoughts began to swarm, my head turning soft with this crazy idea. A job search might be uncomfortable, but this? This was a mistake. I wasn't worried about whether I'd be different or what would change when I returned. I worried about losing things, being beaten and robbed of everything. I saw calamity, nightmares where my front wheel fell off and I veered into oncoming traffic, the whole thing ending in fiery crash.

"Your question is kind of circular," the ranger said. "I mean, you're sort of asking me to do your job for you, right?"

"Oh no," I said, realizing I didn't yet have a pithy reply, "I'm cataloging questions from others." I changed tack. "I've asked some other people. Do you want to hear theirs?"

"Sure," she said.

"My sister, for example, wanted to know this: *What is the role of the judiciary in our democracy?*" As a judge, my older sister's question spoke to her occupation. But it was about more than just interpreting the Constitution, —she was asking how we hold accountable the governance of our collective experience. It wasn't loaded or political, and answering this question was engaging. It asked, *What do you think about this central tenet of our Democracy?*

The ranger tilted her head back and looked at me down her chin for a second. I waited.

"Now that one is a good question." She disappeared to get a map and envelope for my site.

Not going too bad, I thought, feeling good that I had won her over with some clumsy charm, feeling that this whole interview journey was going to work out just fine.

Seconds later, she reappeared from the shadows.

"Well, do you have a question you would ask everyone?" I asked, smiling.

"Nope," she said, cocking an eyebrow. "Not deep like that." Then she handed me the registration, a map, and pointed the way to my campsite. "Your site is down this drive a quarter of a mile on the right. Good luck with your project."

I drove off to find my site, a little defeated. I admit to clumsiness, but I was pulled into the excitement of getting a First Official Question in the notebook. The older me would have patted myself on the shoulder in that moment, offering assurance; this journey is a process. There are no easy answers. And don't get too hung up on the people who don't want to participate. There's plenty ahead of you that do.

Where are you going?

After a fitful night's sleep at the campground, I packed and drove on toward Kalamazoo, stopping for gas at a sprawling trucker plaza. I decided to try out my interviewer skills again while in the long line to pay for my tank.

"Hey, uh, excuse me," I said quietly to the older man in a faded light blue trucker cap standing in front of me in line. He didn't turn, but I forced myself to be persistent because I needed to see how this interviewing thing would work. I had my blue notebook in hand. *"If you could ask everyone you met just one question, what would you ask?"*

He heard me, I know, because he flinched a little and turned more squarely to the rack of snacks ahead. A spot opened at a second register and he broke the line and walked quickly to the cashier.

Day Two and a hard lesson learned: Don't try to interview truckers holding Hostess products while waiting in line for gas.

Interviewing seemed easy when still an idea, but these interactions must have been outliers: the first two strangers hadn't been interested at all. It was almost like my father had sent out a post to alert the country that once again I was leaving common sense behind and *please, please don't encourage him.*

CHAPTER 2

MICHIGAN TO MINNESOTA

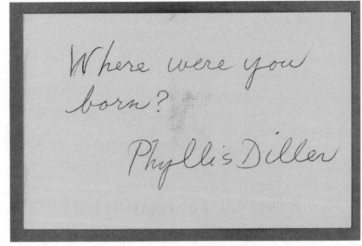

Where were you born? - Phyllis Diller
(Actress and stand-up comedienne)

L ate in the afternoon of Day Two, I arrived in Kalamazoo, my child-hood home. I stopped by to visit some old friends. I brought beer. Mike and Pete welcomed me in.

Sitting on Mike's porch that evening, I filled them in on the project. It was all very new, so I found myself looking for their approval as I laid out my plan.

Mike cracked a beer and restated my question. "What one question would I ask everyone if I could?"

I looked out at the street lights, waiting.

He eyed me, squinting, thinking, then replied in a calm, even tone, enunciating each word: *"What. The. Fuck."* His curly black hair sprung away from his face. He stared into mine.

I was confused. "Does that mean you don't like it?"

He leaned in close, smiled impishly, and repeated: *"Whatthefuck?"*

Looking away to avoiding his gaze, I set my beer down. "Yeah, I guess you're right, I am opening myself up to a lot of challenges."

Mike shook his head side to side slowly; his message wasn't getting through. *"What the fuck?* That, my friend, is my *answer* to your question." Big teeth appeared in his smile.

But quickly he turned serious, uncrossed his feet from beneath him on the chair and stood up forcefully. "And I think it should be your question…" He made a grand gesture with his arms, throwing them wide like wings. "…for this whole project, too."

He was drunk.

"I don't know, man," I said, quizzically. "I don't really know what you mean."

"I don't know is right!" Mike said, eyes wild with excitement. "That's not the point. Your project isn't about *knowing*. Go! Imagine all the experiences you're about to have. You like questioning things, and you've gone and put yourself in a situation where you're about to get paid in questions. You will start living questions and breathing questions!" He nodded as he concluded. "It's almost perfect." I couldn't reel him in. I didn't even want to. "I kind of want to go with you. You could ask your question first, then I'll be like your hype man asking, "*What the fuck?*" He smiled a broad, heart-of-Saturday-night smile, so big I couldn't help but laugh in return.

Pete looked silently out over the dark lawn. "I've got one," he said, flipping a bottle cap into the darkness beyond the yellow halo of our porch light. He turned to me. "I would want everyone to reveal a secret." The bottle cap bounced on the sidewalk. "So I would ask, *What's something you've never told anyone in your entire life?*" He nodded slowly. "Yeah, that's what I would want to know." He smiled in a far-off way. "Imagine the interesting stories you'd hear with that."

Pete imagined and the questions started spilling out. "How about these: *What are you most afraid of? What do you think you are doing here?*"

"Oh, man, what about this: *What do you truly believe in?*"

Mike jumped up to the balcony ledge to pee and turned his head back to shout, "You're going to hear all kinds of crazy questions!"

Smiling to myself, I realized yes, there would be fascinating questions in abundance. Crazy questions.

What in your life would you change if you could?

Mike and Pete and I were rock stars once. The three of us played together in a local band on the rise, hoping to make it beyond the small, sticky tables of Midwestern dive bars. And we almost did. The world called, and I left to study abroad before finding out if we would have. They replaced me with another drummer and kept going. They got close, oh so close. They played in front of 10,000 people once.

But they played in front of 137 people many, many times.

Offstage, Mike could be the same keyed-up, charismatic lead singer as onstage, but he also had the presence, the magic. Under the hot lights he could draw you in as close to him as any other being on Earth. This guy—he made you feel like he knew you, like you knew him.

Pete, meanwhile, lived out the role of the quiet guitarist, often looking off into the middle distance, carefully picking the right word, the right note. These two were almost opposite personalities, but they shared this: they were caring and smart, funny and loose. Neither got nervous onstage. They both had such confidence in their instruments they were magnetic to watch.

We met early in our youth, Mike from the neighborhood, Pete from across town. We became close by setting up and breaking down gear, playing our hearts out in an abandoned factory that we used as a studio, smoking cigarettes and talking about life in the pauses between songs. We thought we were doing the work of professional musicians, with regular practices and putting in time on the road, but really we were doing the work of getting to know each other.

They continued after I left, but the band broke up in the early 2000s. The scene grew up; the long hairs became short hairs—or no hairs—and Mike and Pete dropped off the rock 'n' roll radar and into a second act filled with diaper changes and domestic concerns.

Each time I returned to Kalamazoo, a new card in the deck of life revealed itself. Someone had gotten married, someone had another new kid on the way. It repeated like a mantra: Stay in town, settle down. Find yourself a solid, loving woman. Have kids. Give them a good home. Visiting Kalamazoo lulled me into those rhythms. Both Mike and Pete were happy. I could be happy, too. It was not when I was in Kalamazoo that I wanted to leave Kalamazoo.

At that moment, I needed reassurance. I worried they were going to tell me some version of my father's truth, that I was supposed to stay. Find a job. Settle down. Get married. Make sure you have benefits. The answer that I feared the most. Though I could shrug it off from him, or pretended I could, I wasn't so sure I could shrug it off from these two.

"Don't worry about anything." Pete smiled, as if reassuring some version of himself. "Do it! This is a good idea. Listen, man, here's the best-case scenario—life-changing experience. And the worst-case scenario? You get lonely. Turns out people suck. Easy answer: Follow the dream. Go."

How can I understand you?

An image of my father sat on one shoulder throughout the journey, skeptical of the premise. He encouraged me to drop it all and get a professional job ASAP, one with benefits.

A different character sat on the other: Brian, a wildly creative, but reckless friend from high school. As I eased the car onto the highway to begin the journey, his memory appeared. A situation he orchestrated back in our teens had opened my mind to possibility, led me to think big and imagine things as big as the Question Project at all, really. As much as I was traveling to find where I existed between adult and middle age, I felt myself pushed and pulled between the values of my conservative father and the influence of this outrageous childhood friend, Brian.

Rail thin at sixteen, with long, stringy blond hair, Brian was a provocateur. I was curious about many things, but Brian was the only one who actually cracked them open, ate from the shell, let the juice run down his arms.

Our sophomore year we both sat on the debate team, winning the majority of our competitions and going all the way to State. And each time we went to some new city for competition, Brian would pull a new stunt. The first time he told everyone he went by a different name. Another time he convinced me to jump onto another team's departing bus after a state-wide competition, just to see where it would take us. *Why are we doing this?* I remember asking as we climbed across the black vinyl seats. He just pulled one of his sneaky smiles to mollify my worry. We'd meet some new people, he said, they'd take us in and feed us. Don't worry, he said, we'd figure out how to get home. But first we'd have a great time with a whole bunch of folks in a place we'd never been before.

The plan with Brian was always: No Plan. It was intentional, and his kind of thinking blew my mind wide open. Confrontational, challenging, and improvisational, Brian strove to become everything my father was not. Together we came up with lots of bad ideas.

As much as my father tugged at me hard to straighten the path, Brian's peripatetic curiosity had its own discomforts. There were plenty of drugs around for these adventures, often leading him down paths I didn't want to follow.

His first year into college, Brian died. In the dead of night, riding home from a concert, two tons of metal hit a tree, flew high into the air, and churned drunkenly, psychedelically, into a molten heap. When I told my father, he expressed condolences and shook his head as he grimaced, "What a sad way to end your Saturday night." My father was right. But I'm sure, as sure as I am of anything in the world, Brian laughed as he flew.

Unlike my father, I'm sure Brian would have asked me very pointedly about the journey, "How far are you going to go with this thing?"

Or, he would've said exactly what he said when we stood at the door of one of those busses as they rumbled to life, ready to take our high school debate selves to some unknown destination.

"Is this scaring you?"

When I nodded and wrinkled my brow in uncertainty, he smiled. "Good."

What's unique about your area?

The concrete side lot to my father's house sat full of cars—my grandmother's huge burgundy Crown Victoria, stepsisters' minivans, uncles', aunts', and cousins' station wagons and SUVs squeezed into every possible spot. A summer gathering of family in town. I parked my little red Honda around the corner and down the block to make room.

My father and stepmother had all beverages chilled, and hors d'oeuvres on the coffee tables. The house was bright and inviting. All the guests entered through the back door, crossing the same brick patio, rather than the large ceremonial front door reserved for very special entrances. Or the pizza guy.

My father might give me guff, but I felt comfortable around all these family members, so I decided to introduce my project at the party: six months on the road interviewing people with a single question.

On the kitchen island, I smoothed out a AAA map of the United States and carefully traced my intended route in black Sharpie. Outside Denver, I placed a star. "Car catches fire here," I wrote. Pretty funny, I thought, but no one seemed to notice. As I traced the line, my need for emotional support became clear; I could feel my father anticipating failure. To keep things moving, I began to ask The Question.

My uncle Don lumbered over and handed me a beer. He smiled. Barrel-chested, with a full shock of white hair, he resembled a modern-day Andrew Carnegie. And like Carnegie, he lived a comfortable life and let others know his opinions. But unlike my father, Uncle Don didn't care what I did. He didn't see me as a failure or not a failure. I was just his nephew, and he was more than happy to think deeply about a question he would ask everyone.

I relaxed a little, though I could see my father out of the corner of my eye.

My uncle considered his glass for a moment before responding. *"What's unique about your area?"* he said. "There's always some story about where people live, and I always want to know that story. You know, out where we live"—he gestured vaguely west, but we both knew he meant Gun Lake, a shallow, float-boat lake that housed many happy cousins— "there are stories I still don't know about our history." His question made me realize how little I knew about Kalamazoo and about my own history, and I realized we take so much for granted just trying to sort out the details of our own lives.

Off to the side in a high-backed chair sat my grandmother. She wore a soft, white sweater and would laugh at jokes, but often sat quietly, listening and absorbing. In her nineties, Grandma Sassaman was the family's last-surviving member of her generation. She could be tough in her opinions, but they were always meted out in a loving way. She had raised five kids through a program of straight talk, and all went on to be successful. Her hands sat on the arms of her chair, her demeanor remained relaxed.

"Tell me who you are." She looked me in the eye after I asked The Question. This direct confrontation caught me off guard, forcing me to look away. But she worked through the question the same way Mike had, simply saying her first thoughts aloud. There was something to learn from this. She paused, looking beyond me, out on the yard. *"Who are you?"* she said, turning back. "That would get me there." She broke out into a warm smile, a new thought floating into her mind. "But that's not my favorite question. If I had a choice, I would ask a different question to each person, depending on whether they were seven or twenty or fifty or ninety-five." She took a sip of her white wine. "But *Who are you?* is really the question I would like to have answered."

My cousin-in-law Steve sought me out when he found out what I was doing. *"What would you do if you could do anything you wanted for the day?* That's what I would want to know." He smiled. "You have a free day and nothing planned. What would you do?" As an airline pilot with a newborn, I'm sure he dreamed of his past uncluttered life, a life with large, open days.

Tall and skinny, and mostly just shy, my nephew Kenny broke out of his teenage shell, asking, *"What is your favorite food?"*

Someone from across the room yelled, "Chicken!" Which cued Celine, Kenny's mom, to offer her question. She asked, *"Is a chicken wing light meat or dark meat?"* We all laughed like a family, and Celine gave a mock frown. "What!" she said, scowling. "That's a valid question, and I'd like to hear what people think!" The conversation continued to happen among the group, but I quietly stepped off to the side, starting to get into the swing of things. This isn't so hard, I said to myself. You don't need to be an interviewer with a capital I. *Just keep asking.*

While they talked, my niece Hallie had been thinking. A high school joker, she leaned in with a straight face and said, *"If you had a mustache, would you wash it with shampoo or face wash?"* We all laughed again. This was good. Even better than expected.

Later, Jack, her father, walked over to chat. *"What is your first memory from childhood?"* he said confidently. "As a teacher, I think that says a lot about who you are."

Every time I asked The Question, each person looked at me in expectation right after they responded with their question. Was I supposed to say something more? I found myself doing my best to give nothing, looking at a neutral point and nodding when they seemed to be done. "Are we done?" asked Jack. I made eye contact, smiling weakly and half-shrugging an answer. Was I supposed to validate each asker? Was I supposed to ask them their question?

My father sat in my grandmother's inner circle, laughing with the grown-ups. *"Is the world round?"* he lobbed. No one picked it up, and he smiled vacantly for a second before changing the topic.

I strolled into the kitchen to get a fresh beer.

What's the biggest mistake your parents made?

Of course, he was kidding. My father loved to laugh and joke, and I'm lucky he passed that quality on to me. But often his humor obfuscated his true intent, and here, it stung. He had heard and seen the plan, and now I sat in the middle of his dining room interviewing the whole family. His point remained unclear. Turns out it was his validation I needed as much as my old friends.

In middle school, my father wrote a double-spaced five-page paper titled "Ophthalmology." It has been passed around the family, and now I've got it. The essay is meticulously researched, grammatically perfect and typed without error. At its end, he proclaims his desire to become an ophthalmologist. Here's the thing: I've taught writing to middle-schoolers, and, trust me, this paper is a goddamn Lourdes miracle. And to top it off, for something like five decades, he *was* an ophthalmologist. It's as though a series of dots connected his career path. An actual path, lit before him.

In financial and professional matters, my father appeared a solid man—earthbound. Each of his thunderous steps resonated through the hills as he walked about—whole villages founded in his footprints. His opinion mattered; this is why you do this, and this is why you do that. As a doctor, he always seemed to be right. I had always been something else entirely, buzzing about him, swinging on nearby branches, always asking, *But why?*

Sartre once said, "Had my father lived, he would have lain on me full length, and would have crushed me." My father did not pass away in childhood, like Sartre's, and it was his approval I sought above all else.

Cancer would appear shortly after I completed the journey, and my father was swept away quickly in its grasp. But we can never know these things of the future; in the moment, it bothered me that he chose to be so noncommittal, so oblivious, convinced that I was driving away from common sense itself. In his mind, my plan consisted of going nowhere, accomplishing nothing, wasting both gas and money.

My father and I laughed and joked on any islands of common ground we could find, but I baffled him, just as he had baffled his father before him. My grandfather, the work-means-getting-your-hands-dirty small-town printer and furniture maker, sat on my father's shoulder all the way through medical school, proud but suspicious. *There's no callouses on those hands.*

My father followed the developments of my road trip planning with little attention to the details and even less to the theme. He didn't ask questions about any of it, probably because he worried I didn't have a plan, just like the time I moved to Japan without a plan. Or when I rode my bike across the United States without a plan. These previous adventures left him confused about my life path. He doggedly pursued his parental line: *What are your work prospects? Will this lead to a job?* His questions seemed to miss the very center of the trip. From his perspective, my trip had no center.

What games did you play as a child?

When I was six or seven, I climbed the white pine tree in our front yard to the very top. The very top, in this case, being only around thirty feet—but it did exceed the height of our roof and it did, surprising to my sense of fear and my small body, sway quite a bit in the breeze.

I remember the soft carpet of grass in the front yard, the hushed underside of the tree, and the large branches like spokes radiating out from the trunk. To me they looked like a variation on the monkey bars, offering an easy way north. Surprised by the open views, I wanted to get higher to see more. I climbed on.

While I must do my best to reconstruct specific memories, there is one fact that remains stamped into the leather of my soul. My character—the me, as I knew it—disappeared. I wanted to get higher. I wanted to see more.

Enthralled, I paused between limbs. Parked cars looked small, and I loomed large—a giant to these ants. Looking up to see more tree, I climbed on. As I ascended, the thin trunk swung to and fro with the wind, and I clung happily to its swaying support. Finally, I arrived at the sparsely branched top of the tree. A bird chirped in my face. Look at how big that bird is, and at the large red stripe crossing its beak. I stood in the kingdom of birds!

Between gusts in the strong wind, my mother's voice could be heard in the yard, coaxing me to return to solid ground. A strident panic entered her voice though she attempted to appear calm. The euphoria of height and solitude burst, and instantly I knew I had done something wrong.

I don't remember what kind of trouble I got in. But by that afternoon, all branches lower than six feet from the ground were gone. To this day, my mother talks about the day she saw the fuse had been lit. She realized then she needed to be careful what she encouraged me to try. I needed no coaxing to explore.

Though I wouldn't arrive at my mother's house on the west coast for three months, I revealed my plans on the phone while still in Cambridge. She paused for a moment.

"This sounds crazy, and as your mother I'm not supposed to say I think it is OK. But it does sound like fun, and you're going to meet a lot of interesting people. An adventure like this will stick with you for the rest of your life. I kind of wish I was going, too. Now, stop barking!"

I held the phone away from my ear and looked at it. "Barking?"

"Sorry, I was talking to Pepper. Have fun, honey. I have to take the dog for a walk. I'll see you when you get here."

She supported me; my mother liked to get to the heart of the matter, and my brief description assured her this trip would drive straight to the heart. I knew that when I arrived in California, we'd walk the dog and she'd ask me how it felt and how many people I met, especially the most interesting. We would talk as close friends.

How's my hair?

Stopping by Mike's house again to say goodbye on my way out of Kalamazoo, my father's dismissal following me around like exhaust. Mike invited me in and played with his baby on one side of the stark, white kitchen while his wife, Josephine, stood at the sink and washed dishes. Tall and willowy, she could be intensely focused, like many new moms, on the safety of her baby. No loud noises, no dirty hands. Watching Mike live the life I had deliberately chosen not to pursue while struggling to maintain his rock star spirit, I wondered if I would ever find myself in the same place.

As she finished rinsing the last sippy cup, I asked her The Question. She stood there looking upward but not at anything in particular, her mind far away from childcare duties and a busy husband. Finally, she turned to me and said flatly, *"How's my hair?"*

She pulled a sly smile, and it took me a second before the laughter began. I realized she was turning my assumptions on their heads; parenting wasn't all seriousness. In that moment, she set me free from the heaviness of what I was "supposed" to be doing. Once I started laughing, I couldn't stop. I laughed all the way to my car and all the way out onto the highway. Tears rolled down my face. I laughed, reveling in my new resolve, and I laughed with the possibility of more questions like this.

Why do humans see patterns in everything?

I'd only interviewed a couple dozen people by this point, but already a stark pattern began to emerge in their responses. People either took The Question very seriously or used it as a set-up for a joke.

The humorous questions were almost always immediate. The serious folks almost always asked for more time. They sighed, cocked an eyebrow, and said something like, "Hmm, that is a big question." And if their question was serious, you could bet that they'd be looking you dead in the eye. Humorous and serious intertwined in my mind as I drove out of Michigan toward Minnesota, recounting the questions of Kalamazoo:

What do you think is the role of the judiciary in our democracy?
What are you doing here?
What do you think is the future of our country?
Are we going to have sex later?
What are you most afraid of?
What's your real phone number?
What is one secret you've never told anyone?
If you had to choose between two superpowers, would you choose Invisibility or Flight?
Where did you originally come from? What brought you here?
What's been the highlight of your life?

What is something you regret, and what have you done to change that?

Driving across the upper Midwest, weaving my way toward the North Woods, I called another childhood friend, Karin. We were talking and laughing about some crazy escapade we'd gotten into as high school students in Kalamazoo. We reminisced for a long time before I told Karin about my project.

"That sounds fun!" she said, and then she paused, thinking. "Here's my question: *What is something that you regret in your life, and what have you done to change that?*"

This seemed like an interesting question, so I asked her about it. As we talked, blue and green highway signs sped past in a blur. Karin started answering her own question and telling me about her relationship with her mother, when I started to see signs for cities I didn't recognize. "Lacrosse, Wisconsin," I read. I'd driven this highway many times, but I'd never been to Lacrosse in my entire life.

When Karin asked about my answer to her question, I was already on the side of the highway looking at a map. "Well," I said, tracing my finger along my route, "I could say something from my childhood, but right this very minute would do just fine."

Instead of heading north on Interstate 94 when I reached Tomah, Wisconsin, I had continued straight west adding almost two-and-a-half hours to my drive, but unlike my father's wrath at these kind of navigational failures, I found myself enjoying the added time spent crossing the north woods into real wilderness. Eventually, I swung north. Norway pines thick with green needles crowded the two-lane highway as I left the last big city, Duluth. I knew this rural highway surprisingly well; I'd driven it for years as though pulled by magnet from whichever state I lived at the time.

The last stretch of the drive from Duluth always shone with unique warmth. Up beyond the Twin Cities, my car wound through a lush green carpet of plant life to the very edge of Lake Superior's onyx chill. Thirty miles of stunning shore and then turn a sharp left, straight across marshy boreal forest. Evidence of humans thinned out, apartment buildings and chain stores replaced by long, quiet stretches of black asphalt and blue sky. Purple irises shot up and exploded in vibrant patches out of money-green bogs. Cell signal disappeared. Getting out of the car to pee late in the afternoon brought the whine and whir of many bugs. The dusk, when I arrived, was filled with the sounds of crepuscular animal calls.

Buoyed by friends, I left Kalamazoo floating on laughter over the confusion. I arrived at the Outward Bound base late, the twilight-dark wood of the buildings welcoming and warm.

I had stopped shaving when I left Boston, and now, two weeks into the drive, I had the outlines of a short, full beard. Before unloading and becoming a part of this stop on my journey, I sat in my car for a moment alone. The Question Project was bound to flourish here.

CHAPTER 3

THE NORTH WOODS

Happier? - Atom Egoyan
(Canadian film director, writer, and producer)

H ands together and eyes expectant, I sat across the table from Jenny, the Executive Director of the Outward Bound Base thirteen miles east of Ely, along the northern edge of Minnesota. We had just eaten lunch on a screened porch that overlooked the large wooded lake of the base. She had hired me and had nurtured me over the years into a competent instructor. I was honored that she would take part in my project.

She looked blankly at her plate for a moment and then gave me a thin-lipped smile. "I don't want to be a wet blanket, but there just isn't a single question that I would ask everyone." I sat, waiting for her to continue, not realizing she had said all she had intended. Professionally, Jenny dealt with all manner of people, from at-risk youth to outside funders to veteran instructors in the field. Surely she would have something profound for me to reflect on. I decided to push.

"Come on! Really? Nothing?"

"Nope. What's most interesting to me is discovering each individual person's unique question, what makes them tick, what they want to know about the world. And for that to happen, I'd need to get to know each person before finding out what one question I wanted to ask them." She stood up and looked out through the porch screen at the vast wilderness before us. She smiled again apologetically, arranged her dishes to take them into the kitchen, and turned to look me right in the eye. "Sorry."

A new wrinkle appeared in the project. As she walked away, I sat flustered; was she copping out? She challenged so many people to express themselves that I was surprised she didn't do the same. It turned out I would have plenty of time to investigate, but not until I returned. Jenny was the only staff member I would engage with before

I jumped right into planning and leading a twenty-two-day expedition in the wilderness.

"*What do you think of Canada?*" a guy had asked in a bar in Kalamazoo. A question like that didn't require any special reflection. It was funny. And questions such as, "*What brings you happiness?*" and, "*What are you most passionate about?*" led others to think about their lives, too. But Jenny's response differed from these; it cut the project to the quick.

I carried my own dishes to the washer, thinking over our interaction. Then it hit me. She had left me confused and reevaluating my assumptions. And it made some kind of sideways sense; she wasn't going to give me something wrapped up neatly in a bow. Seven years earlier I had come to Outward Bound for this exact perspective.

Why are you here?

By the time I became a senior in high school, Brian had moved on to college and his influence had blossomed in me; I ran reckless and more than a little wild. I made a list of all the different drugs I'd taken, and I'm a little surprised, to this day, of the generosity of the contents. But unlike Brian, I wasn't seeking to self-destruct. Instead, I sought new worlds. This world seemed too confined; I wanted to ride a Hendrix haze to Outer Space. I wanted to hop on a bus to a destination I couldn't even pronounce. The difference between Brian and me was that I always wanted to come back. Brian wanted the trip more desperately than I did. He partied like he wasn't interested in the return portion of his ticket.

I joined him, traveling into the haze, going far enough to fail out of college. Passing all my belongings out to friends and walking to South America barefoot comprised my entire life plan when I returned home that summer. This is what I told my father when we looked over my zero-point-eight grade point average on the flimsy white grade report.

"Please don't do that," he said, wincing, just as I came to the no-shoes conclusion of the plan. A few days later at dinner, he tentatively placed a catalog down in front of me. On the cover, a group of teenagers stood on top of a boulder-strewn mountain peak, grimy with dirt, each one deeply sunburned. They had red helmets on and huge packs by their sides.

"Your mother and I want you to do this," he said.

I agreed just on the adventure principle of the thing and made sure I enrolled in what the admissions guy told me was the most remote and challenging alpine mountaineering course Outward Bound offered. I spent twenty-two days in the Northern Cascades hiking narrow ridge-line trails, camping on remote moraines, and climbing and sweating. But something else happened over the course of that expedition. Something deep. Something I had been searching for.

What drives or propels you?

"Why are you here?" my instructor asked me on Day One.

"My parents sent me," I replied.

"Why did they send you here?" he asked, curious.

"Because I failed out of college."

"I'm sure that's an interesting story. Why did you fail out of college?" He took off his shades. It wasn't a challenge. He seemed genuinely interested. Surprised, even.

I wasn't prepared for someone to ask me *Why*. Up to this point, everyone had just been disappointed or angry by my failure. My mother cried.

This negative reaction to my failure was so common that I became defensive. I reflected the anger and pessimism, absorbing the disappointment. But out here in the wilderness, things were different. This time, someone wanted to hear things out.

Just because my instructor listened didn't mean the expedition was easy; we grunted up the sides of mountains and ate tough, dried food during the day as huge North Cascades panoramas unfurled from every switchback. But every morning we left camp with a question.

"As you go about your day, I want you to keep in mind one single question," our burly guide would say as we packed up. "Today it is this: *What has helped you get through the most challenging experience of your life?*" He adjusted the straps on his pack and turned to the trail. "We'll discuss it at dinner tonight." He looked back smiling. "And keep in mind, your story might be about your experience today."

And discuss we did. The other students in my brigade would talk about the question all day, as we forded streams and double-checked maps to navigate. We'd dissect and analyze and come to our evening circle prepared. But never prepared enough. When we'd sit, faces glowing yellow from the fire, satiated from dinner and feeling open from sweat and nature and exertion, the stories would come tumbling out. Chad came to fend off alcoholism, Jerry fought low self-esteem, I was a dropout. And always the instructor would parry back:

"How did that decision feel?"

"What did you do about it?"

Everything didn't change overnight upon my return, I still had some rebelliousness to work through, but something internal had righted itself. I was more self-confident. Problems that came up in life were not to be avoided, but dealt with. And, most importantly, I fell in love with nature. I vowed to return.

"I'm going to be an instructor one day," I said to my leaders in my exit interview.

"That's a great goal," said one, smiling at me, "but that's what everyone says at the end of a course. What's something you plan to do in your immediate future?"

He didn't realize I was serious. Ten years later I became a house painter to earn the money needed for the 58-day instructor development course in North Carolina. Soon after I was offered my first course to instruct, one of the proudest days of my life.

If you could go one place on Earth, where would you go?

Something happens when you get out into the woods, away from the constant barrage of televised images, the bombast of radio, and the blue radiance at the electronic altar, the Internet. In the outdoors, you relax, your guard gets lowered, and a spirit of playfulness, curiosity, and adventure overtakes you. You feel part of the natural order again. The great gulf that exists between the city dweller and the natural world disappears, and you return to *you*, able to revel in the world as a part of it, instead of trying to be its master.

You become aware of the beauty, and tenuousness, of existence. You re-form the bond between you, the planet, and all the creatures in it. This awareness strengthens the connections with those around you. Friendships are easier to make, and they're tinged with a more profound connection than those made elsewhere. Throw in the element of challenge, in this case disaffected teenagers, and many conversations dig more deeply and span more of the confusions of being alive. Life in the wilderness speaks to the core.

I arrived at base while teenagers were preparing for three weeks in the wilderness, packing to make their own journeys from all corners of the country. They flew into the small Duluth airport from Florida, Connecticut, Colorado, points all over the US. Two arrived from Brooklyn. We gathered in a circle by the luggage carousel for introductions. With caps on backwards and lumpy duffle bags, they looked like a rag-tag baseball team out of a movie.

Over dinner at the base, we went over gear and then I set up brief individual meetings. 10 yards from the group I set two empty camp chairs and had students come over one by one.

"So, what brings you here?" I asked each of them. Alexa was worried about starting college in the fall; Dani wanted to experience the woods, something not available from her apartment in Brooklyn. I saw myself in Chris, who had "screwed up pretty bad back home." But the lesson for me came from Tom. He sat cross-legged in front of me, leaving the seat empty, and played with a stick while we talked. "Why am I here?" Tom asked me quizzically. "I'm here for survival skills." He flicked the end of the stick at some leaves. "I'll put it this way: if I don't have the ability to live independently in the wilderness then I will never be asked to join a roving band of survivors in the post-apocalypse." He drew the stick across his throat like a knife. "I'll be dead meat." I wasn't sure what question to ask next.

The next morning at dawn, we put canoes on the water. Day One. Paddles quietly pulled us into the boreal geography of the Boundary Waters. More than a million acres of wilderness lay before us, and while many of the logistics were mapped out for safety, there were still many unknowns. It was, for everyone, a journey. We were to leave everything of comfort and embark on a true expedition. With all our food and gear packed, we left self-contained, on a route that posed many challenges. The students would need to rely on themselves and their interdependence for emotional sustenance and happiness.

As we pushed off from land and paddled into that wilderness, the students' true needs became clear. This was not about my question, or my journey, but about other, more basic, more pressing questions of immediate need. As we lost sight of land, I quickly remembered that when overseeing a brigade of teenagers, your life becomes theirs. Unlike the meta-reflection of my bigger journey, more elemental questions came alive in the wilderness. Questions such as:

Where are we going?
Will we make it?
Is it lunchtime?
Can it be lunchtime again?
Or my favorites:
You know I didn't sign up for this, right?
And:
What is this crap?
I hate it here!
That last one's not even a question.

What's the story of your life?

In many ways, the youthful faces that asked each of these questions did reflect my own larger journey in the world. A journey within a journey. For them, faced with so many challenges in the wilderness, life itself became a question. Just as it did for me. Seeing them coming to grips with the challenges of our expedition, with who they were and what their real motivations were, I too ended up looking at deep questions of self—deep human questions. On this expedition, I engaged some of the questions I had, until then, only documented. I watched the students go through the very trials I worked through.

The days passed quickly in navigation lessons, setting up and breaking down camp, cooking, and leadership experiences. Mixed within were some beautiful moments. One evening halfway through the course, loons appeared in the moonlight. We camped on a long and thin lake, far from regular paddling traffic. Glassy and smooth, sparkling ebony under the moon. The plaintive wails of the loons broke the silence, calling to lost loves or to the deepest reaches of the universe with unanswerable questions.

I appreciated their calls. Loons are one of the few creatures in the wild that seem unconcerned by human presence. By day they popped up next to our boats, scaring students, surprising me. Their blood-red eyes peered at us briefly, and then they dipped back under in search of food. They seemed so confident, and—unlike my teenage brigade, unlike me—so self-assured, so free of the need for answers.

"Did you hear those loons last night?"

I nodded.

"Weren't they beautiful?"

I nodded again, knowing that now, midway through the course, the student experience had changed. They were concerned with beauty.

It rained as the first student offered an answer to The Question. We were huddling on the shore in rain gear, off the lake because of incoming lightning, when Dani, a small girl from Brooklyn, leaned in. "OK," she said, "I have an answer to your one-question project. It's something the whole group can discuss while we're standing here: *What's the story to your life?*"

She presented it more to her brigade than to me, which, honestly, I found refreshing. Her question set the others into a wonderful, deep conversation about what brought each of them to this particular spot in this particular moment. Chris said, "The first thing you'll probably want to know is where I was born, and what my lousy childhood was like, and all that crap, but I don't feel like going into it, if you want to know the truth."

Dani laughed. "*The Catcher in the Rye*! We just read that in Mrs. Lutz's American Lit class! But c'mon, I want to know *your* story."

We stood close for warmth, cold rain falling hard around us, but the students seemed barely to notice. Chris looked down. "The truth is, I didn't even know I was coming here. My parents packed my bags and took me to the airport so early it was still dark out. And put me on the plane, for here." He looked down. "I've been not doing so hot. I did have a great childhood, but lately I've been skipping school and stealing stuff. I'm not a bad person, but it's so easy, you know? You just get up and walk out of school! Done." He smiled, but ironically, it seemed.

"I threw a massive party at my house when my parents were out of town. The police came and everything. That's what *really* got me sent here. At the airport, my father said, 'You go do this and when you come back, clean slate, we'll start fresh.'" He looked from person to person. "But I don't know if I can make it. I really hate it here."

I could've jumped in right there, bulldozed his sadness with advice on how to live his life better and all the misguided, kind-hearted thoughts I could muster. But as I held my tongue, Alexa the tallest, spoke up. "That sucks," she said pouting, "but we're glad you're here. If you weren't screwing up in school, you wouldn't have been sent here and we wouldn't have gotten the chance to meet you!" It was perfect.

"Thanks," Chris smiled, sheepishly. "Oh yeah, I forgot the part about how I stole my parents' credit cards and charged a bunch of pizza and clothes and all kinds of stuff to the account. They're probably just getting the bill now." Well, OK, that slate is going to need some scrubbing before it comes clean, I thought to myself.

After the rain died down, we paddled. At dinner that evening, Elena shared her thoughts. "Hey, I've got mine: *What advice or details about your life would you tell your five-year-old self?*"

"Quit being so worried about what everyone else thinks," Tom responded almost immediately.

"Even if the food looks yucky, you have to try a little bite, and you might find that you actually like it!" Chris said, stirring his bowl of warm mush, his sarcasm palpable.

Everyone laughed, and the conversation amongst the brigade sprang up again. Answers tumbled, some deft and some inane, over and over each other, fighting for attention.

As the fire died down, Jeff jumped in with one last question for the day: *"How would you describe yourself, and how would your friends describe you?"*

The course went on and on like that. At the approach to the sheer cliffs of our rock-climbing day, Alexa asked, *"What would be your credo statement?"*

While we ate lunch, Harry shared his: *"When you saw me for the first time, what did you think?"*

Portia ended the day with hers: *"Have you lived your life to the fullest?"*

Each time one of the students asked his or her question, everyone discussed, engrossed. They wanted to know so much about each other, yet the questions they were taught to ask didn't get to the information or the exchange they yearned for. They didn't want to know what adults and teachers seemed to think; they didn't want to know what everyone's favorite color was, or what video game people liked to play, or what movie rocked. Even more than most adults I asked, they wanted to know the core of it all. *What makes you tick? What do you stand for?*

What are you really afraid of?

Humans—ice fishermen, astronauts, sewer inspectors—find ourselves in all manner of unwelcome environments. As I helped the group push boats through a deep channel in a bog, I realized we were in that category, too. We stood in a narrow and murky channel, so tight and the reeds so high that we lost the path often in the tangle of floating peat and bent fronds. I'd been there once a few years earlier, and instantly remembered the disquieting nature of the place. Often a foot hit nothing, and the entire leg, followed by the whole body, would slide into the muddy, coffee-colored water, weightless.

Up ahead, Jeff, the tough kid from New York, slipped and began yelping in terror. "Help me!" he screamed frantically, clawing at wet, muddy plants, feet scrambling for purchase. I offered a hand and he pulled like he was trying to remove it. Yes, it was scary, but he was safer than he had been any day of his life in New York City. Anything down there in the bog swam for its dear life at his thrashing feet. And nothing down there would rob him of anything. Or worse, shoot. Most Americans live barely knowing that in the city they are in danger of losing their foothold at any time.

For a moment, waist-deep in muck and supervising, I felt centered: I knew this world. I knew what to depend on. The overreactions of these city kids kept me calm.

How do you find peace?

At lunch on our last day, I paused, dipping the fiberglass tip of my paddle in the water. Small, concentric circles formed on the surface, expanding as they pulsed away from the blade. With every movement of the paddle, however slight, another ring extended, but all the rings were contained within the initial, largest circle, the first ripple, the first stroke. Every event fit into that wobbly circle. All was contained within. A metaphor for life itself. I sat hunched and studying, like a primitive scientist discovering meaning in water. Entranced in the center of the lake, gently touching the tip of my paddle in the water, removing it, touching it again, watching rings expand and collide.

Jeff laughed, and slowly I remembered where I was. Paddle in mid-ripple, I looked up to catch all of them staring at me from their boats. They smiled back and laughed out loud. One shook his head, side to side. It wasn't worth explaining to him what I'd seen, *This is where questions come from. I was just there.* I wanted to say. But his thoughts were plain on his face: *You crazy.*

After five years of instructing, Outward Bound gives you a pin. It's not much, but there wasn't anything that made me more proud in the world. I immediately put it on my favorite, well-worn visor.

One visit back to Kalamazoo, my father took the faded visor off my head, playfully. "How about we throw this old guy in the trash here?" But then, looking closer, he paused.

"Hey, what's this?" he asked, fingering the shiny, multicolored pin. The visor was warped and stained from five seasons in the outdoors, but the button shone new. My father appreciated what Outward Bound had done for my college career, that I had actually graduated, but he didn't quite know what to make of the place itself. Though I corrected him, he still referred to me as a "counselor" and to the school as a "camp." When I explained the five years of service and my recent promotion from assistant to lead instructor, he smiled. "Does that mean that now you make the big bucks?" I shook my head to say, "No." He tilted his head as he smiled more imploringly, "Benefits?"

The truth was more painful. I made a little more than a hundred dollars a day. And benefits? Yep: free rent. The meals were free, too, as long as you ate them with a group of sunburnt and bug-bitten teenagers in the middle of the woods. I would never be able to show him, in his language, that I had found success beyond what I had ever thought possible. Chasing questions in the wilderness was its own reward.

What'cha got cooking?

On the first day back at the base, the whole brigade cleaned and restocked gear. Then the students packed, said goodbyes, and began their journeys back to points all over the country, home. By lunch, they were gone. Though everyone counts down to the last day as the big brass ring and says loud goodbyes and hugs and waves, sadness ripples through it all.

There's a certain kind of emptiness that sets in as you go through your own cleaning and restocking routines at the end of an expedition; all the people you've spent the last few weeks living with are gone. The conversation and laughter disappear and your world becomes really small again: just you. The radio offers little comfort, and the friends you want to see are often off leading their own courses.

I wasn't lonely during our expedition—that wasn't possible living together as we did—but sitting on the porch to my cabin the afternoon after the students had left, I realized, once again, that I was single and alone. No one waited for my call.

Heading down for a meal, I bumped into Sam, a first-year instructor, in the cafeteria. Her soft blue eyes were alight with playfulness. I envied her tribe of women. She cooked her own food: organic, black cast-iron skillet. She listened to punk rock on cassette, drank wine from the bottle, and danced topless in her apartment in the city, shouting joyfully out the window at the people on the street below. This is what I believed, anyway, looking at those eyes. This belief gave it a sort of truth. The way she laughed reminded me that I was traveling solo.

We arrived at the big kitchen at the base to find it empty, but for Sam. She smiled. I smiled. "So you are Sam, Queen of…what country again?" Feeling playful, I decided to start the conversation with an odd-ball tack. She looked confused for a second and then smiled.

"Samanthaland," she replied, with a nod. I looked down. I asked her The Question.

"Oh," she said in mock thoughtfulness. "Let me think." She paused for just a second and said, "How about this: *If you could punch anyone in the face, in the whole world, a celebrity, someone you know, maybe a political figure, who would it be?*"

Her thoughts came out so fast, it felt as if she had been waiting for someone to ask her a question like this. I loved it. Finally, one of those questions that through sheer ridiculousness gets people talking.

"Would I get in trouble for it?"

"Nope. You'd be anonymous."

"Would it hurt as much as usual?"

She looked at me sideways. "Getting punched in the face? *Hello!* Of course."

Then a light went on. "Actually, I have two questions. Here's the second: *If you could go back in time and take a dump on someone's floor, who would it be, when would it be, and why would you do it?*"

I crinkled my nose at the imaginary smell.

"Now that's the Ultimate Revenge Question," she said. "What could be worse than that? She paused, scrunching up her face to mimic mine. We both giggled at the absurdity. I liked her freedom, and her absurdity. We finished lunch and parted ways, but something remained.

The next morning, I walked down to the main building, got a cup of coffee hoping to "accidentally" run into Sam again, having noticed her name in marker on the scheduling board. She had already started that morning planning for a new multiweek expedition. She smiled and waved as I walked into the big logistics room, but she would be gone in the wilderness for longer than I. When she returned, I would be back on the road. Not that I cared. It wasn't a big deal. I mean, who cares? Seriously. I barely even knew her.

Disappointed blossomed. This driving around America on a big adventure helped me to forget that my last serious relationship had occurred more than two years prior. The flirting over lunch, and the attraction of Sam's unique humor—for the first time on this journey I had an emotional horse in the race. Our brief interaction made me realize that I would continue on the road without any friends.

I would leave the base alone, and the claustrophobic potential began to settle in. Connecting and disconnecting reminded me of the ever-present possibility of loneliness.

What do you plan to do with the rest of your life?
(Tom Regan, American Philosopher
specializing in animal rights theory)

After a first shower and change into clean clothes, the functions of the nose are reset and one becomes acutely aware of how pungent life is in the wilderness. I needed to do laundry. To counteract developing feelings of loneliness, I roped my friend Tonder into coming with. "C'mon," I said, mustering up enthusiasm, "it'll be fun."

"Watching you do laundry?" she responded with a cocked eyebrow. Tonder and I had been friends for a long time, and I hoped she would come along just for the companionship.

Instructing for Outward Bound was recent in my professional work, but Tonder showed up as an intern at nineteen and never left. That meant she had spent two decades trudging through swamps with at-risk and adjudicated youth, at base camps all over the country from the middle of Florida to the northern reaches of Minnesota. She'd been on dozens and dozens of courses, accruing thousands of days—years, in fact—in the wilderness.

When I think of Outward Bound, I think of Tonder, out there in the field, mediating fight after fight, sitting through hundreds of dinners with morose teenagers, emboldened through long, hot days of sun-ripened anger, and, somehow, having a pretty good time. Somehow she stays happy and light. And with all of her experience, just being with her feels as if you're living a story.

As we drove, I asked her The Question. She took a minute to think. "Well, I have two questions, partner. I know I'm supposed to do one, but whatever. That's how I roll." She smiled and looked over at me, winking comically. She wasn't going to hang me out to dry. "The first question: *What is your cure for the hiccups?*"

I gave her the sideways glance Sam had given me when I asked where she was queen of, but Tonder remained serious.

"Come on! That is something we need to know about. Think about how different society would be if we could solve that?" I agreed.

"OK, here's my second question: *What are you most passionate about?*"

We rode quietly along in the car, as I found myself lost in thought. Driving in silence through the countryside with an old friend holds a unique kind of reassurance. The conversation still felt alive, not suspended by lulls. No need to fill the silences.

But as we rode, my mind wandered back to Jenny, the school's director. Her polite refusal bothered me more than it should have. It stuck with me for weeks out in the wilderness. Finally, I spoke. "This project," I said, knowing she hadn't intended for me to respond, but it just kind of spilled out.

"Tonder, I need some advice. I'm on this journey, right, where I'm asking people just one question. And suddenly I'm feeling lost in it. Jenny dismissed the whole thing."

She looked at me intently. "Nah, she was just answering your question. Those are her honest thoughts. That's just how she operates. But I think you're struggling with something deeper. Are you doing this project so you can get some specific question answered, or are you doing this because you want to know about people?"

"Both," I replied. "I'm doing this journey for fun—I want to see what is on people's minds, what do they want to know about everybody else? But I'm also seeking an answer for me. I'm hoping I'll hear that one question that will resonate with me, one I can rely on, one that makes sense in my life."

She nodded. "I hear you, there's so much out there to believe in, it can be hard to arrive at just one."

I looked out the window, the yellow sun seemed to hang fixed in the sky. "But I'm doubly confused because Jenny said, 'There isn't a single question that I would ask everyone,' and yet that's exactly what I'm looking for, one single question. This challenge doesn't come up in spiritual traditions, there is often just one: *Do you believe in the word of the prophet Mohammed? Is Jesus Christ the son of God?*

Tonder paused, processing. "This all goes back to your purpose with this journey. Do you think the world has a message from other people to *you*? Or do you think you are supposed to be cataloging the thoughts and dreams and fears of *other people*? It boils down to this: Are you talking or are you listening?" Trees whizzed by as we entered a developed two-lane highway. We were no longer on the dirt road, the one that brought me into the base.

The tires made a dull echo as we rolled over a metal bridge looking out across a languid and brilliant river. "I feel totally lost in my life. Four months ago, in Cambridge, I was in school and I was sure that when it ended I'd have a clear purpose. But I didn't. I don't."

"I gave you two questions," she said, "now I'm going to give you two truths. Here is one: *Everything is That Big.* What you are worrying about is important, no matter how minuscule it may seem. Problems bear examining, and while there may be no solution that is clear and present, everything you do is important and should be treated as such.

"Here's another: *There is no solid plan.* Anywhere. Ever. Get used to it. If you let yourself truly experience it, everything in life is chaotic, liberating, and terrifying all at once. So now you're doing a traveling project, interviewing America, and you throw yourself into the very den of deep questioning: 'What should I be doing? What's going to solve the riddle of the unknown path?"

She paused for emphasis. "Nothing is going to answer this for you. You must inhabit your confusion. It will take you to another place. These questions feel big, because they *are* big. So often our lives appear set in stone, the path before us supposedly clear. But here is the problem: Too many people use their 'plan' as a crutch. To let go of all that and embrace the complete not-knowing means that all you're left with is yourself. That's where you'll find your answer." She smiled, "Or, your question."

I had to admit, even at that very moment, all of that sounded strange, to live without a plan and to intentionally continue not having a plan, waiting and watching until things became revealed.

But she told the truth. I'd counseled others in this same way. You alone make the meaning of your life and your actions, and you need to make meaning of them continually, at every juncture.

Tonder looked over and smiled, pulling me back from my thoughts. "And with no plan, there's nothing defining you. It is scary as hell. I understand, man, believe me, I can relate." By relating the problem, she offered friendship, not consolation. We both nodded together, in the moment together. We rode in that car in silence for almost an entire minute.

"I think I get what you're saying," I said, breaking the silence. "Do you know what Mike Tyson said about plans?"

"Enlighten me," she said.

"Everybody has a plan until they get punched in the mouth."

Tonder laughed, "That's what I'm talking about."

Why is money so important to you?

We arrived back at base just in time for dinner. Around the large wooden dinner table I posed The Question to a group of instructors, both ones I knew well and newly arrived interns. A red-bearded instructor sat next to me and immediately chimed in. "OK," he said, thoughtfully. *"What's the most valuable lesson you've learned, and what's the story around that?"*

"That's two questions, jerk!" someone needled from another table.

"Yeah, but they totally fit together," he defended. The table turned to me as judge and arbiter.

I shrugged. "Valid points, both." I said, not interested in being the Ruler on this one; I wanted to hear what others thought about it, to watch how they processed it. This group, like all the others I'd asked, was more intent on finding questions than answers.

Nancy, the basecamp cook stepped out of the kitchen and stood at the head of our table in her white apron. One corner of her metal spatula rested on the table pointed down, as it did when she asked for feedback on the dinner. "I've heard about your project," she said, addressing me, "and I've got a question to add." All heads turned. Here her announcement was of a different sort. "I've never been quite sure if I'm headed the right way, so I find myself asking: *Do you think you are on your right path in life?"*

The air was still, everyone contemplating all past and future choices.

"Some people seem to get it and somehow know they're flying right, but then there's all the rest of us, so I follow it up with: *Have you been able to find your right path?"*

"Well, I'm going to jump in with an answer that goes for everyone," voiced a barrel-chested, flannel-flying instructor. "To the first I say: No Idea. And the second: Probably Not."

The cook smiled. "And you are working with the youth of America." She let out an exaggerated sigh and returned to the kitchen.

Nobuo, a quiet instructor with long black hair, chimed in when the volume diminished. "I would like to know: *Why is money so important to you?"*

Most folks stood up and began clearing their dishes after hearing Nobuo's question, but his thoughts resonated with me. I had just deposited my paycheck from my weeks in the field at Outward Bound, and it would float me all the way around the United States and back to Boston if I played my cards right. Slim, economical cards, that is. And I had to play them just right.

I didn't worry too much in the moment though. It was my first night back on base, and a portion of my paycheck would be devoted to frothing pitchers of beer.

Later that evening, in town at a booth in the Kwazy Wabbit saloon, questions went around and around. But the more instructors I asked, the more it became clear that The Question had yet another layer that, up to now, had eluded me. It seemed to ask: *What do you think is true about everyone? What do you think we all have in common? What do you want to know about other people?* After so many answers, I found that that seemed to form part of the central core to The Question. You had to ask *everyone*, and this is what made The Question both liberating and confining. It was one of a number of ways that The Question was beginning to reveal itself.

What do you want to be when you grow up?
What happened to that dream?
What happened to you?
What is the biggest mistake your parents made?
What makes you most happy?
Who do you blame?

What is something that you know will never change?

In my simple pine cabin at the base, a revelation struck as I dropped off to sleep my last night there. I was alone in the cabin, in the quiet woods. In my half-asleep state, I reviewed all the questions I had heard; everyone wanted to know about something that had caused change, but no one wondered about that which remained constant. I continued to ruminate, dazed; if I could get a grip on the constants of the world I might have an inroad to my path.

I sat up in a half-daze, made it over to the desk and sat, pencil in hand, until I came upon the right words. Not just an interview question but the question I want to ask everyone. My own question. It hit and I wrote it down: *"What is something that you know will never change?"* Anchored and firm, I knew immediately I could hold onto it while it answered the challenges of Brian and the challenges of my father. I felt good about this development, a byproduct of interviewing so many people. If I could find the things in the world that never change I could connect to them myself. Those things would be my rock.

A-ha! I thought, now I would be able to recall clearly when this journey took a turn, when it moved from a survey of the population to a personal exploration. I would continue my journey, but now I had a purpose. I studied English in college, and this was one of those transcendent moments from the stories of antiquity: the hero accepts the path before him.

The next morning, the group from the previous night reconvened at a restaurant in town. We put in orders for greasy plates, and I had a chance to try my new question over my last meal before I left. I let loose my brilliance.

"What do I believe never changes?" responded one long-haired, rock climbing instructor, eyeing me quizzically. He spun his coffee slowly, spoon clinking the mug. "That's easy: Gravity." Another answer followed. "Love." And another. "Need for shelter." Now fully awake and drinking coffee, my new question didn't feel as solid.

The table stayed silent for a beat until another instructor chimed in. "Change," she replied.

What's your angle?

"We thank you for your submission and look forward to your presentation," read the thick cotton invitation from the conferring committee. My paper had been accepted. It was official. I would present my grad school research on a unique Boston high school at a conference in Texas. My final stop was confirmed. I felt like I was faking it as an academic, peeing outside and averaging approximately one shower a month, but so what? The work at the school was impressive in dismantling traditional teacher power structures and giving voice to students, and I knew it was important to get this work out to the world. Besides, starting conversations was the point rather than trying to be the final word on a topic. The acceptance had waited in my box back at base while I traveled out in the wilderness, leaving me only a week to mail my response.

I drove away from Outward Bound on a rainy, slate-gray day in August, excited for what lay ahead but sad to be leaving such a rich and thoughtful environment.

CHAPTER 4

THE PLAINS

Why? - Country Joe McDonald (Musician, lead singer of the 1960s psyche-
delic rock group Country Joe and the Fish)

I loved the driving. Sometimes as I traveled, I got so excited I could barely contain myself. I'd crank up the music. I started to kind of vibrate. I'd yell. I'd roll down the window. I'd stick my arm out and bang on the outside of the door. *Yeah! We're doing this!*

Through all my waving and honking, no one on the road ever reciprocated, and I could see why: it's strange to have someone careening toward you, waving like a maniac. Especially when that someone is unshaven, unshowered, and riding in a car packed with what is obviously his every belonging on Earth. Waving back was the last thing anyone wanted to do. After enough quizzical and horrified looks, I decided that when that feeling washed over me, I'd bang a little bit and then do the wind-current-hand-surfing thing. At the height of my excitement, I'd twirl my finger and go:

Woo

Hoo!

My hand rode the gusts of air. It would pop up at unexpected moments, pushed flat to the door in the next. This simple act always reminded of how much I enjoyed hurtling through geographies at seventy miles an hour. As my hand flipped and flopped, I was thrown back to my first day on the trip, back to all the confusion burying me then. That had been only two months earlier, but now this trip seemed so possible, so interesting. I had broken the spell; the scope and scale of it just made it that much more fun.

Where did you go to college?

There was a time when the question-asking became my downfall, when I started to question everything. Driving south into Iowa meant encountering other, unwanted memories. Pulling into Des Moines for gas, a sign for Drake University appeared, next exit. It was at Drake that my need to question things veered negative. Not only that, but Drake represented the biggest disconnect between my father and me, and until this trip, I had tried to avoid the state of Iowa altogether. For some reason, a force pulled at the wheel, tugging me in. I took the off ramp.

What can't you forget?

Parking on the edge of campus, I turned off the engine and sat for a moment, surveying the scene. Though it had been sixteen years, I could name every building I saw through the windshield immediately. I opened the car door and walked toward my old dorm, the cafeteria, and a group of buildings where my classes had been held.

It was a Sunday morning in summer, which meant the entire campus sat barren and eerily silent. The sidewalks emanated the humid heat of August in Iowa, and all were empty. I walked to the center of campus and stood looking around before beginning a self-guided tour. Moving like a ghost, I made my way from building to building, then crossed the main yard, floating the stairs to the hallway of my freshman dormitory.

They say college is a time to find yourself, to experiment, and to question everything, so I did. *"What does college do that consistent, intense personal study cannot do?"* I asked one night, stoned out of my mind. I was sitting next to my best friend at the time, Mike, both of us in pajama pants, watching TV. It took a minute, but then his eyes widened and his mouth circled. He turned to me. "Whoa," was all he said.

We laughed, but I stayed lost.

"How am I supposed to know what to do here?" I asked many others.

I began skipping classes and then assignments and by the end, the school year fell apart like soggy cardboard. In spring, grades were posted: I had failed out. The next morning, I met with an exit counselor. It all happened very quickly.

"Mr. Sassaman," she began, chin raised and pointed toward the door, "why are you here? What is it you want from this institution?"

"I don't know," I said quietly. Her desk sat heavily on the lino-leum-tiled floor. From each heavy foot, cracks emanated in slow motion, making their way towards me.

"What did Drake do, or not do, for you that led to this?" She motioned to a copy of my transcript.

"I just don't know." I wished I could've said what I know now, that this was a time when I was asking too many questions. What did I need? More structure? More encouragement? Drake was a fine school, but instead of finding my own path, I was trying to do right by my father's expectations, by society's norms. I looked back at the cracks.

"Well, I hope that you find better luck at your future institution." She was curt. We sat silently for a moment. Then she stood and walked to the door. I stood up slowly, the enormity of the decision settling in. She waited by the door, unsmiling, with an outstretched hand.

"I wish you the best of luck, Mr. Sassaman," she said, as she shook my hand. With that, she sent me home.

Being back at Drake, many years later, I realized that my questions were too scattershot. I needed to refine my searches. I needed just one.

What is the most beautiful experience in your life that isn't related to birth or marriage or death?

I continued westward. By midafternoon, Iowa sat far behind, but the miles and miles of Nebraska landscape were becoming deadeningly familiar. Flat, treeless miles lay before and behind me.

It all reminded me of other journeys I'd taken across this landscape, sometimes out of necessity, such as when I moved from Oakland to Boston, my little red car packed to the gills.

It was not that I drove to discover the geography of America; I had done that ten years crossing the country on spinning bicycle wheels, covering more than 4,000 miles in 105 days. The childhood dream of so many young bike riders became real then; it wasn't about carving some new path, but inhabiting the spirit of the Adventurer. I wanted to find what Kerouac had felt. What William Least-Heat Moon and

Lewis and Clark and MacKenzie and Remington and Bowie and Evel Knievel and that guy from the Marlboro ads all had felt.

When that ride ended, I slept in the boiler room at my sister's college dorm in Rhode Island. When I began to overstay my welcome, I found I didn't want to leave the worn corduroy of its embrace—that boiler room, America, the journey itself. But this, this was different. Here I made my way across America as an adult, bucking the career path in Education that my father had grown proud of me for.

As I drove across the endless, dusty highway, I thought back to the beginning, when the Question was still just an idea.

Cambridge was in early spring then, green leaves developing into a full canopy. Even though I knew I wanted to ask a single question, it was difficult to find the right wording. I mulled over simple ideas, trying out questions that engaged more than a parlor game. I wanted to see if I could reveal a whole process of thought through a single question. *You have an opportunity to ask everyone a question.* This felt right. *What would you ask?*

I found that subtle changes in the phrasing of my question led to wildly different sorts of answers. *"What question would you ask, if you were going to ask everyone that ever existed one single question?"* This version contained the actual idea, but it floated too rhetorical and too wordy. The responses also tended to be more imaginary:

What was life like before fire?

Is there universal consciousness?

How do we achieve World Peace?

So then I tested out, *"If you could ask everyone on Earth one question, what would it be?"* And suddenly the responses switched to practical, but they stayed grandiose: *Why is there war? What is evil?* I liked the depth, but I didn't need months and months of that. I needed the wording that would allow for interpretation. The project seemed easy enough on paper: just drive around and ask people a question. Not rocket science. But the trick was finding a question that could break free, stay weightless. Keep it simple, but make it soar.

Here's the thing: You can ask everyone you meet the same question. But there is something about the "could" that made it right. *Could* is

Can's imaginary friend, and *If you could* turned out to be a magic trap-door. Suddenly a wide variety of questions arose: serious, silly, deep, funny, and sad. I knew the right version arrived when a friend wrote his response in an e-mail: *"What is the most beautiful experience in your life that isn't related to birth or marriage or death?"* Suddenly the question wasn't determining the answers.

Night drifted in as I rolled into Lander, Wyoming. A long, monoto-nous day of driving had left me exhausted, and I decided to spring for a cheap motel.

The next morning, I got up, still tired, and went for a jog, run-ning for exercise and wherever my feet might take me. I ran through an industrial area and emerged in a low-lying, rough neighborhood, moving through it and on to the town center, big storefront windows sagging with dust. The whole place could've used a restructuring, a face-lift, a caring hand. I jogged around the town square, which hap-pened to be not only the center of city, but the center of the entire state. This Wyoming downtown looked like hundreds of other crum-bling downtown squares across America: a couple blocks of shops, a Carnegie library, and then a wasteland of For Sale and For Lease signs boarding up the rest.

I chatted with the clerk as I checked out, using my uncle's question from back in Kalamazoo:

What's the best part about living here?

He smiled through crooked teeth.

"Nothin'."

CHAPTER 5

THE DESERT

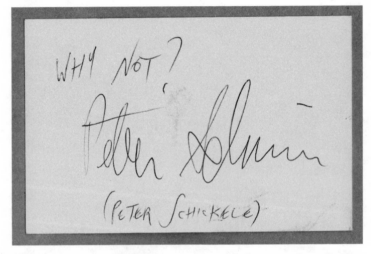

Why not? - Peter Schickele (Composer, musical educator, and parodist, best known for his fictional comedy persona P. D. Q. Bach)

"You are going to Burning Man." Gutierro stated, standing in front of my bike on the walkway as we crossed paths on campus. Gutierro was always a study in casual, flip-flops and shades.

"What the hell is Burning Man?" I asked. The only thing I knew at that point was that it had something to do with hippies and, well, burning a man. Hopefully not alive.

"Here's the website," he said scrawling an address on a loose piece of paper from his pocket. "Just get a ticket, man. Join us." He smiled, letting me know that mystery surrounded this event. "It's a week long, and it's out in the desert. We've got a camp to join, and we'll figure out the rest later."

How did you arrive at this particular place, and why did you come?
(Lois Lowry, Newbery Award-winning
author of *The Giver* and *Number the Stars*)

Back home, I checked out the site and, on a whim, paid the entrance fee for the event.

"Dude, it is going to be off the hook!" he yelled into the phone when I told him I had a ticket.

Gutierro had stuck around Boston for most of the summer. He worked as an instructor for some summer events, but mostly he had just hanging out. Now that fall approached, he was on his way to UC Santa Cruz, to beginning work on his PhD. Burning Man was his final stop before a new round of academia. Now out on the road heading west, he drove exactly one day ahead of me.

"If you don't want to camp tomorrow night, there is a Red Roof Inn that has the cheapest rates I could find. I'll call you back when I find the address and I'll tell you where." His voice sounded Martian through the tinny cell phone speaker. "Start watching when you pass the pink motel on the left two hundred miles from now." Hours later, I would pass the pink motel. He was the *déjà* to my *vu*.

"Tomorrow's going to suck," he said the next day, "after you leave Salt Lake City. Make sure you've got food and gas. It's pretty for a while and then…" His voice cut out. I closed my phone way back in Cheyenne, in a diner surrounded by buildings and with a pancake breakfast in front of me. Then his voice came back. "You're wearing sweatbands, right?" He laughed heartily and cut out again. With the vague warnings and the technology breakdown, I realized I was getting all the trappings of a bad horror movie. Whatever, I wasn't freaked out by it one bit.

OK, a little.

I finished my Waffle House breakfast, took a last slug of coffee, and paid the bill. A small bell jingled as a pushed through the glass door out to my car.

The hotel clerk was wrong: Cheyenne to Laramie is beautiful. The landscape rolls with occasional trees and then builds to carpets of forest, round low hills giving way to mountains in the far distance. Leaving Wyoming, however, everything changes. There is a point, somewhere outside of Rawlings, where everything turns to dust, and driving across the great basin of Utah is a true test. The constant flat, hot air blowing through the window, the unbreakable will of the sun, and the dead-sea riverbed all conspire towards insanity.

What did you learn that the teacher didn't know?

As we made our way through grad school, Gutierro and I shared most of our classes. I'd never met someone as fiercely extroverted, as fearlessly friendly, or as impervious to embarrassment. In one of the first class sessions we had together, the professor asked if there were any final announcements. Gutierro stood up and invited the entire room out for a beachfront barbeque.

"It's casual. Just bring yourself, food if you want. We'll have fun on the beach, and we'll get to know each other."

Before I left Oakland, California, where I'd been living, my sister conferred essential advice. "You don't have any pressed, collared shirts, do you? Get some. You can't just wear whatever you want in a place like that. It's no California." I scrambled in fear to join this enterprise requiring new clothes.

After comparing what my sister told me about the Ivy League with this character standing before me, inviting sixty strangers to his buddy's —not even his own— beach house, I opted for the latter. I was sold on this guy. He wasn't Ivy League. He lived with his heart.

Through Gutierro, I realized that my desire to meet people wasn't bad. I had always felt that extroversion was somehow uncouth, that by always seeking to know and befriend everyone around me I denigrated the relationships I had with others. Gutierro understood that liking many people wasn't an either/or proposition. Of course you want to hang out with everyone. Just talk to them, ask them questions. Everyone has something to teach you. Everyone.

While I didn't know anything about Burning Man, I knew that this unique environment, so saturated with creative people, would be the perfect place to ask The Question, and Gutierro would be the perfect guide.

Would you rather live in a society on the rise or in decline?

As the Ice Age ended and glacial extrusions ground to a halt across the North American shield, a curious event happened: the melted ice caused massive runoff that poured down long troughs in what is modern-day Nevada. These deep-cut reservoirs dried and became the hot, desiccated geography that comprises California's Central Valley, and the baking heat that typifies the state of Nevada.

In the northwest corner of the state, one of these large runoff lake beds is known as the Black Rock Desert, formerly Lake Lahontan—also formerly under five hundred feet of water. Now utterly dry and pancake flat, this massive basin is a recreation area visited by occasional rocket enthusiasts. It is also home of the World Land Speed record, set in 1997.

The surrounding desert is populated year-round by poor local Sioux tribes and supports a post office, convenience store, and bar. Life at the edge of the grid is phenomenally quiet until late August, when a purple cloud arrives, filled with multicolored buses, glow sticks, and body paint. And then, for that one week of the year, the entire Paleolithic tendril becomes a seething mass of fifty-thousand-plus revelers known as Burning Man.

What's your greatest travel adventure?

I was running behind. I'm always running behind, but I needed to catch up to Gutierro and friends. All day, I drove, fretting. I made a quick stop in Fernley, Nevada, for some last items: batteries for my headlamp, more socks, and two ten-gallon water jugs. Lastly, I pulled in at a liquor store for a week's worth of booze. Quick: You like to drink and you are going to Burning Man: *How much is a week's worth of booze?*

I only asked myself this question, but I stood confused, scanning the aisles of alcohol in the local Liquor Barn. How much beer was I going to drink at this place? Should I be bringing alcohol at all? Would there be drugs there? Was I going to lose my mind?

Standing in the aisle, I was jarred back to reality by the buzzing of my cell phone. It was Gutierro, and he started talking before I even finished hello, feeding me details about a meeting place. I hung up, paid, and headed outside to scribble down the notes on an envelope on the hood of my car before I forgot them. Then I hopped back into my car and onto the highway to meet up. At that moment, it felt incredible that we could designate a spot in the world and then meet there at an exact time, plans coming from months earlier, from thousands of miles apart. But we did it. Standing in front of a roadside flea market, Gutierro and two friends waved, all of us smiling. It all seemed so strange, that after driving for weeks, it was possible to meet up at a specific location at the side of an unremarkable road in the middle-of-nowhere Nevada. I bought a cowboy hat for shade, not realizing it would become part of my persona, almost part of my sweaty head itself throughout the journey.

I chased Gutierro across the country, one day behind him since Iowa when we first talked, and now a pickup truck a few miles ahead carried him and two friends to our meeting point. At an agreed-upon roadside vegetable stand, we all got out and hugged.

"Ty, meet Macy and Corey. You guys, this is Ty."

They both smiled warmly at me, already in sun-bleached clothes and bandanas. It was late afternoon and hot.

I don't know why it struck me as so unique; we are all on our trajectories. We bump around and carom off each other incessantly. That a butterfly could flap its wings and cause a tsunami sounds ridiculous, even as a logical chain. And the odds that we as humans whipped around by that same chain is also ridiculous. But we are not butterflies bouncing around. Instead, we meet. Somehow we always meet.

Dude, seriously, what is your problem?

Dozens of miles from the entrance, things began to change; cars started appearing in our lane, and then we began to slow. For hours, I had zoomed along the remote two-lane highway that funneled into the ticket gate, but as we approached, the outgoing left lane remained empty, but the right lane slowly packed in with cars and trailers and bikes, all heading to Burning Man. Ancient mountains rimmed the horizon and framed a singular dust cloud far in the distance, a tumultuous moving fog created, in part, by the endless stream of traffic into the area. My stomach knotted in anticipation. What would The Question be like in this environment?

We introduced ourselves quickly, and Gutierro hopped in my car to lead the way. Plus, he and I had some catching up to do since our last meeting in May. A good friend in the car was nice.

"Are you still doing that question project?"

"Yeah," I said.

"Dude, seriously." He started shaking his head. *"What is your problem?"*

"What do you mean?" I crinkled my brow. I wasn't rattled like back in Michigan. At this point in the project, I was confident. Something unique was happening. But still, it seemed a strange greeting.

"That's my question."

I cocked an eyebrow at him, and he started howling.

"I've been waiting to say that for months."

He stopped laughing, and with a faux serious face, turned to me. "I mean years."

Unlike with Mike, way back in Kalamazoo, this time I smiled.

We had a lot to talk about. For Gutierro, the project was still an idea being tossed around back in Boston, a party conversation one night at a small party at the end of graduate school when we all sat on the floor laughing about our plans. I resolved that evening to determine what question I should ask. We were drinking beer, laughing and saying goodbye for the third or fifth time that week, when one of them looked right at me, head bald, eyes shining, and said, "Why don't you just ask everyone *that?*"

"Ask everyone what?"

"That," he said. "Ask *everyone* what question they would ask *everyone.*"

Gutierro watched me nodding then and was first to put his hand up for a high five.

Now he filled me in on what lay ahead; more than just a gathering in the desert, Burning Man had evolved its own unique culture, and with that came norms and its own unique set of guidelines. Other than the price of admission there was, for example, no money that changed hands. Groups of people formed into camps that pitched tents together and offered some form of service or entertainment to the greater community. But again, no trading. You simply offered services or food as a gift.

"So what will our camp be doing?" I asked him.

"We'll be serving pancakes," he said.

"Like…Magic Pancakes?" I said, still trying to get a handle on the festival.

"Nope, like a plate of boy-am-I-hungover golden and delicious pancakes." Gutierro said. "With syrup on top."

Have you been here before?

As we arrived at the gate, I turned my cell phone off and placed it in the glove box. Gutierro folded his newspaper and slid it under his seat. With those two simple acts, the outside world disappeared. Like pushing off solid land for an Outward Bound expedition, I was again off the grid.

Gutierro pulled a beer from a dusty knapsack, cracked it, and handed it to me. He looked out the window at a gathering dust storm, smiling. "We're so close, man." He cracked and sipped his own warm Pabst Blue Ribbon. We were off the roads and crawling at ten miles per hour toward the entrance gate. Once inside, I'd park the car for a week. With this in mind, I readily accepted the beer. It's fun to drink and drive, if one beer is all you are drinking and the driving is slower than walking. We clinked aluminum as the dust continued to swirl, picking up to a howl as we crept along, snaking towards the entrance. As the dust gathered, the vehicles in front and behind the car began to lose their definition, lines of form fading in and out.

At the gate, greeters in full dust masks and goggles emerged periodically from dusty silhouettes and directed traffic. Anything we could identify quickly disappeared into dust and darkness, sometimes reappearing, sometimes not. More than an hour later, we reached the end— our true destination. No more roads. Our beers empty.

Lighted kiosks appeared through the white-gray haze, beacons in a storm. A woman wearing a green WWII gas mask and a black bodice stepped out of an entrance gate. Her black-gloved hand made circular motions and pointed to my window as she approached my car. I rolled down my window only a couple inches. Dust shading the sunlight. She pulled the mask up to speak but the winds swirled loudly. She pressed her mouth against the window crack. "Have you been here before?" she yelled into the car.

"Nope," I yelled back to be heard.

"Al-right!" she hollered, cowboy-style. Greeters at other kiosks gave us thumbs up.

"Hey, I've got a question for you."

"What's that?"

"If you could ask everyone you met one question, what would you ask?"
She laughed heartily.

"Well, honey, I've got a few of those, and I'm going to ask each of them to you, one right after the other. Ready?" I nodded, unsure of what she meant.

"Do you know where you are camped?"

"Yeah, uh, actually he knows." I thumbed over at Gutierro. He fumbled for the map.

"Do you have enough water?"

"Yes. I brought more than two gallons per day."

"Are you sure?"

"Yes." I pointed back to two light blue ten-gallon water containers in the back.

"Do you know where the emergency station is?"

"Yes." By this time Gutierro had located our campsite on the map, and he raised it to the window with his finger on it. Then he pointed to the emergency station at the very center.

She yelled each question through the window, waiting on each until we nodded. At the end of the list, she yelled to the winds, "I hope that answered your question. We got a newcomer! Welcome!"

She pulled a cord that rang a bell at the top of her gate. The resonating sound left the bell and swirled into the consuming winds, immediately turning to dust. A lonely ring in a gale. Into the blinding dust we drove off, squinting through the windshield, looking for our way to the camp.

To save humanity are you ready to joyfully give your life for peace, justice, and care for all people and nature, knowing we must end market capitalism?

(Patch Adams, American physician, comedian, social activist, clown, and author)

The dust storm subsided soon after we arrived. We set up our tents, met back up with Corey and Macy, and walked over to the center of our camp, feet crunching on large gray-brown flakes of dried seabed. After about thirty yards, we stopped to stand under a faded sign that read "Pancake Playhouse" in multicolored paints.

"So this is it!" I nodded, excited.

"Yep," said Gutierro, smiling back. He waited.

"OK," I said, after a pause, "but what is it?"

"It's Pancake Playhouse, bro." He kept smiling. "We make pancakes. We're going to flip pancakes from the time it's too hot to sleep until it's too hot to eat."

Gutierro's obliqueness made things more mysterious. We said hello to some of our campmates and decided to go out walking. Corey leapt out of his chair to join us.

"There's Center Camp, the true heart of Burning Man," Gutierro said as we walked, motioning to a beacon of light pointing into the sky. The beam split into many swirling lights, making it feel like we were strolling to a movie premiere.

"And there's the Man," pointed out Corey. He grabbed my shoulders, twisting me to look down a line of sight between the tents, off into the distance. "It's made of wood, and we're going to burn him on the last night of the festival."

I could barely make out the Man in the distance, but it turned out it didn't matter. Nothing we did the entire week had any bearing on the quiet wooden effigy.

Gutierro and Corey continued to point out landmarks, but I couldn't find any of them through the ocean of tents and giant stages pounding out electronic music. Eventually, we walked beyond the tents to the large, flat, open lakebed. Tracks crisscrossed the dried dirt, and lights blinked from numerous art cars cruising in the empty blackness. To be able to drive at the festival, you needed a permit. To obtain a permit to drive, you needed to show that your car contributed to the art of the event.

A long passenger van rolled by, sides covered in colorful caterpillar fur. The three of us stopped in our tracks, eyes wide at the sight. It even had antlers.

"Folks took this permitting very seriously, huh?" I asked.

"Yep." Gutierro smiled.

Bucking and swaying, a large pirate ship rolled up beside us, brown sides built on the metal skeleton of an old double-decker bus. Brown cloth insinuated the thick brown planks, and brown paint filled out the illusion. At the helm sat a disaffected DJ, cigarette hanging out of the corner of his mouth as he pushed bright buttons, cueing the electronic beats from an array of small silver boxes. Techno blasted from large speakers. A handful of people disembarked. "Let's jump on here!" I looked at them excitedly.

"There's room for one," growled a sunglassed bouncer at the entrance.

Corey and Gutierro looked at me. "You take it, Ty. We haven't seen each other in a while. We'll catch up." I looked back hesitantly, but excited for adventure.

"Go." They both smiled as I stepped on. "Have fun!"

I climbed aboard the converted school bus and I was on my own.

The ship lurched into motion as I made it up to the top deck. The flat expanse of the playa rolled under my feet the higher I got. The ship traveled miles across the entire expanse in a matter of minutes, a route that would have taken hours on foot. Only, we weren't on a route. Rather than heading to a specific location, the pirate ship steered a course for nowhere in particular. Occasionally we'd stop, but with no clear signal for when, or how. No one seemed to know. No one seemed to care.

The open, upper deck of the ship was full of people, the mood an affected calm. Quite possibly everyone was stoned. We sailed by all kinds of gatherings and parties. After hearing far-off sound systems since the moment I arrived, I got to see it all up close. The scale of the gathering at this height and speed became apparent. Huge. There were thousands upon thousands of people. Night settled in, black and peppered with stars, which made me smile. Here I sat with a group of techno pirates, house music blasting all around. Acrid smoke drifted up through the floorboards. Someone handed me a warm beer. I had no idea where I'd gotten on or where my tent was.

"So, who ye be, matey?" The hippie next to me looked like a Keith Richards Pirate, and one of his drunken eyes crossed lazily. He nodded slowly as he spoke.

"Hi," I introduced myself. "I'm Ty." I stuck out my hand.

"I'm Mark." He grabbed my hand and shook firmly, though his eyes remained gently unfocused.

"What brings you aboard?" he asked inquisitively, dropping the pirate accent completely. With relaxed inhibitions, I decided to just jump in. I told him all about The Question.

"Whoa. Man, now that is deep." He wanted to know the funniest question, the strangest question, my favorite question. Our conversation attracted the attention of the British couple next to us.

The techno music that at first seemed only to surround the boat now engulfed it. Slowly the DJ had turned the music so loud that it filled all the spaces around the speakers, the lock-step techno destroying all conversations. We yelled to each other.

Can after can of warm beer appeared from all corners of the ship, and the silly paradox of Burning Man came alive; a pirate ship traveling on a dry lake bed, its innards filled with liquid. I strained to hear the English couple next to me, because, not only were they quiet and clearly out of their element, they seemed very sober. I tried to engage them in our conversation.

"So," I said, yelling Mark's question, "What are you guys doing here?" She smiled half a wince; he looked sheepish. "I'm a writer," she said.

"And I'm with the BBC," he said.

"The NBC?" I yelled back.

Like anyone has ever called it "The NBC."

"No," he said even more quietly, "the British Broadcasting Service."

I wanted to hear what they had to say. Clearly, their reluctance belied the importance of their jobs. They were interested in The Question, but after they asked, the techno pounded even louder, swallowing their voices in the gale. They didn't appear to be interested in screaming the rest of a conversation, so we both shrugged and smiled and turned away.

His question, *"What is your ultimate goal for happiness?"* stuck with me. It was the first time I'd heard a question repeated. I didn't know how many times I'd heard it in the past, but I became aware in that moment that others had wondered something similar. I wasn't in the business of judging the merit of individual questions, but I couldn't help wondering about this one-sided happiness thing people were seeking. Wasn't happiness the Yin to sadness's inseparable Yang? *"What's your ultimate goal for balance?"* seemed to be more rational, but rational wasn't what people were seeking. Happiness seemed important, and I wanted to follow up, but his wife started to speak, and under the din, I had to lean in close to hear her. *"What helps you get to sleep at night?"*

Now here was a question that needed answering.

If you didn't have to work for a living, what would you do?

Though he declined to offer his own question, Mark watched intently as I talked with the English couple. When they leaned away, back to their own silence, he jumped in, telling me how my interview reminded him of an interaction he'd seen earlier in the day where a microphone became a tool of seduction. After seeing this, he thought my project could also be a great way to pick up chicks. Mark laughed describing it, "This guy was unreal! He would just hold the microphone inches from her lips without moving it back and forth. And for some reason his hand seemed immobile." He imitated, his hand wobbling all over the place. "And it worked! She swooned as she stared into his eyes."

I laughed at the scene he enacted. Then he scrunched up his face, revealing his true feelings. "And I wanted to shove that goddamn mic down his throat!" Here he paused, eyes twinkling, "Though I have to admit it looked genius." He tipped his chin, acknowledging me. "Is it working for you?"

I pulled a comical grimace. "I don't know yet," I said with a shrug, though deep down I feared the answer. "Guess we'll just have to see."

Do you like to party?

The next morning, I awoke sweating in the heat. The twists and turns of my night drew the outline of a body in damp relief on my sheets. I opened my tent fly, gasping for air. Finally, the techno had fallen silent, but its replacement was worse: Hall & Oates, blaring out of rotten speakers, distorted and fuzzy, like my breath and my mind. *She's a man-eater, man-eater, I know.* I tried to get my bearings. I poked my head back out to confirm the hallucination. Gutierro poked his head out of his tent at the same time I did, smiling mischievously.

"I forgot to tell you, we're making pancakes *and* jamming out to soft rock hits of the '80s." This was absurd and perfect in equal measure. Instantly my mood lightened. I laughed like a seventeen-year-old popping whippets. We guzzled some water, brushed our teeth, and walked the fifty yards to the pancake booth, blearily wiping our eyes and yawning.

Under a large white tent—a summer-weight carport—stood the entirety of our camp. Eight grills crackled with sloppy mounds of spreading batter, and camp members hustled around, cheerily flipping pancakes and singing along with Air Supply into the backs of spatulas. Loud music with a hangover is a bad combination. But here it functioned differently; instead of exacerbating the bad, it made me feel free and light.

In grad school, any semblance of a hangover during a productive study session would have been unacceptable. Teaching in the classroom, it meant doom. With parents calling, field trip details to finalize, and the principal wanting all copies of weekly lesson plans, life was busy and demanding well beyond the act of teaching. Here I could just be hungover and flip pancakes. It was, in fact, exactly what I was supposed to be doing. Maybe I had finally found my calling.

I considered contacting my father to get his thoughts on the matter. Ha! I knew exactly how that conversation would go. I did wonder several times during the festival what my father would've thought of Burning Man. He hadn't paid any attention to my proposed route back in Kalamazoo, and I didn't see any value in sharing the joy of riding a bicycle buck naked or that I'd been experimenting with body paint. I was not only off his radar, but off the actual grid itself, and I didn't have to take his perspective into account. I didn't have to feel self-conscious or explain myself to anyone there. Brian would have loved it, and I half expected to bump into his spirit animal, or something equally absurd. I soaked up the freedom, liberated.

The sun beat down hot as I walked to the service end of the tent to see who we were serving. From where I stood, it looked like a couple dozen hungry mouths. Someone jostled me out of the way, "Hey, man, we're busy! You can't stand in the middle right there if you're not flipping pancakes!"

"OK, got it," I said, lazily scratching my chest, "but it doesn't really look that busy." I gestured at the six people being served out front.

"Oh, yeah?" He pointed outward, but still I saw nothing to be alarmed about. "We're one of the biggest food camps at this entire event."

He curved his open hand through the air to indicate the side of the tent, encouraging me to step out the back to look. A line of partiers with paper plates in their hands stretched far down the dirt road, neon clothing and sunburned skin as far as I could see, easily a few hundred Burners shifting from foot to foot, waiting for hot, syrupy pancakes.

Laughing at my own naiveté, I ran back into the tent and put on an apron.

And that became the everyday routine: stay up until too late, sleep until the sun burned too hot, flip pancakes until the midday heat, nap, make a simple dinner over the pancake stoves, and then go out and ask The Question.

By day four, deep in the bowels of Burning Man, I had totally forgotten that there were other concerns going on in the outside world. The confirmation paperwork for the education conference in Texas remained due, for example. This would not have been a problem in the real world, but finding a single first-class stamp bordered on impossible. Might as well ask for a gold brick. Or a shower. I asked around to find the ramshackle, spray-painted boards that formed the Help Desk Central Office. I checked in with my campmates on what I should do to get a stamp.

"They might take a bribe," said one.

"Cover it in syrup," said another.

An hour later, I stood in front of the Help Desk Central Office window with a plate full of warm, syrupy pancakes.

"What are you sending there?" the dusty, dreadlocked woman asked me from behind a square cutout in a plywood wall painted orange with a small wooden shelf nailed to it. She looked straight out of a Charlie Brown cartoon with a short red dress and black and white striped tights. The Post Master Is In.

"Well, this funny thing happened," I said. "I totally forgot that there is this Outside World, and even though I'd like to continue forgetting it, I won't be able to present a paper at a conference if I do."

"OK," she said, "so do you have a question for me?"

"Yes," I said, conflicted; I needed the stamp but wanted to ask The Question, too. I don't know why, but I went with The Question first: *"If you could ask everyone you met just one question, what would you ask?"*

She smiled at me again.

"Here's the obvious answer: *Are you going to hand me those delicious-looking pancakes or what?"*

It was ridiculous, me standing there with a plate full of pancakes, asking her this question out of the blue.

"I can tell that you want some sort of favor from me but are embarrassed to ask. So, I've got to be direct."

I offered them up. "Is there any way I could get a first-class stamp for this letter?"

She took a bite of the pancakes and nodded.

"For pancakes like these? Absolutely!"

I rode away happy, but bigger questions lingered: Why didn't I send the confirmation off earlier? I should have considered it a miracle that I even found the envelope tucked under the front seat of my car in the first place. How could I be so careless with something so important? The responsible voice of my father echoed in my head.

Those concerns would prove to be foreshadowing. But for now, it was enough to just watch this woman smile and reassure me, between bites of fluffy, yellow pancake, that the letter would indeed go out in the next day's mail.

Walking back to my camp, I happened to cross paths with a woman, nude, in full body paint. She wasn't decorated as a sea creature or even anything identifiable. Each limb painted a different color, she almost looked like a doll sewn together. The way her eyes shone white through a dark blue face, she looked alien, otherworldly.

Shirtless in my patchwork skirt and sandals, I got swept up in the energy of the event. Instead of introducing myself I just looked directly into her eyes and asked The Question. She, in return, did not chitchat but walked a few paces and offered a question that was an answer to itself: *"What's the farthest you've been from home?"*

And on she walked.

What makes meaning in your life?

A group lit out from camp later that afternoon to explore, even though the heat of the day was still startling. I thought that would mean actual exploring, but what it actually meant was walking a few hundred yards over to the loudest possible DJ and planting themselves in front of the stage. I didn't find any particular magic to the lock-step House beat, which was my loss; it seemed to pulse at the very core of the whole gathering. When I realized that standing there was the plan in total, I opted to take a stroll and explore the desert. That's when I met the Artic Traveler.

When he asked *"What's the meaning of life?"* I wanted to hear his thoughts, it is a valid question for us all to ponder, but on this journey I found myself consumed with what was the meaning of my own particular life, my own particular purpose. I still needed to find my own question.

What could you do this very moment to feel astounding aliveness?

The next morning, I ventured out after making pancakes and ran into some old friends from a co-op I had lived in years before.

"So good to see you!" Ethan said as we hugged. I agreed. We chatted for a minute about crazy things we had seen or done over the week, and I told him about my project. When I asked Ethan The Question, he thought about it but said, "Hmm, I'll have to get back to you on that one. But you know who would love to answer a question like that? Samuel."

I hadn't seen Ethan for five or six years, and the only Samuel he could've possibly meant was Samuel Burns, a mutual friend from the co-op. Samuel and I were great friends back in the day.

"Samuel Burns is here?!"

Ethan smiled. "He sure is. You can find him at the Pants Camp." By this time, I knew how to get around, and finding Samuel's camp would prove to be easy. I hugged Ethan, and we promised to meet up again.

I parted the canvas flaps of a big tent and looked around inside. Sure enough, there stood Samuel, all six-and-a-half feet of him. A big smile stretched across his face when he saw me.

"I know I shouldn't be surprised to see you here," he said, laughing, "but I am."

I smiled back.

"Welcome, my brother!" Bear hugs. "Are you up for a walk?"

While there is a lot of work that goes into the event, everyone shows up at Burning Man for a week with no schedule. The days are so big and bright and empty that they take on their own meditative rhythm. So, we walked.

Samuel and I sauntered out a fair distance beyond the gathering to a small landing field used as an emergency airstrip for the event. Supposedly Sting had flown in on this strip the day before.

"I've got to go pick up my shirt and pants," Samuel stated drolly, as though he had left them at the dry cleaners. I realized the shorts he wore might have only been boxers. "I'm pretty sure they're over there." He pointed vaguely to the horizon line. We walked.

Sometime later, we reached an orange cyclone fence, the enforced edge of Burning Man. A striped shirt and drawstring pants fluttered flat against the plastic like a hovering, invisible body. Samuel peeled them off the fence and put them on.

Finally, after walking what seemed like miles, we came upon a big blue cargo container. "This is where we stop," Samuel said. I looked at him quizzically.

"For a swim," he said.

It turned out that this cargo container held water. "Box of Rain," it read along the side. A rusty ladder led to the top. Samuel climbed it.

"A couple days ago we were out here and found this box," Samuel said, reaching the top. "We opened this round cover," he began twisting the round portal, "and jumped in."

The cover didn't budge, and Samuel leaned back. "It was the strangest swim I've ever had in my life, a pitch-black box of water with a bright shaft of light piercing down from this hole." He climbed up and sat down on top of the box. "Looks like they sealed it. Darn. It was like swimming in a dream."

The heat was intense, and I would have loved to have swum, in a dream or otherwise.

I climbed up and crossed my legs. Samuel stretched his long legs out across the bright blue container top. The child of Back-to-the-Land folks, Samuel grew up running around a ramshackle northern California yard with a tire swing and all kinds of interesting homebuilt contraptions for moving water and dirt. This led him to engineering and surfing.

Though eight years younger than I, Samuel's insight into life always proved valuable. The son of Sonoma grape-growers, or as he called them, "the last sharecroppers," Samuel exuded an amazing ease, at comfort in his own skin. Smart and thoughtful, evenhanded and adventurous, Samuel did not let life pass him by.

From his Sebastopol beginnings, Samuel had been nurtured to think for himself. By the time our lives crossed at a co-op in Santa Cruz, he was already studying calculus and building silly, impractical machines. We lived together for a year in a big, sunny house on the hill that overlooked the most popular, beautiful beach in Santa Cruz and one of the best beaches in all of California. Samuel built a human-powered blender for the house, and one of my first memories was of him on a converted Exercycle, spray-painted yellow with a blender contraption attached to the front. I couldn't help but notice it out in the backyard.

"Samuel, what the hell is that thing?" I remember asking, confused by the apparatus before me.

"A blender," he replied, looking off in the distance, thinking about alterations. "I'm going to take us off the grid one appliance at a time." His eyes twinkled at the thought.

"Good luck," I said.

Later, after errands, I walked back through the backyard past the new bicycle blender. Chunks of fruit were sprayed on every wall within ten feet. Rivulets of red, sticky juice trickled down the yellow bike frame.

Samuel had in him the big pushes and pulls I had in me—always questioning relationships, unsure of the right path. But where this energy became tight and anxious for me, Samuel seemed able to contain this discord within a comfortable California balance. In the face of big decisions, he remained relaxed. When he felt untethered, he lived unafraid.

One day he rode away from the co-op on a week-long touring adventure, his bright red accordion laced to the back of his bike. Needless to say, an accordion doesn't fit well on a bike, never mind the weight. I'm sure he did it because he wanted to play music each evening at camp, but this also served to tempt the gods of chaos.

I liked that Samuel was an engineer and a surfer. I was an educator and a writer. They were different pushes and different pulls.

Samuel produced an orange and skinned it while listening to The Question. He offered it to me before putting slices into his own mouth. His jaw worked the pulp side to side as he considered his response. Then he spoke. *"What could you do this very moment to feel astounding aliveness?"*

I relished this time with Samuel. I knew he would let The Question resonate through his entire self, where it would continue to ring across his internal landscape. And he would say it just like that, too: "I want to see where it rings across my internal landscape."

When he spoke, he spoke about the orange, about getting up in the morning, he spoke about Right Now. He sat facing the seemingly endless, flat brown basin off in the distance beyond the orange cyclone fence, not even noticing the techno bomb that had detonated, with fifty thousand revelers half-naked and dusty behind him.

Neither of us had an answer for his question. After some time, we got up and walked back to the party. We said goodbyes, and he split to take a nap before the evening. I knew I would see Samuel again, but neither of us made any plans. It might be six more years before that would happen. Or longer. It didn't matter; we would meet up again. Somehow, we always do.

Samuel offered a transcendent presence in my life, and his astounding aliveness was what I sought on the journey. His question didn't need my thoughts; it was an answer to itself.

Would you like to dance?

Blond hair twirling like a dish mop while she danced, the swirling Sophia smiled at me the minute I walked into a bustling techno tent that evening. She wore a long multicolor skirt and glow sticks around her wrists. It wasn't clear if she traveled with our group or if the glow stick fashion sense was just coincidence. I would never find out. About the girl, I mean. Glow sticks were definitely everywhere.

We left the techno tent between DJ sets in search of more dancing and more partying. Sophia quietly became part of the group.

As we walked, we talked. She bumped into me.

"So what brought you to Burning Man?"

"I'm on a road trip, and I thought it would be interesting," I responded.

"A road trip, huh? What are you trying to discover?" Curiosity gleamed in her eyes. Something stirred in me. This wasn't how the interviewing usually felt. In the moment, the aching aloneness that had started developing on the way to Burning Man evaporated.

I felt connected, as if we two were in on a joke. She offered a smile that brightened the more she talked. I smiled back, not sure why. Even if my smile raised it all to Goofball Factor Four I didn't care. I was drawn to her, excited.

"I'm on a big interview project." I quickly explained my journey from Boston and some highlights along the way.

"Oh, that's cool! So, what's the best question you've heard?"

"I can't tell you." I smiled.

"What? Why not? That's not fair!" She grabbed me by the bicep, tossing her hair. Even though she had said earlier that she had ditched her girlfriend for the evening, she made it clear she was flirting. It was fun.

"I can only reveal what others have said after you answer The Question. That's my policy."

She loved the idea of my journey and answered excitedly. We sat down outside the curtained entrance to our next stop, a busy rave tent, to address her thoughts. She crossed her legs and straightened her spine, stretching her head from side to side. People walking by looked down at us quizzically.

"First off, I've been drinking all day."

"Do you want to answer right now? We can do this later," I said, motioning to stand, but she shook her head as if to say that this may be ridiculous, but we would be pushing on.

"I'll make something up on the spot," she said, smiling, "and it will be *awesome*."

Then she closed her eyes. "OK," she said, "I'm going to try and say this somewhat eloquently." She set her hands in her lap and then leaned in, opening her eyes wide. "Are you ready for this?"

I nodded.

"Really ready?"

I nodded again more vigorously.

"What is your favorite sandwich?"

"Wait!" She grabbed at my wrist, laughing. "That's not my actual question." Then she got up and walked me a few dozen yards out to the desert. We stood, looking at the stars. There were reflections of them in her eyes when she said, "Here's my real question: *If you could make any movie, what movie would you make?*"

She smiled a huge, wonderful smile, and we stood, looking at each other. We stayed in this silent reverie for a minute, and then she turned and walked back into the bustling tent to dance, melding with the crowd. And with that, she disappeared.

I looked over the tops of the dancing throng for any clue, but she was gone. Why did she leave? I continued dancing, lost in my own thoughts. Where did she go? Even surrounded by friends, I felt far away, like on the moon. A man in an astronaut suit dancing alone.

How do you defend the hypocrisy in your life?

On the last night of Burning Man, a group of us went out. Corey, Gutierro, myself, and a small gang of others, lightly connected by flipping pancakes. Other camps joined in the stream, emptying out onto the front road dividing the camps from the endless, flat desert. We walked down the Esplanade, a wide boardwalk thronged with people.

Considered prime real estate, the Esplanade featured flashing lights, large colorful dance parties, and fire jugglers. A Vegas Strip with dreadlocks. Even with the lights and all the people, I didn't find it especially inviting. We popped into a few tents and danced for a couple songs, but the techno started to grate. Between the repetitive, electronic kick drum, the heat, and the dust, I readied to move on. I took off my glow stick necklaces and put them on the person dancing next to me. A gift. A salutation.

Corey had heard me ask The Question. "Man, I really want to answer that," he told me one afternoon, "but I need some time."

Now covered in his own glow stick regalia, a thick necklace with multiple bracelets, Corey slowed to walk beside me, a slightly confused look on his face. It was time.

In front of a human gyroscope, he paused, putting his finger to his lips. "I've arrived my question. It's something I truly struggle with." A shirtless man in cutoffs stepped into ski boots at the center of the gyroscope and his arms were strapped to the upper curve. The ride began to spin, and he groaned loudly. A small group around him cheered.

Corey stopped dead, oblivious to the gyroscope and the spectacle and the fact that the others had continued walking. "This question is especially for Americans." Then he started strolling again. A Stanford graduate, he followed in his father's footsteps through law school. Covered in ridiculous-looking glow, this wasn't the lawyer talking. Corey offered me his true question. Now I was receiving a gift.

"My question revolves around this idea: How can you be pro-death penalty and anti-abortion? How can you work for justice all day and then leave in a Rolls Royce? I see it all the time, and it comes up in even small, little things, the interactions between people, the racism, and the sexism, and on and on." As Corey spoke, a mellow, ambient techno began to float in the background, pervading his conversation like a soundtrack. "I'd like to ask everyone this: *How do you defend the hypocrisy in your life?*"

We stayed in proximity, but our group slowly splintered and fragmented over the course of the evening. In the cold, predawn hours we stood yards apart, dancing or talking with strangers or sitting in triads. Tired and ready to head to bed, I decided to sit. Immediately I realized how deeply exhausted I was. I would watch the sun rise over the desert basin, I decided, sleep for a short time, and then leave this place.

As I watched the sun ease into the sky, I walked around the desert, taking last photos of lone sculptures birthing shadows in the dawn light of an immense desert. I had sucked the marrow from the festival. I needed to sleep. And even if I had the energy to stay longer, I had no choice. I'd met so many interesting people in the desert, from the Arctic Traveler to Sophia and reconnecting with Samuel.

When the journey began, I focused completely on how I would enjoy my travels. And now, it seemed, my project became twofold. The journey, what had started out as a series of interviews, was becoming more. A chance to listen. I had made the choice not to respond directly to people's individual questions, but that didn't mean our interactions were only one-sided. On the contrary, each time I encountered a new question, I found myself thrown into reflection. *What's the farthest you've been from home? What principles do you live by? What are you most passionate about?* I'd sit, trying to appear passive, my mind working away on my own answer.

My job wasn't to analyze, but to evince and offer the space to help each question unfold for others.

The sun's rays shone magical, but more still lay ahead, continuing deeper into America, meeting its people. With my final bit of energy, I packed up my tent and looked over the map to find my way to California.

CHAPTER 6

NORTHERN CALIFORNIA

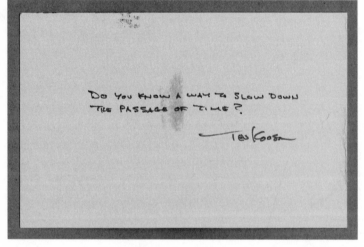

Do you know of a way to slow down the passage of time?
- Ted Kooser (former Poet Laureate of the United States)

My wheels rolled onto solid pavement as I pulled out onto the highway from the festival. I reached into my glove box and turned my phone back on. Though I only glanced down briefly, I had to swerve when I looked up as a car honked and veered around me. Life came rushing in as I merged onto eight lanes and raced downhill toward Reno slots. The return of civilization, an even more jarring experience than arriving at the base after the wilderness of Outward Bound.

My little red car wound through beautiful, steep-carved Tahoe valleys stuffed with green trees. The sun easily beat through the windshield, and I sweated. My goal was Tahoe. There I would unpack and clean all my gear, shake loose a solid layer of desert party sediment, repack, and collect myself. But mostly, I looked forward to sleep.

At the first large, red plastic sign that said "Motel," I pulled in and got a room. There I washed my clothes. Washed the car. Slept in. Watched TV.

Lying on the bed, I realized again that I was alone—totally alone—with no immediate plans. The Burner comrades I left didn't ask where I would go next, and no one in Oakland expected my call on any certain day. The rare times when anyone asked, I deferred to some ambiguous future date, "early in September."

The TV reminded me that nothing changed in my week offline. The world still spun on its same old axis; it was I who had stepped out the side door.

Tahoe was reprieve; for three timeless days, I took a break from the big project. I explored the southern curve of Lake Tahoe by bike, stopping for a whole afternoon to swim in the clear, cool water of Emerald Bay. I swam, lay out and warmed by lakeside, and swam again.

Standing chest-deep, I leaned back in the water, shoulders, then head submerged, letting measured bubbles escape until I floated down backwards through the blue-green layers, sinking. I lay flat on the bottom looking up at the distorted world until I thought my lungs would burst. Being so alone was meditative, time was suspended and I was off anyone's radar. I enjoyed that freedom. But lying there on the bottom, I floated alone, as if in space. Too much freedom. Too far from others. I pushed off the bottom and broke the surface gasping for air.

Back at the motel, I spent the rest of the day emptying the car and vacuuming dust. Floor mats, the glove box, between the seats—any loose remnants were shaken free. I washed and wiped the omnipresent dust out of every edge, line, and crevice, and then carefully put the interior of the car all back together. I hand-washed the outside, careful to buff my hood ornament to a nice shine.

Are you in the Matrix?

A couple years before my journey, I called my friend Ed, a metal sculptor. We both lived in Oakland, though we were friends from growing up in Kalamazoo. Ed left in his early twenties to pursue his love of art and metal. It was spring, and I had a thought out of the blue, so I called him.

"Hey, man, I want to spruce up my car. Would you make me a hood ornament?"

Ed accommodated. He knew I'd be looking for something unique.

"Just come down to the shop. I've got a box of ideas we can look over. See what strikes your fancy." I headed over and when I arrived, Ed pointed to a box of small metalworks. "Help yourself to anything in there," he said. It was a very kind offer, and I perused various strange metal shapes, evaluating each. I rolled a rhinoceros around in my palm, then a replica of the Millennium Falcon. At the bottom, I came upon a figure with two faces, one looking away, one looking forward. *Janus*, I thought. Always peering into the past, always looking out to the future. This god knows the dizziness of being placed in both directions at once. I had much to learn from his perspective. I held him up to the sun, looking for any cracks. Finding none, I nodded. "This is it." I said to Ed.

We walked out to my car, Ed handing me a hammer and metal spike. "OK, man, let's get this thing on there." I've never been a big fan of corporate logos and it felt good to watch him remove the H insignia plate and set spike to hood.

I remembered standing at a punk show at fifteen, an older punk giving me a lecture about how, if you really liked a band, you didn't buy their T-shirt. You cut out stencils, got out the spray paint, and you made it. His heartfelt harangue stuck with me. I loved my car, so I decided to make it mine.

My hand replaced Ed's on the spike. I raised the hammer. Bang! A jagged but round hole appeared when I removed the punch.

From there, we tapped and soldered. When we were done, a four-armed figure appeared to be tromping up the hood of my bright red car. At five inches tall, the size of an action figure, this diminutive statue did not seem powerful. Small dents around his feet from the metal punch gave the impression that he had just landed heavily—from another planet? —and was about to make his way up the hood. Or down the hood to see what lay beyond. As the talisman, he held this trip in his strong arms. He was cast bronze, and with his two faces pointing in opposite directions, he traveled with me, reminding me always to stay in the Now.

At the Tahoe motel, my inbox pinged with a message from an Outward Bound school on the West Coast, shaking me from my reverie. They needed an instructor in South San Francisco for a high school day group in two days. I replied immediately. My restlessness and need for connection were starting to tap me on the shoulder. I needed to go. The next day I would drive to Oakland. The desire for a new adventure hastened my departure from this paradise.

What question would you ask everyone, if you could ask everyone just one question?

"We're here with Andy Wiles," I said, turning on my small recorder and pointing it towards to my old roommate and friend, Carl. I had pulled in to my old house just in time for lunch, but looked up "Greatest Living Mathematicians" before I arrived in Oakland, just to make a connection; Carl was in doctoral studies in Theoretical Math at Berkeley, and Andrew Wiles had recently solved Fermat's Last Theorem, a 350-year-old unsolved math problem. Before we made sandwiches, we sat side-by-side on a small brown two-seater couch that had recently been found sitting beside a dumpster. It fit just right under the window in the nook beyond the counter. Carl smiled at the Wiles reference.

"My friend the famed international mathematical legend." I waved the recorder majestically. "Will you reveal to the world what are you working on at school?" Among all the housemates when we lived together, no one understood what Carl studied, but even his mention of "Topology" seemed impressive, especially when he told me it had nothing to do with maps. He often took professorially long pauses when answering questions, which, combined with the word "Topology" was proof enough for me. The house was only partially inhabited by the folks I had lived with just before I headed east, but even with some new residents, sitting on the couch with Carl still felt like home.

Carl had joined me on the drive to Boston from California a couple years prior. I dropped him off with friends in Fargo, but we spent those days together laughing and driving and talking. Although I had a big, bushy beard and Carl shaved clean, I always felt we had a lot in common; we both loved to compost, ride bikes, and laugh. Carl played out the introvert to my extrovert, but I think sometimes you're drawn to what you aren't. Oh, and—side note—I don't know anything about math. That always intrigued me about Carl—his other world, one almost mystical with numbers. Carl remained notoriously close-mouthed about his research, and I always tried to get him to talk about it. I never wanted to miss out on opportunities to learn some things I would never be able to understand. "What is the hardest problem you've encountered so far in your math work?"

"I don't know," he said. "I would say the problem of focusing on a good problem and getting something done about it."

I laughed. "So the problem of finding the problem is harder than solving a problem?"

"It sounds ridiculous, but right now, yes, that's it, pretty much."

I wished I could've spoken with him about the nuts and bolts of his math questions, but leafing through one of his Topology textbooks, I realized that he thought on a different plane. If not a completely different galaxy. For me to begin to understand him, he would have to lecture me for thirteen or fourteen years, starting with tenth-grade geometry. This, of course, was contingent on the highly improbable assumption that I'd be able to understand tenth-grade geometry. I could picture myself, having sat and listened for fifteen years, with a long, white-flecked beard and tattered clothing: "OK, I think I got it. Mostly."

Carl didn't give me any more to go on, and our conversation slid toward general questions. I decided to ask him mine. He rubbed his chin thoughtfully. "I would try to figure out something to ask that would get people to say what they would do with their time if it was up to them. Something to get people to say what they were really interested in." He squinted and then said, "A question that would do that sort of thing might be: *What question would you ask everyone, if you could ask everyone just one question?*" I raised an eyebrow. Was he messing with me now?

There was no chance to follow up, as just then Barb walked in.

This is not the proper way to get a response to your request.

**(Maya Angelou, author,
poet, civil rights leader)**

Carl and I both lived with Barb when I still resided in Oakland. She was, at times, the smartest person I'd ever encountered. Like Carl-level smart. One day, while I sat on the couch studying vocabulary flashcards for the GRE, Barb walked by. "Flashcards!" she said cheerily. "Hit me." I turned the stack facedown, and she squared off in front of me.

"Enervated," I said, flipping up the first word. Without a second's pause, she gave the precise definition.

"Worn out, tired."

For me, each card required some thinking time, so it took me a second to flip to the next card.

"Acarpous."

"No longer fertile."

"Attenuate."

"To reduce the power of, or, perhaps ... to *enervate*." She smiled, slyly. This went on and on. She nailed each definition, making little jokes, enjoying the experience. After a lifetime of imperfect test-taking and months studying these terms, I got frustrated. *Doesn't she realize how difficult this is?*

And yet, at other times Barb could be strangely disconnected and infuriatingly obtuse. Not dim like dumb, but *off*, like the wires weren't connected. She saw events through a unique and, to me at least, baffling perspective. Often I would find I didn't get her objective, where she was coming from, or why she had made a particular point. She, in turn, would get flustered by my lack of understanding.

It was, come to think of it, almost precisely the same problem I had with my father.

Carl watched Barb while I asked her The Question. She thought for a moment and twirled around to sit on an upside-down white five-gallon bucket. "I would notify everyone of an open-ended call for advice; a request for submissions," she said neatly, then stood, opened the fridge door, and casually looked for something to eat.

I wrinkled my brow. "That's not really a question."

She looked over her shoulder from the fridge and smiled mischievously.

So, I asked again. "I mean, how might you form that as a question?"

She pulled out some pickles and sat back down with a crunch. "It would just look like a newspaper article with, you know, an open-ended request for advice or submissions."

I felt misunderstanding approaching, but I pressed on. "OK, but point is to ask a question. Would you say something like, 'This is a request for advice'?"

Barb crinkled her brow. "It wouldn't say, 'This is a request.'" She threw out a frown that said: *That's just stupid!* "It would probably just look like a newspaper ad requesting submissions or advice in any language in 100–1,000 words. Maybe I don't want a question. Maybe I want an invitation."

I got it. Barb was not going to ask a question. Maybe from her per-spective, asking a question of someone felt too confining, both for the one who asks and the one who answers. Maybe for her, simply by asking a precise, direct question you became constrained to that limited topic.

In this we were not dissimilar. In starting this trip, I couldn't narrow my question down to one simple subject. My quest became a simple search for what people wanted to know, what troubled or confused them. Inverting this process, Barb saw all this from the exact opposite perspective; she wanted to learn what people know, what they might share voluntarily.

If all of this were stone, Barb would build for herself a temple of all the world's knowledge, sturdy and strong.

I, on the other hand, was drawn to the unknowable, the uncomfort-able. I was more interested in how we interpret the truth than in finding truths. I would build a tower, miles high and wobbly, one that terrified all those around it with the threat of collapse. But, oh boy, the views!

"So, Barb: If you could ask everyone you met one question, what would you ask?"

Why did I ask again? I don't know, I just did. She nodded along with the words as I spoke, and without hesitation, she asked, *"What question do you want me to answer?"*

Another housemate, one I had just met, entered the kitchen and started cooking while the three of us talked. She looked over the scene as she turned on a burner and opened a can. "So serious! What the hell are you guys talking about?" she asked, pouring the contents of the can into a little pot. While she stirred, I asked her The Question. She looked up at the ceiling. "Whoa, that's a pretty big question." She continued to stir soup and pursed her lips. "Now I see what the hubbub's all about."

I pulled some cooled water from the fridge and began making a sandwich before she spoke again. She said, "Hmm, I could come up with a question, but really this idea makes me more interested in the questioning process. Like, thinking of it as asking a question rather than getting an answer." This was new to me.

"What's the difference?"

"Well, getting an answer implies you will be getting what you want, and sometimes that's just not how things work. Expecting to get what you want kind of feels like a forceful means of communication. I'd like to give someone the option to not answer, or say anything they'd like without worrying about the lens of The Question."

I'd not heard someone say anything like this before. So far, evincing an answer from the questioned was always the imperative of the asker. Not yet, I realized, had anyone brought up this way of looking at things, that the setup of my question might be restrictive rather than my goal, expansive. My mind opened.

Barb, listening, winked as I bit into my sandwich.

What is working for you today?

I had rolled into town happy, satisfying the need to find some work; only my second day in Oakland, and already I looked forward to early rush-hour traffic on the way to earn money.

The sun shone strong through the walls of my tent next to the compost pile where my old roommates offered a place to sleep. The pile was layered with hay and didn't smell strongly, plus I got to stay near the people I liked. Most importantly, it was free.

In the shower that morning, stark, bright beams of light pounded through the small rectangular window, making me squint while I lathered up.

Out of the shower, clothes on, down the stairs. I put a piece of toast in my mouth as I struggled with a coat sleeve. I walked down the empty sidewalk to my car, birds lightly chirping in the hedges, climbed into my car, closed the door, and turned on the radio. Voices began chattering through the speakers, and the muffler puttered a low hum into the quiet, dewy morning.

As I pulled onto the 880, the too-bright sunlight glanced off the river of metal hoods in a slow-moving sea of Bay Area commuters. The brightness of the early light cut so intensely, I could barely see through the windshield, so I squinted, coffee in hand, hand as a makeshift visor.

The commute was the same as I'd done for years as a teacher. Everyone just trying to get to work. It didn't matter where I'd come from or how I composed my worldview or anything else, really. Being on time was paramount. We jockeyed on these streets to not be late, all the millions of us. I'd joined the Mad Parade once again. I laughed, wondering how many lost travelers like my current self I had driven by over the years in my rush to get to work.

As I pulled up to park, my engine began to emit a loud grinding noise. One of the instructors set down his orange flag used for the border to a big group game and walked over to listen. I winced in reaction to his own wince and shut it off. A second instructor walked over to help. They winced together.

"That didn't sound too good," said Ron, the older of the two. "Why don't you turn that thing on again, and let's hear it one more time?" said the other.

I cranked the engine, and the grinding started up again immediately. I popped the hood, cocked an ear, and listened for a loose part, something broken, something trying to destroy the engine. We all winced together. I shut the hood and let the decisions for next steps continue in the background of my thoughts while I went to work.

The day of team-building activities went well. The students would be in much better shape than my car—that was for sure.

I called friends over lunch to find a good repair shop and drove away from the school and directly to a spot in my neighborhood. Turned out the culprit, a dying alternator, was an easy fix. Luck smiled on me with an appointment open for the very next afternoon.

One day and one thousand dollars later, I was back on the road. Ouch.

As a former public school teacher recently out of one of the most expensive universities on Planet Earth, I was not swimming in money. And the check from my work at Outward Bound in Minnesota, supposed to float me for the rest of the journey, disappeared by half with these repairs. I had to keep justifying in my mind: car trouble is just something that happens, and this, or something worse, could happen at any time. Good thing it happened here and not in the middle of the desert. I wanted to not worry about what might happen and stay on the adventure, whatever form it took. I also wanted to live Nobuo's question from Outward Bound: *"Why is money so important to you?"*

That evening, in my tent next to the compost pile, I lay on my back and thought about the day. It was great to work, and I was lucky to have the money to be able to get my car fixed so quickly. I had my health, the freedom to travel. I was pretty goddamn blessed, actually, and grateful to be able to do this journey at all.

Being back in the East Bay surrounded by great friends was another blessing. It also made me realize how much I had given up when I left. I got to sleep in the backyard of a home I loved so much. Inside, the others slept, half of them old friends, half complete strangers. When Carl and Barb left, so too would my connection to the house. It would just be a place I would drive by decades later and point out, "There's my old house." I wonder how many other people drove by slowly and said the same while we lived there.

What does family mean to you?

It was refreshing, halfway through my journey, to be on the West Coast, back in the Bay Area, back to where I lived before Boston. Back to the place I had lived before any of this, back when I was still a harried, but happy, elementary school teacher. My sister, Jo, lived here and had staked out SF as her territory. I had always felt most comfortable in Oakland, over in the East Bay. We had our separate geographies and yet lived close enough to see each other often.

Jo had come to visit the East Coast while I was studying, and we talked over a project as big as America. She had helped me come up with the idea of the journey in the first place, one afternoon in the spring before I graduated. Now that I was back in the Bay Area, I called her up. We met at her co-op house, situated above a Chinese restaurant in the heart of the Mission District.

We sat in her room, afternoon sunlight streaming through her picture window looking out over her busy neighborhood in the Mission. I had one foot up on the arm of a worn couch. Jo leaned back in a comfortable desk chair she had found in the street. I was excited; here was a chance to bounce my ideas off someone known, someone trusted. I sought guidance. I wanted to better understand why I was so confused and yet compelled to keep going.

When I asked, Jo scrunched her eyebrows, clearly having forgotten The Question. She leaned farther back in her chair, looking at the ceiling. "Wow. I'll be honest, I had forgotten what your project was all about. Last time we talked, you had decided to ask a single question, but I didn't know what you'd decided on. Let's see, I feel like I could come up with some general starter questions, but they would change." I sat, listening.

"OK, I've got it: *If you had a couple of cats and unlimited access to small outfits, what would you dress them in?*" I frowned, anticipating a conversation with more depth.

She paused. "Ty. That was a joke."

I sat, stunned. "That was a joke?"

"Yes. Seriously, c'mon." She smiled widely in response. "If anyone is going to get a really bad joke, it's you."

And then, regaining her composure, she turned serious. "Have I ever told you about Fresh Talk?"

"Nope," I said, shaking my head. "Never heard of it."

"Well, last summer I created a radio show at design school I called Fresh Talk," she said. "I named it after Fresh Air, the interview show on NPR."

"When you're working on projects in design school, you end up spending countless hours sitting at these large drafting tables. Covered in to-go dinner containers and big enough to tuck under for a nap during an all-nighter, these tables become like a second home. One night in the middle of a big project, around midnight I just started going stir crazy.

"On a whim, I asked a friend to be a 'guest on the show.' He agreed, and I walked him over to the middle of this open space and began to interview him. I pretended like I was at the console of an actual radio studio, except in reality everyone was just sitting at drafting desks and there wasn't a piece of electronic equipment in sight.

"To my amazement, everyone stopped what they were doing that night and listened in. They loved it. People asked me about it the next day, 'Are you going to do Fresh Talk again?!'

"It was fun, so I did more. Without fail, whoever I asked would always say, 'Sure!' Then, at 10:57 p.m., I'd usher the interviewee to a table in the center of the room, sit down, and stage-whisper, "Fresh Talk is on in 4-3-2-…Hello and welcome to this episode of Fresh Talk!'"

"And you never recorded any of this?"

"Nope, not a single recording. That was the point. The sound projected well, but only to the students working at their work stations in close proximity. That was it."

I smiled, "That's more pirate than pirate radio."

She smiled back, laughing. "Yep. One day I even walked into a completely different department, and introduced myself to the *director* of that program. She walked through the design space often to get to her office. I was like, 'Hey Harriet, I was wondering if you would be willing to do a short interview and be on my little program called Fresh Talk.'"

I knew Jo had a penchant for the absurd, but it was starting to sink in: this was crazy. I was incredulous. "Are you serious?"

"Dude, totally. And she was like, "Yep. I can give you about 15 minutes."

I was still trying to get a visual on all of this. "So wait, did other students really listen in?"

Jo leaned back in her chair, gearing up for the payoff. "Everyone. They were all just working and listening to Fresh Talk like it was on the radio."

My eyes were wide. "Ok, but back to this director; she didn't think you were crazy?"

Jo fed off my incredulity. "No, you don't understand…she just totally *went for it*. She started out being silly, talking about whether orange or lemon trees are best for landscaping, but I quickly cut out any of that monkey business, asking questions about what it is like to be a woman in her role. She was open and honest and it was a blast."

Jo leaned in, ready to pull things together for me, for my journey. "The truth is, Ty, the reason she and all the other people participated wasn't because of some special power I had, or anything I offered from my radio show."

"Radio-*style* show," I interjected, laughing.

"Yes, radio-style show. No one cared if it was being recorded or not. Everyone jumped at the chance to participate because someone expressed interested in what they had to say. People love to be asked questions. They enjoy being interviewed, even if it's only for the twenty or thirty people sitting around them. This program director? She loved it. After the first interview, when it was clear I was just giving them a forum to talk about their lives and influences in front of a group of interested, listening people, they chomped at the bit. I'm telling you, *everyone* wants to be asked interesting, insightful questions about their life."

It's true, I thought to myself, most people I engaged with The Question were happy to be asked. Many talked at length about their question and how it was formulated, or what it meant to them.

"So Fresh Talk was quite a life lesson, huh?" I said smiling.

"Yeah, but it wasn't just that experience. I used to work as a news researcher for an actual independent radio station in San Francisco, a really small one. It was my job to record the interview and edit it down to sound bites. I'd show up at a specific address with a list of questions and interview whoever was on the docket for that day. At the end of each interview, I'd wrap it up with one last question: *Is there anything else you want me to ask you about?* When I got to that point, the interviewees would seem to sigh a Thank You, relieved to be asked something open-ended."

Jo continued. "I think a lot of people in the world feel unheard and they don't have anyone in their lives who really listen to them. Because the truth is, at work, there is usually only the administrative few who do all the talking and the decision-making."

She offered a new insight: just by asking questions we are engaging people. It doesn't take a background in psychotherapy to understand. Simply by asking a question, we were not only getting people to connect, but to talk about their actual lives. I nodded in agreement.

"Everybody wants to be interviewed and have people hear their unique take on something they care about. And most people don't ever get that."

Yes, I thought to myself, this connection-making with others was exactly the reason I embarked on this project. By talking with Jo, I found myself analyzing my own motivations.

"I'm telling you, everyone wants to talk about their lives, and the answers I've heard so far make me want to ask this question even more. Definitely my question for every person I met would be: *What have you been waiting for someone to ask you?*"

What dessert are you having?

Gutierro and I had split ways after Burning Man, but I knew he would be stopping by San Francisco, so we made sure to plan a get-together with our classmates who had moved to the West coast. He drove over to pick me up. We were all going out to dinner, an invitation that sounded enjoyable and a little intimidating. Other than Gutierro, everyone already had a great job.

"Have you ever intentionally broken something over somebody's head or hit somebody in the nuts with something?" Gutierro leaned in. "That's my new question." The waitress approached our table. "And I think you should ask our server that."

Another round of drinks appeared. We sat, facing each other at a small table in a hip German restaurant in another hip part of town. While the mood stayed light, situationality hung in the air, as in: *What's your situation? Did you negotiate a great salary situation?* My father would've been right in the fray: *How's the benefits situation?* Everyone seemed, already, to have a good job.

Gutierro would leave San Francisco to begin work on his PhD at UC Santa Cruz, and the others discussed their situations. As we sat around a table, all of them excited and nervously discussing recent career conquests. I mostly just listened, hoping I wouldn't have to reveal that eating dinner out was a luxury and—barring any more car repairs—I had just enough gas money to get me back to Boston.

To change the subject, I brought up The Question. They picked at it hungrily before our food arrived, interested in clarifying details and gauging how soft the target.

Do you mean asking people that I've already met?
Yep, everyone.
Everyone in the world?
Yep.
Are the people who respond going to be honest?
That is definitely an assumption in this question.
Let me think about it and get back to you.
OK.
Do you want a really well-thought-out actual question, or do you want me to say something that doesn't mean anything to me?
Up to you.

Who loves you?

After dinner, Gutierro dropped me off at my sisters' place, and I drove back to the East Bay, back to my tent. I lay on my back, thinking over my visit so far—my friends in the house just a short footpath away, my sister, and all the folks I had known when I lived here. Over the five years I had lived in Oakland, I'd developed a real sense of community among friends. In my brief two week return, I was invited on bike rides, invited to dinners, invited to sleep on couches. The gravity of friendship was strong here. Interesting, fun people. People who knew me well. It seemed foolish not to move back. For that brief period, I remembered how great life was.

I wondered on balance if it was worth it, moving to Boston, having ripped myself from this fertile ground of community. And yet, a funny part of me still pushed on, needing to explore more. What I said I didn't love about Oakland—the traffic and insane prices for food and even more outrageous rent—were the reasons I gave whenever anyone asked. But truthfully, the issue was me, always seeking something more to discover. What had pulled me to Oakland, I realized, was the same force that pulled me away.

Why can't human beings learn to love?

Damaris informed my whole understanding of Oakland, of the whole Bay Area. She taught high school History, directly from Howard Zinn's *A People's History of the United States*, and often raised challenging questions of race and class in everyday life, always examining, and seeking, justice. We met online and hit it off immediately. We analyzed privilege and power, went on our own road trips, and shared the joys and frustrations of teaching. It was sweet and light, but carried some gravity; she represented my first Adult Relationship.

Because we were both well out of college, we navigated our way with the other looking for more than companionship. Our courtship raised the idea that this might be The Courtship. Behind our petty disagreements loomed bigger questions; it wasn't just dating, we asked about future children and mortgage payments. Just as often as we affirmed each other, we looked into each other's eyes, as if to ask, "Are you The One?" The stakes, in everything we did, felt awfully high.

"I don't know if we are right for each other. Maybe we should call this thing off," she said one night, three years into the relationship, for the one-hundredth time. "I just don't think I'm the right person for you. You're looking for a cigarette-smoking, hard-drinking woman covered in tattoos. I'm none of those things."

That night, I listened carefully. The next morning, I stopped arguing with her that we should be together. As soon as I conceded defeat, the relationship ended in a blink. It all seemed so easy, *We're just different people*. But it left behind a confusion that has yet to clear.

"Just wanted to drop off these clothes," she said a few days after the breakup.

"Great, thanks," I said, trying to gauge the level of distance we were attempting to maintain. "And I don't want you to forget this," I said, handing her back a T-shirt she loved, and then we each stepped back a pace, silently snapping the cords of connectivity; it was too civil.

The corrosive challenge to our relationship came mostly from her grandmother. Her grandmother got mad at Damaris for jumping from one guy to the next, seeking perfection in her relationships, perfection in love. By contrast, her grandmother's life had its challenges, living with a man who wasn't always a True Love, at times someone she barely even liked, trying to make it work. But her grandmother's point stood strong: Occasionally one might find a match made in heaven, but that was like winning the lottery. Everyone got someone they liked well enough and then just plain worked at it, like a full-time job. From her point of view, marriage wasn't about perfect matchmaking—it was plain hard work.

Our generation expected the opposite. Why would you be with someone who isn't your perfect match? Love was the magic dust that made marriage a fairy tale.

Damaris and I would argue about the best qualities of cars that we didn't own, whether to prioritize recycling or composting, where to shop, where to eat. Instead of making life blissful, we were cataloging each other in Platonic profile: *Are you the form of my one true mate?*

We questioned often if we were truly, deeply in love, and yet, the whole time we also questioned whether that knowledge could ever be certain.

In her grandmother's generation, love meant the basics: living through life with someone else, sharing resources, having children, fighting, and, in some moments, experiencing vulnerability and tenderness. Love, for her, was about a whole family together, not about each of us alone trying to find absolute synonymy.

Damaris and I were individuals, and we stayed individuals, and before too long we split—around the time I went to grad school.

Though I wondered if I would ever find the familial love her grandmother talked about, I still looked in my rearview mirror as I left Oakland for grad school, on the off chance that she too might be fleeing the city at that exact moment. Wishing for certainty or familiarity in the face of more change, I hoped again to see her on the highway as I left. Wanting to not drive on alone, I checked the rearview mirror once more as I left the Bay Area.

CHAPTER 7

SOUTHERN CALIFORNIA

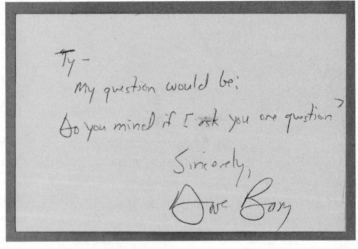

My question would be: Do you mind if I ask you one question?
- Dave Barry (Pulitzer Prize winning American author and humorist)

The trees start to thin out to brush as you leave the South Bay and enter California's Central Valley. The hassles of trying to negotiate the traffic of the heavily populated bay dissipate, and Highway 101 becomes an unbroken ribbon of asphalt traversing a valley miles wide, with soft-edged green and brown mountains on either side. It's much easier on the brain for reflection, and I found myself lost in thought.

At a stop for gas in Gilroy, eighty miles south of San Francisco, I thought of one of my former classmates who had recently started working for the New York City Department of Education. Her name had come up at dinner in San Francisco, so I called, curious to hear about her situation.

Within moments of answering the phone, she had spilled all the details: she worked an important job in the largest school system in the country, excited by the size of both the responsibilities and the salary. She showed interest in my trip, but we were both impressed with this new world she inhabited.

While she talked, I stepped up onto the curb. I padded across it as we talked, heel to toe, like on a balance beam, with one arm straight out and the other with the phone against my ear. With each detail she revealed, I thought about how things could have been different if I'd gone her route after graduation. I was still sore about the car repairs and the state of my finances, and when she guided me room by room through her new Manhattan apartment, the gulf between our realities could not have been wider. In contrast to her solidity, I found myself on an emotional balance beam, in danger of falling off. She, above solid ground being whisked skyward in a career elevator. Me, hoping for some comfort in asking people questions, trying to find just one. Jump-and-the-net-will-appear was my safety net and all I could see in the moment was a distinct lack of netting.

Emily started telling me about the great benefits that came with her new job when a massive engine revved in the parking lot, drowning her out.

"Sorry," I said. "What was that?" I pushed the phone deeper into my ear. "Can you repeat that?"

"Sure," she said. As she spoke, the engine gunned again—a bright red Ferrari in the MacDonald's drive-thru. I stayed on the curb, using all my balance, turning to see a couple in the soft leather bucket seats, tanned and laughing. They didn't look over to me, but I scowled regardless, pointing to my phone.

Emily and I chatted for a few more minutes, but I remained distracted. After I hung up, I walked back to my car. It sat in the open sun, melting in the heat. I opened the door with the bottom edge of my T-shirt to protect my hand from the black plastic door handle. As the door swung open, a stinking sigh of hot clothes and dust billowed out. I climbed in and sat still for a moment, stewing and sweating. Even though Burning Man was a success, deep questions surfaced again, and I regressed. Primitive doubts bubbled to the surface.

Why are you doing this? My father patiently asked, once again, in my ear. Heat lines emanated from the blacktop, hot enough to boil water. Why had I chosen to be here, instead of looking for a job in the professional arena I had toiled so hard to join? I squealed tires out of the lot and lurched back onto the highway.

After a few miles, I let myself calm down, and a new meaning washed over me. Along with the miles and the questions, I was growing in my understanding of the human experience. Through the journey, I had deliberated on my own past and future, forced to confront my shifting feelings about the project as I moved through it. I looked out the window at the mountains that edged the floor of the Central Valley, undulating and green to the horizon, my little red car inching along the floor of the valley. Those mountains stood through rains, erosion, and sun. Just by persisting they were beautiful. I had to keep going. Just keep the car in Drive.

What's more important in life, money or happiness, and what have you chosen?

(John Huston, first American to
ski to the North Pole unsupported)

That night, I wrote this in my journal:

I've started using my credit card for groceries. I'm going to be honest with myself: All but the gas money has run out. I'll have to pay it off when I get a job back home. When I get a job.

I'm not scared about getting a job; I just don't know what I want to do. I'm excited about getting started on writing a book in November and then looking for a job. I think both of those things will be good. I just have to make it home without tapping into any retirement savings. That's my last straw. And it's a small straw.

I'm not flat broke, but when my gas money savings run out, I'm down to zero. Then I've got nothing. I'll get a job pretty soon upon arriving home. Hopefully. I'm going to continue to Trust the Magic. Something cool has to happen. It already is.

In retrospect, my naiveté is hilarious. I spent the next year with growing debt and student loans deferred on piecemeal hand-to-mouth wages. Little did I know that my East Coast job search would take so much effort and so much time that I would eventually just move to Minnesota. Or that my payments and credit card charges would balloon to $7,000 and it would be two years before I could pay it off. I was so cavalier! And yet in the moment, I could only live on hope, traveling in the same threadbare clothes, meeting so many interesting people.

I'd worn the same pants every single day for weeks, since Burning Man. And more often than not, I slept in them. Standard brown Dickies, soft with wear. An easy lifestyle, living in your clothes.

My beard grew big. In only ten weeks, it had blossomed into an unruly mass. As I drove, lost in thought, my fingers would weave and dart through its tufts.

Is a chicken wing light meat or dark meat?

Driving down from Oakland, I stopped in Cambria to have dinner with my cousins. Jack, Celine, Kenny, and Hallie were all at the family party back in Kalamazoo, and here they were, home, on the other side of the country.

The meal was ready when I arrived, so immediately I helped set the table and pour water into juice jar glasses, each a different size. As we began to eat, I asked them if they remembered what questions they had offered back in the spring.

Celine squinted as she tried valiantly to think of her question from before. While she sat lost in thought, Jack started talking. He had taught fourth grade for years, and his thoughts were always around kids. He was a creative and fun teacher and a wonderful, caring father to his own two children.

"It had to be something that throws people off a little, because I like that." He moved some food around on his plate. "It couldn't be, *What's the highlight of your life?*" He paused, in thought. "What about, *What's your favorite memory in life so far?*"

"Bingo!" I said.

We all laughed as I reminded them of Hallie's question, *"If you had a mustache, would you wash it with shampoo or face wash?"*

It had been one of the first truly funny questions, and it reminded me so much of that family party. I was unsure of myself in such a different way back then, like an over-earnest student. I wanted to conduct a textbook interview and always fell short. Through the laughter, Celine hit on her question: *"Is a chicken wing light meat or dark meat?"*

Everyone laughed as she turned the lens to Jack. Still chuckling, Jack said, "Don't look at me; *I* don't know!" Celine scanned the table, nodding.

"See," she said authoritatively, "I'm serious, you guys. That is a good question."

Anyone who ate chicken would have an opinion. It would start everyone talking. I nodded in agreement.

After dinner, we stood in a half circle in the driveway and hugged goodbye. I climbed into my car, rolled down my window to wave, and headed south to Santa Barbara.

At the end of the day, what kind of tired are you?

Now late September, I found myself home, standing on the top rungs of a ladder in the tiny side yard of my mother's house, tucked thick into the upper branches of her fig tree. The large green leaves spread from the tall side-yard fence to her roof. In contrast to my open-ended, open-road adventure, I found solace in the small jungle the fig tree created around my laddered perch. Hundreds and hundreds of figs hung in fat, juicy bunches from these branches, and I spent hours each day, picking and eating the warm, sweet, ripe fruit relentlessly, recklessly. They seemed to multiply overnight.

Each morning I would climb the fig tree. Resting the ladder against the trunk, I'd move upwards through the winding branches, up above the roof. Leaning on the larger branches as I picked, the tree swayed a little with each step. Each day I climbed, and each day I leaned farther off the ladder to reach the laden branches, the tree shaking in disapproval. *This is how I will die*, I thought. *This is the last time I will do this. I might die for figs.* But the next morning I would awake and look out the window. Those plump little fruits would be hanging there, bidding me to come to them. *No, this time I will resist. It's too dangerous.*

Making my way toward the upper branches, I entered my own green, secret world, the roofline of the house beside me. From there, I could see the yard, the neighbor's yard, and then, rolling down the hill, all of Santa Barbara, dispersing in the soft yellow sand of the beach and the white foaming surf.

Small, errant branches stretched into the sky, shoots reaching heavenward, so healthy with tendrils, exploring and growing. I wondered as I picked: If this tree could answer The Question, what would it say?

It would probably ask me why I ate its babies.

I spent too much time in that tree.

I picked figs until my fingers were sore, ate them until my stomach bloated, until my teeth were numb with sweetness. In the early afternoon when I finished, I would go inside, wash them and pack them into a crate, and then turn on the TV. While my mother stayed busy at work, the days of my life were reduced to these simple acts.

Do you feel loved?

Each morning, my mother would get up and go to work, leaving me alone and free to soak in the lazy warmth of the day. Then, promptly at 5:30, she would return home. We'd make dinner together, talk, and walk the dog. A nice routine developed, but short; she'd often be in bed by ten.

Somehow, even though I had a sense that I should be accomplishing something—I drafted a fine To-Do list—I'd managed to do nothing for entire days except pick and pack figs.

On day three, I went a little stir crazy and decided to deep clean the final remnants of Burning Man dust off my car. I went online to address the hundreds of e-mails accumulated, and washed all my gear. In the repacking, I gathered a pile of unworn clothing in a box at the far end of my bedroom. I decided to ship back to Boston anything I hadn't touched since I left. The box filled quickly; I'd been wearing a combination of three or four shirts with those brown Dickies since I'd left.

Life had been pared down to the essentials; out of hundreds of e-mail messages, only a handful truly needed a response. Being home offered its own stasis, a place to stand still, safe from moving, safe from confusion. But reducing my life's sphere to a car and its contents made everything more simple. The sun shone every day in California, and any need could be met with flip-flops.

Looking up my long-lost high school friend Andy was one of the items on my to-do list. It had been years, but Andy turned out to be very easy to find. I just walked into the bar where I last saw him several years earlier, and there he was! Only this time, he stood behind the counter.

He still had a mane of long black hair, and within the first five minutes I found out he still surfed and still raced mountain bikes. The very definition of laid-back southern California ethos, I'd always enjoyed Andy's perspective on life. He visited me once in Kalamazoo, my only Santa Barbara friend that had made the effort. I had fun taking him out in the snow to tromp around and introduced him to the host of Midwest characters that populated my childhood.

As we sat down, Andy grimaced in pain. He'd been having chronic back pain, and he seemed uncomfortable even in the soft restaurant chairs at brunch

"Man," he said, still grimacing, "My lower back is messed up. I went to yoga, and I think I just got too deep into it." He leaned over, wincing. "Even my knees hurt."

Accordingly, Andy had gone to a doctor for this condition and had gotten a "prescription" for the pain. I had no idea why he emphasized that word; people get pills for pain all the time. And then it dawned on me what we were talking about exactly. This wasn't a new condition. And the condition wasn't in his back. He had strained his Party.

I threw my head back, laughing. "You got a prescription for *weed*? Are you kidding me?" It was clear to me right then and there: America was at the dawn of some pretty big changes.

Andy smiled. "Yep, I did." Then he stopped smiling. "And keep it down, will ya?" I realized I had laughed pretty loudly.

What is happiness?

Before we left brunch, I asked Andy The Question. He looked at his fork and then out to the street. It took him only a few seconds to respond, as if he had been waiting for someone to ask him this question: *"What in life would make you happy?"*

He continued, "The answer, obviously, is going to take you your entire life. But, the process of answering this question on a daily or weekly or monthly basis would get you thinking about the things that contribute to making you happy. Ultimately, I think it would make you a much happier person to be around."

I listened but was distracted by the mention of happiness. Everyone in California attempted to achieve happiness and, to the rest of the nation, it appeared to be the very epicenter of the stuff. But from the housing prices to the smog, the rush hours to the droughts, and the very threat of breaking off and sliding into the ocean, California wasn't the idyllic land it so casually projected. And here in Santa Barbara, a kind of moneyed superficiality sat atop that beach culture like an insistent, attention-seeking child.

The idea of happiness had me taking stock of my own emotional state at this point in the journey. Though often confused and traveling with almost nothing, I still felt more like my true self than ever before. Even with the ups and downs of the project, I was still glad to be a part of it. Was I happy? Was happiness a moment-to-moment condition, or a longer-wave state? I had run across these Happiness questions before, and I wanted to understand the idea.

"Sorry, but would you repeat your question?"

"What in life would make you happy?"

The more I considered it, the more lost I became. I couldn't get my head around it. Like the difficulty of trying to define Jazz, or Obscenity; what does happiness really mean? I wanted to know. I wanted Andy to nail the concept behind his question and clarify the deeper meaning. I wanted some answers—dispense with the platitudes already. I knew Andy well enough, and I hoped he wouldn't mind, so I challenged him.

"Do you want to know what *would* make you happy?" I asked. "Something that you don't have now?" I tried my best to stifle irritation; it was one of the only questions that came up regularly, and I just couldn't help but feel it was misguided.

He looked out over the downtown of Santa Barbara. "Obviously, we have limitations in life: you're not going to be able to run a marathon if you have no legs, but you can take whatever faculties you have and put them to the best use to achieve your happiness."

He was doing a pretty good job, but happiness seemed to float in the air, still unexamined. Maybe I was the misguided one. I had a feeling that finding the answer to happiness might explain why I was on this journey and why my relationship with my father was so confusing.

"Can you clarify this: Are you asking what *would* make you happy, like what do you *need* to make you happy? Or are you asking how do you *measure* happiness, or are you asking what do you *utilize* to make you happy?"

Andy looked at me quizzically. "The question I asked is, *What in life would make you happy?* Are you doing things in your life, on a daily basis, to achieve happiness? I guess, in a nutshell, I'm going for that in my question. Is that like, good enough?"

I realized I sounded pushy with his contribution. He hadn't thought about it, and I came in sideways with deeper questions. It bore more analysis, but not from Andy, and not over brunch.

"Yeah, sorry, man. I didn't mean to sound like I'm judging your question. I've just got something on my mind."

He didn't understand my pushing, but it was not his fault. We know the benefits of "being happy." Happy people are more generous, they're better at seeing the big picture, and we just want to be around them. That seems obvious. But how do you develop this elusive thing, happiness? I just couldn't get away from this idea that the generalized happiness people referred to felt like a metaphor for something deeper.

What's your favorite breakfast food?

The sixth night in Santa Barbara was warm, and I was with good friends. As we sat around the kitchen table having a beer after a dinner out, I explained my project to my old friend Hana Jo and her two house-mates: her boyfriend, Matthias, a PhD student in Materials, and Lewis, and MIT-trained LED scientist. When I finished describing the trip, Lewis nodded in thought and then walked into the next room to work on his bike.

Hana Jo leaned in, very curious. "What's the best question you've heard?" As I had told others, I said I wouldn't reveal my thoughts until she offered a question. "Darn," she said, tucking a lock of her short brown hair behind her ear. "OK then, what is the best part and the worst part about this project so far?"

"Interviewing people is actually a lot of fun," I found myself saying without thinking. "You get to hear a million different questions. But as I interview and catalog responses, I've found it's harder than it seems to ask people this one particular question." I paused. "I don't mean the interviewing part, just The Question itself. I want to make sure that people get it, you know? Often I find myself asking it in three or four different ways. And even though I do that, half the time someone wants more clarity, more detail, more parameters."

As I finished, Lewis popped his head back in the room almost on cue, wrench in hand. "Hypothetically, would everyone answer my question?" He looked at me inquisitively.

"Yes," I replied.

"Is this a question you have to ask your entire life?"

"Well, yes, I guess so," I replied.

"Is this a question you have to ask everyone you meet, or is it just for *select* people?"

Here I turned to Hana Jo. "You get the picture."

She looked back at me and said. *"What is your purpose?"*

I thought she was jumping on Lewis's bandwagon, parsing out each rule of the entire question-asking process.

She laughed. "That's my question." A little bell went off in my mind; I wondered if having a purpose is what people seek, not the essence of happiness itself.

Matthias, sitting across from us, leaned back in his chair, extended an index finger, and set it vertical to his lips. "I would ask everyone: *What's your favorite breakfast food?*" He said quietly, very sure of himself.

"Ok, Matthias," I said, going for it, "what's *your* favorite break-fast food?"

"Waffles," he said, breaking into a big grin. "Thank you for asking."

Do you think that you are fat?

The next day, Hana Jo and I hiked the steep and rolling foothills of the Santa Ynez Mountains. Matthias and a group of his friends were there, too, but they had taken off at a startling pace, almost jogging up the side of the mountain.

When we stopped at an outlook, I again asked Hana Jo what she thought about my project. She sat down on a large, flat rock. "I've actually had a similar vision for an art project based on travel, and I made it into a blog called "The Great Blue Yonder." It's the idea that when I first embarked on travels after college everything seemed so far away then, you know, like I was imagining another place I was heading toward. This kind of goes back to my question, *What is your purpose?* I was having this vision of going somewhere, but a cliché kept surfacing, 'Wherever you go, there you are.' The Great Blue Yonder…you're actually never in it. It is always yonder."

We fell silent as hikers often do, light clouds breaking through with sun. Is it a sense of purpose people mean when they talk about happiness? Certainly, some part of happiness seems based on purposefulness, but are they more closely related? Is the search for happiness elusive like yonder?

"A lot of people see the Great Blue Yonder as a metaphor for death, which is the ultimate yonder, although you could argue that madness or insanity is more yonder."

As she continued talking through the idea, I found myself repeating yonderyonderyonder over and over in my head until it sounded meaningless. *Yes, it could be death*, I figured. Is death happiness?

"Another aspect to yonder that is even more alienating," she continued, "is wherever you go, there's always more out there. You can chase it, but you'll never really be…*there*."

I wondered if I would have this problem with happiness. We sat silently for a time, my thoughts running. What is this elusive quality we seek?

She stood up, a sign we should catch up to Matthias and the group. And eventually we did, near the top. Ann, the skinny, super-cute girlfriend of one of the guys, sat on a rock across from us. While everyone was sweaty, Ann, in her short jogging shorts and tight pastel shirt, was somehow not. She seemed the very definition of Southern California ideal. As we snacked, I asked her The Question. She responded immediately.

"Can I say whatever I want?" She smiled at me.

"Of course."

"Do you think you are fat?"

What's the coolest bar in this area?

Dirk leaned back, baseball cap rising gently off his scalp, eyes rolling up, mouth gaping open. He was young, and he was drunk. To keep a tenuous hold on his balance, he put a hand on the bar and splayed his feet out before him. His head lolled forward. I had asked him The Question for fun but was about to walk away when I realized that his mumbling was an attempt to offer a response. He reeked of the thick sweetness of flavored whisky. In that moment, I did not miss being twenty-one.

"OK, I got one," he began, slurring. He raised both hands in devil horns and squished his face like he was in the middle of a guitar solo, *"How do you fuck shit up?"*

Dirk's response notwithstanding, Elsie's Bar turned out to be a great choice for The Question. Being only one hundred miles north of LA, Santa Barbara was largely under the influence of superficiality in the sun-worshipping culture of Southern California and the main street bustled with a mix of tourist shops and high-end boutiques, but Elsie's Bar sat just far enough off the beaten path that only locals knew about it—a refreshing salve from downtown's shallow smiles. Every time I visited my mom, I stopped by. And every time, I made a new friend or had a great conversation with a stranger—a rarity in that town.

Dirk's friend walked up. He mopped at his forehead with the back of his hand and squinted at me, just as wasted. I asked him The Question, then he too chimed in. "Here's my question dude, how about: *We're totally messed up. Are you messed up, too?"*

Laughter erupted, which doubled them over. With hands on wobbly knees, they continued to shake uncontrollably. Though glad for their mirth, I smiled with the knowledge that I didn't have to stick around and party with them.

Funny and strange questions came at me every night I visited Elsie's. I don't know if it was the alcohol or the environment or the characters I met, but questions bounced off the walls, unable to stay still. I could barely get them written down before they disappeared back into the warm night air.

A lively scene thrived at Elsie's, and the questions flew in and out, up and around. Asking and answering came loose and easy.

If you had it in you to write one book, what would that book be about?

Do you believe in infinity?

What kind of drugs did you do before you were twenty?

Do you appreciate life?

What's your angle?

What do you really think of me?

How many people do you think that the person next to you has slept with?

What is one thing that you love?

If you died and were born again as one of your friends, which friend would it be and why?

What's your favorite restraint?

Do you want to see me pee off a goalpost?

What makes you laugh?

What are the ways in which systems of binary discernment—up/down, good/evil, man/woman, etc.—impact your life, and how do you deal with it personally?

Did you forget to bring the hang glider?

Can I have a moment to think?

What would you like to talk about?

The questions at Elsie's often turned into conversations. Sometimes it was hilarious nonsense, and then a group of bar drunks would make me briefly question everything. Take these two guys, for example:

Guy #1: *What is your truth?*

Guy #2: "I don't know if there are any truths, man. I mean, yeah, the whole issue of truth is pretty controversial."

Guy #1: "Well, why would we ask questions simply because we don't have a truth? Do you know what I mean?"

Guy #2 (with a wry smile): "But that doesn't imply that there is a singular truth."

Guy #1: "But if there isn't truth, an endpoint or something, then how do we know…?"

Guy #2: "It doesn't imply we don't know whether there is a truth or not. We don't know that there is no truth. It only implies that we have no idea."

A guy sitting a couple bar stools down leaned in with his own retort. "The Truth could be multiple truths."

Yet another friend who overheard chimed in. "There is only one truth. The answer is 42."

Everyone toasted to *The Hitchhiker's Guide to the Galaxy.*

Don't Panic.

Are you about ready to go home?

A lone, clean-cut, and sober member of this chatty group came back from circulating through the bar. His name was Jorge, the designated driver of the group. Someone asked him The Question. Jorge smiled weakly as his light blue Puma tracksuit hung tiredly, itself ready to leave these imbeciles and go home to rest. He kept his eyes on his group. *"Are you all about ready to go home?"*

Too caught up ruminating on God and Truth, no one listened. He looked at me plaintively and sighed, *"Why did you go and ask them questions?"*

The Question discussions at Elsie's Bar grew increasingly absurd the more evenings I spent there. I started seeing repeat customers. I waved to the bartender when I walked in. I recorded dozens of questions.

And I had fun with it. If someone took too long thinking, I gave them a countdown: five, four, three, two, one, comically pulling each finger down as I counted. Other times I whistled the *Jeopardy!* theme. In any other context, it would've been rude, but in my frequent visits I was becoming known, and folks were eager to participate. Many of the questions captured on my recorder open with peals of laughter.

Often the conversations were drunk-crazy. Listening back to the tape this intro popped out: "I'm here with Rick Springfield, the singer/songwriter of the 1984 hit single, 'Jessie's Girl.' What's your question?"

"What would you do about overpopulation?"

As I readied to leave one night I wondered: *Am I truly looking for an answer to my question, or am I only interested in how people answer it?* I didn't have time to deeply consider. The last person I asked offered this as I walked out the door:

What are your feelings about tomato juice?

What criteria do you use to differentiate between right and wrong?

Dylan's worn brown glasses sat crookedly on his face, the left stem sitting a solid inch above his ear. With his glasses askew like this, he looked loopy. Silly. But with his big smile, it was a good kind of crazy. We were out together, riding bikes through town from party to party, two pleasures that we both enjoyed. Dylan spoke his first question, *"What contributes to your quality of life?"* early in the night, but now, at the end of the evening after we'd gotten split up, he returned. He wanted to amend his previous question. I didn't know what he had in store.

A friend of my older sister, Dylan had moved down to Santa Barbara from Seattle and kind of just showed up in my life. I had heard about him months before we met. He had come bumbling down the coast and landed on the floor of my mom's house, looking for work.

"He's really cool," my sister affirmed. "Here's his number." She told me this over the holidays one year in Michigan, as she scribbled out his number on the back of a card. "You guys are going to hit it off. Trust me. He likes bikes like you like bikes. And he likes beer…like you like beer." She nodded, confirming a truth in her mind, "He reminds me a lot of you."

My older sister had never said anything like this before, so on my next visit, I called him. The first time, we met up at an Irish pub in downtown Santa Barbara. We talked and laughed and made friends with all the people around us. We rode for miles and miles that night, popping in for a drink and then enjoying the whirr and hum of warm bike tires on nighttime streets. From that night on, I called Dylan every time I returned to Santa Barbara, and every time we had fun. His laughter was infectious, and we joked so easily. It was like discovering a long-lost sibling.

On this new journey, I met up with Dylan at an Afterburner party, a post-Burning Man gathering of "modern-primitive" artists at a loft space in the warehouse district. Neither Dylan nor I recognized anyone there until Katja saw me and came over. She was much younger, a German transplant who worked with my mom at the university.

"Ty!" she said, smiling. "Good to see you!"

Katja was petite, with brown hair hanging down to her chin, teeth angling in her mouth in an attractive but distinctively European arrangement. Bouncing and dancing as she spoke, something seemed odd with her; she had not been excited to see me earlier in the day when I visited the office. Perhaps one clue rested in her huge, dilated pupils.

She waved to someone across the room right after we bear-hugged hello. I knew I would lose her to the sea of people any second, so I decided out of the blue to ask her The Question. I didn't know what to expect. Dylan looked away to avoid embarrassment. Katja stumbled a little and leaned in. She crinkled her eyebrows and said, "I would ask this: *What criteria do you use to differentiate between right and wrong?*"

When she leaned back up, she said, "It was great to see you! I'm going DANCING!" and was off. She stated her question quickly, but it continued to resonate with me as she walked away. Just like my childhood friend Pete's question in Kalamazoo back at the beginning of my journey, it was a big question. *What is something that you collect?* Without being direct, it had that magical quality of revealing much about the person who answered. It didn't pose a visceral challenge like, *Who are you?* But it seemed to arrive at the same ends. Without saying this aloud, this is the question we want answered by every person we meet, of every group we participate in: *Does your framework for Right and Wrong match mine?* In some profoundly elemental way, it provides a pathway to another question: *Can I trust you?* Oddly, this question of trust is essential, but only ever answered through behaviors rather than explicitly. Trust can always be broken, and often is; marriages explode, friends become enemies, and money disappears. I couldn't help but wonder what the world would be like if our decision-making process or the criteria we use were more direct, or somehow made visible.

What's your favorite mistake?

Not long after Katja whirled away, Dylan and I left, on to another adventure. As we walked out of the party, Dylan guffawed. "What was the deal with that German girl?" he asked. We both laughed. Two steps later, he stopped me with his arm extended, palm on my chest. We had approached a formidable-looking roadie, a stern-looking bro both tall and wide, loading soundboard equipment into a van. "Oh, man, you got to ask this dude your question." Dylan smiled.

The way he stood right next to the roadie, I figured they were friends, so I did.

"Hey, man, I'm Ty," I said.

"Axel," he said, continuing to load gear, turning away from my outstretched hand.

"Hello, Axel. I'm interviewing people around the United States with one question. Can I ask it to you?"

Axel continued loading. "Sure," he said, talking to the back of an amplifier. I asked The Question. He paused. Dylan and I stood, waiting. Did I accidentally say the wrong thing? Was he mad?

"Look." Following his own command, Axel turned to stand there staring at me. "Suppose that you were not a slave. Suppose that all the limitations, all the controls, all the fears, drawbacks, and impossibilities that you believe constrain your choices in your life, were like a Vietnam vet's phantom limb, the limb through which he feels tingles that aren't there, just like your chains that no longer exist. There was a time when we bent before kings and emperors, now we kneel only to the Truth. Suppose that this is not a supposition and this is true: What are you going to do about it? *If you could do anything, what would it be?*"

The hulking roadie folded his arms over his chest, smiling archly. Dylan let out an exaggerated sigh, and I stood, eyes wide. In one strange, rambling question, this anonymous roadie seemed to be speaking directly to my deepest thoughts.

I stood, slightly dazed. Then, looking down at my recorder and noticed something amiss. There were no red lights blinking. I hadn't even turned it on.

When I played back this recording, months later, the actual tape starts with howls of laughter, the sound of Dylan jumping around in the street yelling "No, no, no! Dude! You didn't get that? Are you kidding me?"

I apologized profusely, standing stock still, reddening. "Axel, oh man, I'm sorry." I looked to Dylan but all he gave me in return was a huge grin and did a little shrug of his shoulders. But he also stood a comfortable seven feet away, outside swinging distance. This dude, I learned later, was a complete and total stranger to us both. Beet red, I asked Axel to recap. "My recorder was off. Would you mind…doing that again?" I smiled meekly. "Please?"

Pausing only to take a breath, Axel once again launched into his question, slowly repeating it verbatim. With the pauses and enunciation, it stood at almost one minute long, easily the longest question of the entire trip.

What contributes to your quality of life?

From there, Dylan and I rode across Santa Barbara to Elsie's, talking and laughing the whole way. When we arrived, we got a round of beers, and then I asked The Question to Dylan and his friend, Shaun. "Now it's your turn," I said, looking at Dylan, rubbing my hands together. He had heard several great questions.

Dylan put two fingers to his chin, a mimic of thoughtfulness. "Here's what I want to hear people reflect on: *What contributes to your quality of life?* That's what really sticks with me." He looked outward, as if speaking to someone at the next seat over, someone we couldn't see. "I mean, what kind of experiences, what kinds of things are important to your quality of life? That's something I really want to know. There's a lot to learn from in that."

I did know. Here I was, driving around the United States—no, circumnavigating the United States—in a fourteen-year-old Honda Civic, compiling question after interesting question. Dylan shot to the core of my own journey. What is important to you? What do you *need*? What does anybody need? Shelter. Love. Religion. Something to gamble on.

Later, on long stretches alone, I'd ask myself this question repeatedly. I would dig into a milk crate I brought for my iPod, cell phone, battery charger, and all their cords and chargers, and I'd ask myself, *Is this contributing to my quality of life?* Would everything change if I just pulled over, set the entire crate at the side of the road, and drove off? Would anything change?

If you could change one thing in your life, what would it be?

After discussing all the questions of the evening so far, we drifted around the bar. I played pool, and Dylan disappeared to the sit-down *Ms. Pac-Man* game.

An hour or so later, he reappeared next to me as I chatted with a pool player. He tapped my shoulder lightly then leaned in. "Excuse me." He stuck his finger up, as if to make it clear he had a point. "I have an addendum that will clarify my previous question." His glasses were still askew, and now he was comically buzzed.

I put my hand up to the pool player. "Hold on, man." I said, fumbling in my bag to get out my recorder. Dylan waited patiently as I got it set up and handed it to him.

"Is this thing on?" he said, tapping the top of the mic. He winked at me, and I nodded silently as he then took the recorder and, dropping his thoughtful façade, yelled like a speedway announcer on full tilt: "*Are you ready to get your ass kicked at* Ms. Pac-Man?"

I put a bill in the quarter machine, then stacked quarters on the table. And we played. And played. It didn't matter who won or lost; we just filled the air with curses and challenges. It was moments like this that sat as gems over the too-long stretches of dry, hot driving. To laugh on a warm night across a cocktail version of *Ms. Pac-Man* with Dylan felt like freedom. I wanted to do it forever. We pressed fresh quarters into the slot and took deep swigs of beer and laughed and laughed.

And then, out of the blue, a bell rang. Closing time. Bright lights came up, and we were ushered out in a herd. Bar closed. Momentarily stunned, Dylan and I walked outside and stood by our bikes. Dylan looked at me, a crooked smile still plastered on his face.

"And so, we RIDE!" he said, his hand theatrically inviting the road before us. We donned helmets, clicking the straps simultaneously, unlocked our locks, and rode the miles north toward our respective homes. Back on the bikes, shoulder to shoulder, we talked in the warm summer evening. As we approached his street, Dylan began to pedal slower.

"Well, this is it, my friend," he said, turning right.

"Happy trails to you," I sang, too loudly down the empty street, "Until we meeeeeeet aaaaaaagain!" stretching out the end of the song in a comic operatic vibrato, my voice full of beery emotion, to his bobbing brown helmet as we separated.

"See you again, Dylan!" I yelled after his diminishing form.

"Goodbye, Ty!" His disembodied voice, now small, bounced through the dark trees and throughout the light, nighttime air.

Turns out, I was wrong. When he peeled off to a hard right toward his home on Mission Street, that was the last time I would ever see him. The very next year, trekking in the Sierras to backcountry ski, Dylan would be crushed to death in an avalanche.

What's one thing you regret?

My mother was sad to see me go. She was a crier. She cried at the ends of vacations, at the ends of plays, sometimes even at the end of a good meal. She'd been known to muster up a cry in the middle of a good movie just anticipating the sentiments she'd feel at the end. I felt guilty for causing this sadness, watching her cycle through a predictable series of emotions every time I visited, and this stage—leaving—was always the hardest. I tried to ameliorate, letting her know beforehand I would be visiting for a solid two weeks, and then, to soften things, I stayed even longer. Still, my departure seemed spontaneous and felt surprising. The guilt of leaving hurt in a strange way, like a joke punch to the stomach that comes in a little too hard.

It took me a few hours to pack, dividing my belongings into that which would continue on the road and that which would be sent back to my co-op in a brown cardboard box. My already lightened load from Burning Man donations just got lighter, the back of my car more comfortable. By the time I left Santa Barbara, I had enough room in the back for my bike.

I said goodbye to my mother at the door to the house. "Ok, honey, go get 'em!" she said, smiling through tears. It made me cry, too. I loved my stretch in Santa Barbara, but it was time for me to go.

I settled into my seat, adjusted mirrors, and turned the ignition key for takeoff.

What's your worst nightmare?

On Highway 134 through LA, I realized by merging east now I headed back. I'd come down the coast and continued heading southwest. The arc was now pulling me back to Boston.

Leaving coastal California and heading straight inland meant going from Hot to Blazing Hot. As I drove into the desert, my engine began to roil. I watched the temperature needle climb, knowing only one fix. I tried driving more slowly, taking short rest breaks, but there was no other option than to roll down the windows and turn on the heat.

I tried to convince myself it was winter as I slid the temperature guide and turned the fan to high. I imagined a cold winter night, my fingers going numb at the end of my gloves. *Brr! Better crank it up!* The hot, dry air made me cough. I remembered my cousin Jack describing an abbreviated cross-country drive he took with his son. They had to cut their journey short because the air conditioning broke down in their rental car. Zipping by dozens of well-known American landmarks, they high-tailed it across the country to get home. I laughed ruefully, sweating into Barstow, the needle edging into the red. Air conditioning?

My little Honda had AC installed, but if I turned it on, the engine would immediately overheat and probably explode. To get the temperature down, I had to invite what I was resisting—invite it in all the way.

CHAPTER 8

THE SOUTHWEST

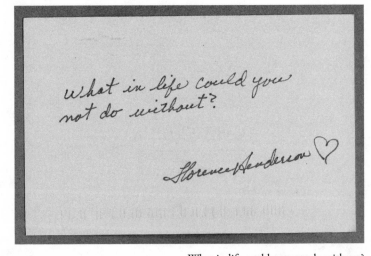

What in life could you not do without?
- Florence Henderson (Actress and singer, best known as Carol Brady on the
ABC sitcom *The Brady Bunch*)

"No car has ever had such obsequious treatment as did Roc as we moved slowly on. Every irregularity in the road hurt me clear through. We crawled along at no more than five miles an hour."

—Steinbeck, *Travels with Charley*

F ortunately, I hadn't read *Travels with Charley* before this trip. I hadn't, in fact, read anything in preparation, which, in its own way, ended up being a good move. I didn't have to measure myself against any metric, especially one as storied as Steinbeck's. Sometimes when traveling, it is good to have physical signposts to measure progress. A cairn here, a mile marker there. But my path remained tenuous, constructed of ideas, unfolding as I traveled. If there was a path, it certainly wasn't apparent to me.

I drove out to a remote plot of undeveloped land to visit some instructor friends from Outward Bound. They owned a few acres of land they used as an experiment to live directly from the earth. Dotted with blue rain barrels to catch water and with shelters made of found materials, they dubbed it "The Land."

Little did I know, as I drove down the rough-rutted road to get to Lucas and Shara's place in remote Northern Arizona, that here my wish to live off the beaten track would be tested.

What does The Land mean to you?

Dusk began to settle when I pulled up to the road that led into The Land, a red dirt line snaking from the highway and disappearing into the horizon, some seventy miles north of Prescott, Arizona.

It was here at the eight-mile entrance road that I started to come to terms with the prospect of no electrical power for the next couple weeks. While living at my mom's, I had been habituated back to the world of electronic devices. How hard would it be to walk away from the reassuring green lights of Full Charge? I wanted to get rid of this stuff anyway. There was a condition, though, worse than Low Battery; being remote also meant having no beer.

I had to make a choice: if I turned back to get beer, my drive on the undeveloped road would be in complete darkness. And all I had to go on for directions was a note scrawled on smudged paper.

What the hell, dark would come soon enough anyway, so I eased off the brake at the snaking red road, pulled a U-turn, and gunned it onto the highway. I checked the map and split north on what looked like a frontage road, but turned out to be an old section of Route 66.

"Seligman, Arizona," the map read, but as I pulled up, fifteen minutes later, there was no town to speak of. A few dilapidated buildings: a cluttered junk shop that sold Route 66 memorabilia, a bar, a motel, and a faintly lit gas station. Pale green paint bleached on tired wood, the gas station also looked closed, but I scanned the windows and saw the baseball cap of a clerk. I popped in, grabbed a couple cases of cheap beer, and paid. The attendant didn't speak but acknowledged the transaction with a slow nod.

Outside, I inserted the gas nozzle and leaned casually against the car. I looked around, the promise of The Land still on my mind. Antiques and roadside kitsch lined the shelves of the shop across the street. In the big front window a big "Route 66" sign caught my eye, stirring something in the deep recesses of my memory.

I knew that sign! I laughed, realizing in a flash that I'd stood at this very dot on the map years ago on another road trip. Back when I was in love.

Damaris and I had stood there, making funny faces, taking photos, and laughing at the fun-house caricatures of ourselves in the reflection of that storefront glass. We were so goofy.

It was bittersweet, standing there, recollecting the smile of a girl-friend on a great adventure. Now alone, I stood silhouetted by the strange yellow gas station fluorescent lights. Not sure what to do with the memory. The gas pump clicked, the tank full.

Pulled quickly from my thoughts, I replaced the handle, screwed the cap on the tank, and drove away. That spring break was so filled with joy; we were certain of our feelings for each other, certain that we'd enjoy the adventures of the road. There, for that brief week together there were no questions.

Almost an hour later, the car topped off with gas and full of beer, I returned to the long entrance to The Land, now pitch dark. My soft yellow lights burrowed not-far-enough into the inky dark, carving only a small halo of light. The road appeared littered with baseball- and bread loaf-sized rocks and long stretches of washboard ripples. The frame shuddered as I sped down the path. Stones pinged off metal. I gripped the wheel. Not how I envisioned my grand entrance to The Land.

This is four-wheeling, I thought to myself, grimacing with the reality that my old Honda Civic was an indispensable piece of luggage carrying myself and most of my material life. I couldn't afford to lose any of these parts, including things like the oil pan. The oil definitely needed to stay in the engine. I slowed down. Rocks continued to bounce and scrape at the underbelly, and I winced as the car crawled over washed-out patches of sand and debris.

Modest Mouse's album *The Lonesome Crowded West* played on the stereo, and I sat tense and anxious. The sad sing-talking lyrics about hanging-it-all-up-because-you're-not-making-any-sense fit perfectly into this drive.

Specters of trees floated, huddling and lost at the periphery of car light as I left the main road and entered an even smaller side road into the canyon. I drove on, finding no indicators, seeing no signposts.

No rain barrels appeared. Why didn't I leave earlier? According to my odometer, I'd gone far beyond the eight miles Lucas estimated and had not seen the entrance. The increasingly steep walls of the surrounding canyon made the air feel close. I drove into a cave, down a well, through time into another era. If I had a mechanical problem, I was stuck, out of cell phone range, far from help. Where were those blue water barrels? Where was that party?

Even as I grew increasingly tense with the mystery of The Land, my hunger grew as well. It had been a couple hours since I walked by the packaged snacks at that gas station and many more hours than that since I'd left Santa Barbara. I looked over at the seat next to me. There sat the grocery bags full of food. I smiled at my mom's care. I certainly wouldn't starve to death. Much more worrying than hunger was the entrance to the property I had just passed. A military helmet sat perched on a spray-painted sign that said "No Trespassing!!! Do Not Enter Under Penalty of Death." Large dogs barked in the distance. If chased, my only hope was to grab a grocery bag and start chucking food in one direction while I sprinted in the other.

Finally, I pulled over, frustrated. I was supposed to be at a party filled with interesting hippies asking The Question, not lost on a strange dirt road who-knows-where.

I cut the engine, reached into one of the grocery bags, deciding to eat before making any other decisions. Inside were several Ziplocs. The first bag held a roll of French crepes. Next came a bag brimming with fresh fruit. And then a smaller one with powdered sugar. I shook my head in disbelief at two lemon wedges in their own mini Tupperware container. If the dogs got me, at least I'd spend my last night eating a gourmet picnic. I filled a crepe with fresh fruit and squeezed a lemon wedge over lightly dusted powdered sugar, raising both pinkies on the first bite. I laughed as I chewed through a couple crepes, feeling deep gratitude for my mother's thoughtfulness.

Satiated, I decided to turn back, give it all one more pass, slowly and carefully scouting the right side of the valley for any sign.

Twenty minutes later, through my soft yellow beams, off to the left, a rope pulled a thin black line connecting two huge blue rain barrels that sat beneath trees, at an angle hidden from drivers entering the canyon. In the center of that rope hung a white paper. I'd found the entrance.

In the beams, I walked up and read the note. Everything silent. Dark.

"Sassypants!" the sign yelled. "Welcome to The Land! We're looking forward to seeing you. We're celebrating a birthday in town, so head on into Prescott!"

What do you treasure and why do you treasure it?

I sighed in relief. I had found it. I turned back around once again, braved the long, rutted, and rocky road, and headed down the highway past the liquor store and on into Prescott.

The endorphins that had been stored in the drive through the canyon were all released upon first sight of Lucas and Shara. They were deeply tanned from the sun and work, and their hugs were strong and smelled of the earth. We met right downtown, across from the courthouse at Matt's Saloon. The lighting was low, but the exuberance was on high, another round of big bear hugs.

"We're so glad you're here," Shara said, looking me in the eye, holding me by both shoulders.

"Yeah, great to see you, man." Lucas smiled.

Their smiles made me forget about the worry and I basked in their warmth.

How do others see you?

The next day in the sunlight, we returned to The Land. Another visitor joined us. His name was Malcolm, and he was a strong-looking rock climber in his mid-twenties. He wore a yellow and brown baseball cap featuring the icon of Bell's, my favorite brewery in Kalamazoo. He was an orientation leader at Prescott College, the closest liberal arts school, in Prescott, the closest real city.

"I like your hat," I said to him as he walked up and we shook hands.

"Thanks," he said back.

"What do you know about Kalamazoo?" I asked, releasing his handshake to point at the brim.

"A lot." He smiled. "I'm from there."

"Me, too," I said, sitting next to him on a log. After a few quick questions, we came to the realization that his older brother and my sister, Jo, were friends in high school.

"Yes, there is magic on The Land." Lucas smiled when we told him of the connection.

That night we made a fire, and Malcolm was excited to dig in to The Question. "*How do others view you?*" he said after some reflection. "I want to know everyone's thoughts on that. It seems to speak as much about the individual's mental state as their perception of others' views of them. I follow up with a second question to flesh their answer out: *Is your self-assessment accurate?*"

I liked Malcolm's method. It reminded me of Pete back at the beginning of my journey saying, "*What is something you collect?*" In some ways, he asked for people to talk about themselves, but not in a pointed way. A few of these questions came up, offering a side-door entrance to the self.

"I have another one," Malcolm said. "It's basically the same idea, but it might be more fun. I ask the students I work with: Describe yourself as an object or animal. It can be a mountain lion, for example, or a hawk, or even a half-eaten pint of Ben and Jerry's." He worked the coals with a stick. "Often the students find some humor in their response, but this question is not the one I am truly hoping to hear an answer to."

This intrigued me. "You're asking a question with the hope of hearing the answer to a different question?"

"Yes, if I ask it right, they are responding with the answer to the question, *What is your essence?*"

Shara, Lucas, and I continued around the circle, answering Malcolm's second question, and we talked and laughed around the fire until late that evening.

"I want to ask you guys something," Lucas said at the end of the night, scanning the faces in the circle. We had been goofing around, so I readied myself for a good joke.

"I want to ask everybody about The Land."

The fire smoldered and popped.

"What is The Land to you?"

"Me?" I couldn't see where he looked in the dark.

"Yep."

I smiled broadly. "OK, The Land is a place where no one ever swears. There is ice cream and unicycles…and enough mustard for everyone." I spread my arms in a gesture of expansiveness. I was in a goofy mood.

Ignoring me, Malcolm leaned in to follow up, his arms wrapped around his knees and glowing in the firelight. "Are you asking specifically about this land and the people who visit, or are you talking about 'land' as a concept?"

Lucas reworded his question. "I'm curious about the experience of this place for you." His dreads hung in circular curves around his face. "A lot of people who visit say, 'I feel totally inspired when I'm out here,' or, 'I feel renewed,' or some other deep spiritual thing. But what is it about this place? What is The Land to people?"

"Is it possible that this is a representation or of what they've experienced in other places?" Malcolm knitted his brow. He didn't know it, but he spoke of me. When I drove in, I was expecting a party to be happening. I put a lot of preconceptions on the place, but it seemed magic so far. I had no way of knowing that my time in and around The Land would offer the biggest challenges of the entire journey.

"I'm curious about this land, in particular. What are some of the aspects of this place that stand out? What is this place to you, being people who have only been here a short period of time?"

"Freedom," said Malcolm.

"Freedom to have mustard," I added.

What makes something natural?

Back at Outward Bound, an instructor friend, Nobuo, had asked, *"Why is money so important to you?"* And the truth is, it's not. I know I am lucky to have grown up in the way that I did, where all my basics were covered and money allowed for extras, but I have found much more happiness in living simply than in accruing money. The wages I earned as a public school teacher were always enough, and kept any grandiose frivolity in check. I found myself drawn to environments where money wasn't the true currency of the experience—with Outward Bound, out in the field for weeks at a time, or in the simplicity of riding my bike across state after state, bags carefully packed with tent, clothes, and provisions. The focus, in these settings, moves away from cultural identifiers such as class and into the personal. Instead of staying in this hotel or that hotel, everyone is sleeping in a tent, close to the ground. The earth itself is part of the journey.

This, at its core, was what The Land represented for me: the chance to spend time with people I cared about, not focused on entrance fees or restaurant checks. We would cook together, work on the structures together, go for hikes together. Lucas and Shara lived there full time, and it was a unique opportunity for me to see people living this way all the time, not just in vacation snatches of preplanned time. The next day as we moved large stones, I explained my feelings about The Land more earnestly to Lucas.

The days on The Land weren't easy, but they were always enjoyable. I helped set the pilings for the foundations to the winter structure and edged a long footpath with white stones. Each day we would hike, and plant, and work on the structure, and at night, Lucas, Shara, and I would sit around a fire cooking, talking, and enjoying the glow. Sometimes others joined us. Life stayed calm, not raucous like I had envisioned. I enjoyed the diurnal rhythms, the sinking and rising sun serving as bookends to our activities.

Lucas and Shara themselves were night and day: Lucas, the physical, and Shara, the intellectual. That's not true; Lucas is also intellectual, but more elemental. He'd ask questions like, *"What makes something natural?"*

Shara, on the other hand, asked if I'd ever read Tim O'Brien, or if I had a favorite poet. But together they would run ten miles on a whim.

I visited to join in their friendship. The Land functioned as a "construct it yourself" place, open scrub and knotty trees. Nothing was built except to serve a useful purpose: the outdoor kitchen area, the garden,

Lucas and Shara's teepee. On a corner of The Land sat a mud hut guest-house, multicolored shards of earthenware pressed into its sides.

The entire spirit of the place contained the character of the builders, a unique mishmash of styles and ideas jumbled into one free-range farm. Nothing prefabricated. A couple of Lucas's old sweaters hung on a scare-crow in the middle of a small garden. The garden provided vegetables even in the heat of summer, because the rain catchment barrels next to it offered consistent hydration. The sweaters, when it began to get cold, would be worn again, of that I was sure.

Shara responded to The Questions first. As we ate lunch under shade one afternoon, she turned to me. "*What motivates you to keep living?'* That's what I would want to know from everyone." She leaned forward to warm a tortilla on the fire grate. "I guess it sounds sort of morbid, but that's not my intent. I think that sometimes we don't remember that it's actually a constant choice we keep making over and over again, to keep living all the time." I stopped chewing, as the depth of her question sank in. "Wow," I said. "I've always thought about life being a result of unconscious processes, like our heart beating without any choice or involvement, but you're right. We don't have to put food in our mouths."

"Or not jump off cliffs," she smiled. "But I'm not as interested in suicide as learning people's deeper motivation for constantly staying alive. We're expected to do meaningful work throughout our lives, but really, what motivates us?"

It took Lukas days to respond to The Question.

"I've gone through many ideas, and I've finally arrived at my ques-tion." Lucas stirred the embers of a dinner fire thoughtfully one night. "Here's what I would want to know from everyone: *Who are you?*"

Who are you?

Second to questions about happiness, this was the only other question that came up regularly. The askers often expressed a certain confidence in having arrived at this question, giving it a profound gravity.

"That one's got to be in the Top Ten you've ever heard," said one of my favorite cousins, smugly. It seems like such a good question, right? Deep. It drives to the heart of human experience. The only question worth asking, one could say. But the truth is, it made me wary.

That this point-blank question, like a finger in the chest, was considered one of the "good ones," fascinated me. As often as not, those direct questions didn't elicit a complex response. They weren't necessarily, in fact, easy or revealing questions at all. Maybe best answered privately, to oneself. Could you imagine summing up your entire self for someone you'd just met? And for those who know me best, don't they already know the answer? Isn't that why we consider them close friends?

But mostly it was the confrontational proposition this question seemed to engage. In real life, deep questions about the nature of the self tend to be confused, or confusing. When somebody asks me, "Who are you?" I'm tempted to answer, *"Who wants to know?"*

Trying to answer this makes it immediately clear that we are composed of myriad personalities, conflicting desires and drives. We are things we can't explain. *Who are you?*

How should I know?

Who are you (really)?

(Corey Flintoff, NPR correspondent)

Lucas and I worked together many seasons as instructors at the same Outward Bound base. I loved him, and yet being around him made me wrestle with my most challenging inconsistencies. Lucas and Shara were unified in making The Land real; they built all the structures, planted the garden, and cooked food for others. They even dug rain catchments to harness and store water from the skies. But where Shara was living out her beliefs, Lucas was a force. I certainly didn't feel that Shara was lesser than Lucas, just that people gravitated to Lucas. He played the role of spokesperson and guide. Being around someone so pure to their ideology, a deeply rooted connection to nature, was infectious. He lived so connected to the very land on which he walked and slept.

Add to this, Lucas was also far and away the most physically adept person I had ever met. At five foot eight, he stood just a hair shorter than I and not as wide, with wild, foot-long blond dreads all about his head. He walked erect and sure-footed. Around his neck hung stones and shells, talismans from expeditions, a charm necklace of found teeth and feathers. His own buck teeth were more pronounced than mine, enough to whistle through in a big, jocular smile. Lucas hadn't cut his beard for five years, and why, he argued, should he? Hair came out of his face; hair came out of his head. *I am me and this is what I look like*, he said directly to the world, *take it or leave it*. In this era of extreme plastic surgery makeovers, Lucas calmly stated his intentions. "Don't change what you look like," he said to me once, "change how you see." That was his answer. Be who you are.

This purity and unwavering confidence drew me in. Funny and kind, Lucas also carried with him knowledge of people. He thought about how people live together and how to make decisions. He took seriously his role as the Base Camp Managing Instructor for the eighty or so instructors at Outward Bound, meeting with each brigade at course end. An amazing rock climber, Lucas was charged with making sure all climbing systems were safe at several climbing sites, and the flow of work at the base ran smoothly.

As much as Lucas had accomplished though, I saw in him the same person I was in youth: the buck-toothed kid in cutoffs riding his BMX bike around the apartment complex, looking for people to go swimming or make up a treasure hunt or go on an adventure. The kid with his vulnerabilities on his sleeve. On this ground, we connected.

Do you believe in luck?

Before every summer season at Outward Bound, Lucas went on a solo trek, the kind that has been a feature of many traditional world cultures as a rite of passage. On a walkabout, a member leaves the community to explore the unknown of the wilderness and to arrive at a new understanding of themselves and their spiritual connections.

One year Lucas borrowed a canoe from the base and paddled deep into the Boundary Waters, on the lakes for weeks, alone in the early spring, as the ice began to thaw. It was late April and, due to the cold, he had the million acres of wilderness to himself. Often the mornings were so cold that he broke ice with the canoe.

When he returned from that journey, he handed me a gift. "What's this?" I asked, looking at the four-inch curved white spike in my palm.

"A beaver tooth with magical powers. A talisman to bring positive energy throughout your travels," he said, looking me right in the eye.

My father laughed, but it came out of my own mouth.

"Sorry," I said sheepishly, "I didn't mean to laugh. I'm just not familiar with talismans, really."

But of course I was: a lucky penny sat in a box on my dresser, along with a shark's tooth I found on the beach in Florida. My father would've laughed at the idea of himself wearing a beaver tooth on a necklace for good luck. He didn't believe in it, and I'm not sure I did either. But it wasn't belief that separated us; he was certainly a man of routine and structure. I'm sure he relied on some elements of superstition as he scrubbed for a difficult surgery ahead. He certainly blew out all his birthday candles and threw coins in fountains. Don't we all? I accepted the gift readily, turning it over in my fingers.

"How'd you find a beaver tooth?" I asked, incredulous; I'd spent years in the Boundary Waters and had never seen a single one.

"They're everywhere," he said. "You just need to get off the beaten path."

I thought I was off the beaten path, I thought to myself.

Why would anyone want to leave a place like this?

The next day I sat cross-legged in the dirt watching Lucas and Malcolm play horseshoes. The sun was setting, and the day was cooling off. Finally.

Red and brown tones completed the landscape, sprinkled with white little rocks, dotted with green juniper trees and shrubs. Flies buzzed everywhere.

The stone path up from the kitchen completed, we began work on concrete pilings. They would become the foundation for their winter shelter.

It is in those ways I knew that what I was doing was Good. I liked who I was on The Land. Everything felt deliberate: the setting of the stones that formed a pathway, the pouring of wet cement, the throwing of horseshoes. There was no "fast." There was only each moment.

I'd been on The Land for almost a week already, and it was halcyon, if hot. Lucas and Shara had only been kind, cooking dinner together, hiking The Land, and laughing. There was plenty of depth and plenty of laughter. The Land was idyll.

Everything, from food to shelter, required preparation. There was no refrigerator, so certain foods didn't last long. Nothing stayed cold. At first I found that frustrating, I brought a box of figs, hand-picked from my mother's tree. Within two days, they began to rot.

Then slowly, once again inhabiting the rhythms of life in the outdoors on expedition, it made more and more sense. There is something to soaking the beans, then frying the beans and mashing the beans and then adding spices that just make them taste better. And while you do these simple tasks, you talk. As much as the big ideas about harnessing power from the sun and water from the sky, I found that the little acts throughout the day made the most meaning for me.

Why would anyone want to leave a place like this?

I imagined my father standing there beside us, gently shaking his head. This is child's play with adult ideas. This life of little money, no retirement, no benefits wasn't only impractical, it exacted a high toll. This voice of reason so many echo: Without the security of these things in place, how could you possibly find happiness through the worry? Lucas and Shara were aware of this voice, too, but they spent their time upending it. Happiness? Look, it's right here all around us.

What's your favorite food?

Late the next morning, a big Ford F-150 pulled up beside one of the big blue rain barrels, and out jumped a cowboy holding two burlap sacks. "Lucas!" he yelled, his cowboy boots pulling his jeans taut in large bow-legged steps around the grounds. I said hello as he walked by, but it went unanswered. "Hey, Lucas!" he said again, a half-full twine sack in each hand. Lucas emerged from the teepee, squinting. "Tomahawk Ron! Good to see you, man. What's up?"

Tomahawk Ron, a thin man of occasional sideways glances, focused his attention completely on Lucas. It was as though Tomahawk Ron found in Lucas, like me, a realized version of his ideal self. He wasn't very interested in Malcolm, Shara, or myself, but kept his gaze on Lucas as he explained how he'd brought a gift of pistachios. "I thought you might enjoy them," he said to Lucas, as though presenting him with an offering.

Lucas reached into the bag and took out a handful of yellow and orange nuts, passing them to all of us seated around. "These are great, Ron! Thank you." He smiled. It made sense to me suddenly, Tomahawk Ron crouching there, keenly interested in Lucas's attention. It wasn't The Land that held the allure of something deeper spiritually; the dirt around us was just that, dirt. The power of the place resided in Lucas himself.

"Yeah, those are pretty cool, huh, Lucas?" Ron said, maintaining eye contact. They continued to speak together briefly. Then, abruptly, Ron stood up. "Well, got to go." He dusted off his faded blue jeans at the thigh and started walking off to his truck. He turned as he opened the door. "I'll bring more just as soon as they ripen!" He clanged the door shut and drove off.

We spent the next couple days skinning and eating pistachios raw or roasting them over a fire in a pan with some oil and salt. They were delicious. The pile of skins next to the bags grew, and both Shara and Lucas commented on how lucky they were to have pistachio skins around to mulch their newly planted trees.

"Anyone who comes to visit will think that we're *kings*." Lucas smiled. "They'll see all these husks and won't believe our good fortune!"

What is the most spiritually inspiring experience you have ever had?

I could have gotten sucked into The Land, become a permanent resident. Life was naive and joyful, and its purity spoke to the lessons of my youth: Don't waste. Money is not important. Have fun.

I noticed that, just like in the wilderness of Outward Bound, I didn't have any contact with the outside world, and that suited me fine. The cell phone had become superfluous, and I realized that e-mail was just a nervous habit, especially on the road. I didn't have a job, so it wasn't essential that I contact anyone. I played one more round of horseshoes, dug deeper the trench for water catchments. No one expected my call.

The freedom was invigorating. The more I meditated in my tent in the mornings, the more it showed me of myself. I felt like I lived on The Land, not just as a visitor, and I wanted to see how far I could go. I had a desire for solitude. At the top of the canyon, a wild carpet of trees and scrub rolled into mountains and back down into wide valleys. Out there, I felt, I might be able to dig in to *Who are you?* and chew on its flesh.

I found I wanted to engage my other self, the one my reckless high school friend Brian would've been proud of, the True Adventurer, so I talked with Lucas about taking a solo hike.

"Where could I go here that would allow me to really be alone?" I asked, imagining my own walkabout.

The request energized Lucas. He ducked inside the teepee, rooted around, and came out with a map. He spread it on the ground and pointed to a few different locations, offering his thoughts on each.

"How about this?" Lucas said, pointing out to the horizon at a small feature off in the distance that only he could see. "Why don't you hike down to the town of Prescott?" He nodded, agreeing with himself that it was a worthy challenge. "It's a good distance, maybe 50 miles. We'll head into town in a few days and meet you there."

"Cool, ok, yeah," I said, the corners of my mouth turned down, my eyes still trying to fix the line, to find evidence of the town he referenced.

The next day was spent packing and going over the map. Adventure consumed me—I looked forward to getting deep with spiritual thoughts and the allure of the trek to far-off Prescott. In that enthusiastic spirit, I passed over some details we call "Yellow Flags" in expedition planning at Outward Bound. What sounded at first like a clear hiking trail in my initial chat with Lucas turned out to be quite a bit more confusing. When we traced the route on a map, I noticed there were no open-access roads to speak of and, worse, there was no actual trail. I had no experience with the physical features of the landscape. In hindsight, it was a bad idea to head off alone with so many unknowns, but I remained excited. This was a chance to give Lucas and Shara some time to themselves, and a chance for me to do my own exploration. Lucas kept interrupting my reverie, giving me instruction after instruction about the route.

"When you get to the end of this fence here," he said, circling a finger over a large, blank spot on the map, "just climb it. Walk straight across this property, and don't worry about anyone threatening you. You've got a twenty-foot easement through which to pass." I wrinkled my brow, trying to remember what the word "easement" meant. "Then when you get to the wash, look across the valley for the three peaks." I asked him what an easement was.

"It just means you can walk on someone's property, as long as you're just traveling through," he said.

"Wait, I have a legal right to cross someone's private property? Is that a Federal or State statute?" I asked, dubious. "Keep Off the Grass" was as American as apple pie and baseball. I gave a skeptical look.

"Yes, no matter how many guns they point at you."

"Guns?"

"Just don't stray off the easement."

If you were an animal, what animal would you be?

Hours later I found myself sitting on the stump of a former telephone pole with aching knees, exhausted, and lost. There were no signs of life, and my pack pulled me towards the ground, leaden with a couple gallons of water. There were several barely discernible mountains to shoot for and little else as far as the eye could see. Fifty yards away, a dozen or so cows stood nonchalantly. They grazed, oblivious to my presence, except for one. And that one had big horns. He snorted, ambling toward me. "Sorry, I'm from out of town," I said, waving and smiling as brightly as I could. He did not break his ominous gaze.

At the beginning of my hike, I arrived at the first gate after only twenty minutes. It hung loose, covered in threatening "No Trespassing" signs, each one dented with buckshot. One was so bent and twisted it looked like it'd been chewed up by something much bigger and meaner than a human. Something that chewed on metal. My mind flipped back to Lucas as he tried to reassure me about these. "Jump the fence but stay on the road. It's an easement. They have to allow access across their land." I couldn't shake the image of a gate I saw on my drive in the canyon to The Land, the one with "Trespassers will be shot" spray-painted across it.

The signs before me were of the more common "No Trespassing" kind, and they swayed gently in the breeze, taunting. *Jump the fence... see what happens next,* they mocked. As I thought about my next move, I looked right and noticed a large, dry riverbed. Barbed wire hung three or four feet above the wash, so that would be easy access. A river would take me to the flat bottom of the valley where I wanted to go, and I wouldn't have to walk right past someone's front porch, eyed through the notch of a shotgun barrel. Of course, I took the riverbed. And of course, I followed it for miles, each step further from the road, further from any easement.

The riverbed led me to the wash, which led me to the stump, which led me to the approaching, potentially aggressive, large bull.

I had hiked for a few hours by this point and looked to stop for a rest. I don't know how long the bull stared at me, but by the time I scanned the landscape, we made solid eye contact. I'm pretty sure locking eyes with a two-thousand-pound creature is something you're not supposed to do. The bull, surrounded by cows, approached, slightly lowering his horns.

As the bull got closer, I began to twist the hair of my beard, a habit from driving. My beard was long, and when my thoughts turned anxious my fingers went to work. I looked around again, this time for safety exits. Nothing on the horizon stood over three feet tall, and the sun's heat compressed everything in the far distance into a sandy hue, leaving nowhere to run or hide, even if my knees didn't hurt. Apparently, power ran through at one time, evidenced by the slowly curving path of the stumps of former utility poles that dotted the dry terrain. I followed these poles after meandering down the wash, because I couldn't figure out which of the peaks in the distance were my three. I was lost and hoped the posts would eventually lead me to a road. Nothing else within sight offered nearly as much possibility.

The bull continued to walk toward me, a well-what-do-we-have-here saunter that drew the attention of the rest of the herd. A dozen or so cows crowded close behind to watch. They circled and tilted their heads like high school students in the curiosity of an impending fight. No one wanted to miss anything.

The bull advanced, nostrils flaring. I took a couple halting steps backwards and found myself in front of the stump of a telephone pole. My left knee buckled. And then I sat, groaning in both pain and fear. I started talking to myself.

Something told me that as I talked I should look away. "I know that you could gore me through, Mr. Bull. There would be no way in hell I could outrun you. And if you gored me, I'd die here."

I tried, subtly, to extend each leg to see how much spring I would have if he lunged. Darts of pain shot up my left knee with every extension. Could I jump far enough out of the way? Nope, revealed my quick assessment, no jumping.

I had purchased the rugged leather hiking boots, excitedly, at a half-off sidewalk sale back in Santa Barbara. My current boots were dead, and these were such a great deal, even if they were a half-size too small. I didn't want to admit that they didn't fit and what I had truly purchased was a future medical issue with a side of potential goring, but I couldn't take them off with this bull approaching. Even if he poked me, I'd still have to hotfoot it who-knows-how-far down this abandoned dirt path, clutching my gut. Best to keep the boots on.

"I would be threatening, if I wasn't so interested in this shrub over here," I said, trying hard not to make eye contact, but I also didn't want to be stuck in the back by a two-ton bull in the middle of nowhere, alone in Arizona, far from an easement.

Several minutes into the standoff, sweat dried to granular rivulets on my forehead. I couldn't continue walking, but I didn't want to sit out in the hot sun all day. And I didn't want to fall asleep before I found out the ending. I gulped water as an idea came to me: *What if I asked this bull The Question?* "Hey, bull," I said, finally turning to look him directly in the eye again. This time I spoke, loudly. "If you could ask everyone you met one question, what would you ask them?" When I got to "you," I pointed at him.

The bull stopped advancing, cocked his head, and kept chewing. It was stupid, but I had to try something. My confidence gathered as I stood up, shakily, an elementary kid suddenly stepping up to his bully. My voice cracked. I almost yelled. "What do you think, Mr. Bull? *What is something that you would like to know from every single bovine on the planet?*"

He snorted a couple times, loudly, and we just continued staring into each other's eyes. My good leg shook and my jaw clenched. We stood together in the moment of truth, that moment where you've played the only card you've got. That moment when you realize that maybe you had been acting foolishly all along and there you are, cornered in a dark alley, or with a bum knee in front of an angry bull.

Eyes locked, he snorted one more time then looked away. He didn't indicate any reaction, merely a side glance. I won! I could tell instantly. He just stood there for a minute, large horns steady, and then slowly turned back, ambling away in defeat. Then the heads of all the watching cattle herd turned. Excitement over, they left in search of more food.

Immediately, I lay down on my back, kicked my boots off, and sighed. That goddamn question saved my life! Endorphins receded, reminding me again of the pain and exhaustion. I continued to rest my knee for a minute, drank more water, and then stood to hobble off.

The difference between the walled-in canyon of The Land and the flat, open valley was dramatic. Instead of closed-in spaces, before me lay an enormous alluvial plain. At some point in history, water had run down the canyons and out into this big, open area, maybe a prehistoric river or small sea. I hiked on in search of road or ranch.

As the sun dropped lower in the sky, I started looking for places to set up camp. I climbed a smaller barbed-wire fence, continuing my way across the plain. Almost everything sat out in the open, and, by scaling the fence, I was definitely on someone's land.

Finally, it turned dusk, and I needed to stop. I crouched behind shrubs to set up a makeshift campsite. Scoping out the scene, I cased the surroundings like a small-time thief. Small, yellow lights of a ranch house burned brightly, and far-off dogs barked. I limped a few hundred yards away, but worried they could smell me. Their barks were vicious, as though whatever had caught their attention needed to be ripped apart. Hoping it wasn't me, I vowed to yell, "Don't shoot, this is an easement!" if faced with the barrel of a gun.

I set up my tarp as discretely as possible, but it is impossible to hide a blue dot on a flat, beige landscape. Was my campsite visible from the farm? I caught sight of a moving cloud of dust and traced it back to its source, a white pick-up truck. A road cut a light brown ribbon right down the middle of the wide valley. I now knew my route out, but other discomforts appeared. That road carried ranchers—people who don't trust people like me.

I cooked a small pot of pasta, stirring it over the camp stove, and poured off the water into a small pit which I then covered. I wolfed down the pasta, as hot as I could stand. No smell meant no dogs, no bulls, no ranchers. Dusk settled quickly, and I went to sleep.

The next morning, I lay in my sleeping bag in the cold, slate-gray dawn, dozing in and out of sleep, aware of rain. Fat droplets hit increasingly hard on the tarp, falling in arcs across the great distance of sky and sleep as I came to consciousness through a cavernous, complicated dream. In it, a rancher had heard that an interloper on a spiritual quest sought to travel through his land. Already this traveler had disturbed the cattle.

The rain continued to pelt the bright blue plastic, tapping loudly, hitting a distance in space miles from me, and yet, very real. The pickup pulled up close, and just as the rancher released the rear gate and the dogs jumped out, gnashing and barking, I awoke. The panic abated quickly upon the realization that there were no actual dogs, but my heart continued to pound. Unfortunately, the rain drops were real, and much of me was very wet.

Falling water splashed on my face as I rolled to look skyward, trying vaguely to assess the storm. With eyes only half opened, I sat up quickly, rolled out of my dampening sleeping bag, and frantically packed camp. My fear of dogs grew in persistence. As I stood, my knee made bolts of lightning flash behind my eyes. As I struggled into my rain gear, my hiking clothes got wet, my boots drenched. Still, the fear upstaged the unpleasantness of being soaked. *This is someone else's land,* kept reverberating in my mind. *They could send those dogs!*

I skipped breakfast, not exhaling a sigh of relief until half a mile beyond and safely down the road. I wasn't relieved so much as profoundly tired. Heavy clouds hung motionless all the way to the horizon. The temperature continued to drop. The rain poured on.

For hours I hiked in stuttering steps, wondering, *Where is that highway?* before any paved road came into sight. The boots continued to hurt, so I switched to Chaco sandals, which showed themselves a worse idea. The straps bit as my feet slid all over the slippery footpad, and the lack of ankle support new pain to my feet and now my right knee. *Well, I found something worse than those boots.* I grimaced.

Finally arriving at the highway, I realized the rain had been pouring all morning without a break. There were no buildings in sight. The dirt road met the highway at a gentle indentation, to my left a rise. No cars in sight. No people. My shoulders sagged.

I hobbled over the rise and far in the distance saw evidence of life: an old convenience store with a crumbling parking lot. Trudging toward it I could make it out more clearly, one large glass window, the interior painted entirely in pink. A cheery little bell rang as I opened the door.

A couple minutes later, a clerk appeared. I had five dollars emergency money, dripping wet in the zippered compartment on top of my bag. I bought and heated a burrito in the spattered, old microwave and looked out the window, soaking wet, waiting for the rain to stop. I sat, defeated like I'd not felt before. It was hard to believe things had gotten this bad after only a couple days of hiking. These two days, fraught with worry and pain, eclipsed the whole purpose of the hike.

What is one tangible thing you can accomplish in the near future that will change your life for the better?

Prescott wasn't that big, and somehow I knew if I could just get into town I would find Shara and Lucas. But that town lay a few dozen miles away, and I had no number to call, no address to point to.

The rain stopped briefly, offering me a chance to formulate a plan. I schemed, walking out back behind the store and peering in the dumpster. It was filled with cardboard, sopping wet. I leaped in. Digging a little, I found the lower layers still dry, so I grabbed a large, dry box and ripped off a flap for a neat rectangle. I threw it over the side and climbed out. Steady droplets started up again. I walked back in the store, borrowed a black marker, and wrote "Prescott" in solid block print. I put my rain gear back on, walked out to the highway, and waited.

Here I was, an experienced wilderness guide in my own right, sitting on my backpack at the side of the highway smarting from a series of bad choices, from the route to the boots. This was definitely not Ivy League decision-making, and neither Brian nor my father would have been proud. The black marker streaked in the rain, like cried-through mascara.

Over the course of an hour or two, a number of cars whisked by, all white families or single men. Not one slowed down. Finally, a small red pickup crowded with Latino men stopped. They pulled over, and the driver said from his window, "Hop in the back...but stay low so no one sees you."

As I lay horizontal across a bed of farm tools, I stared at the sky. At the very corner, dark clouds began to recede on one side to reveal brilliant blues. A curtain was being pulled back, the storm ending just as I had quit, as if a test from Lucas himself. Can you handle the challenge of living directly off the land?

The pickup dropped me off at a Salvation Army thrift store on the edge of town, and the driver waved one hand out the window as a goodbye. I waved back, appreciative. With no map and no clue where I was in town, I stopped in an auto body shop for directions downtown. As I stepped out, someone rode by on an old Schwinn and said, "Hey! You made it!" I smiled and waved. Who was that? They kept on riding.

Twenty minutes later a car pulled up slowly beside me and another person yelled my name, this time out a car window. "Ty!" It was a voice I knew. I turned to see Shara, smiling. She pulled over to the side of the road and waited until I approached, hobbling.

"What are you doing here?" I asked, smiling into the open passenger window. It seemed unbelievable that we would cross paths so quickly, and yet it all made sense; I knew we would find each other. I climbed into her car, exhausted. We drove to their friends' place, where I took them up on the offer of dinner and a shower. I looked forward to the food being cooked, the cold beer the in the fridge, and sleep.

As the water heated up, steaming the room, I rubbed a circle in the mirror with the old towel they provided. I looked like I thought I would; over-tired and frazzled, but my eyes were different, wrinkled at the edges, deep with betraying loneliness.

Can you have pride without ego?

Later that night, after a long nap, Lucas brought me to his friend's bachelor party. As we walked in, Lucas immediately walked me over to his friend, Joshua. As we shook hands, Lucas introduced my project and asked Joshua The Question for me. Nice to hear the words come out of someone else's mouth, I decided. As Joshua thought, I took in the scene. Typical of a summer bachelor party, there were no decorations, just ripped-open cases of beer and rickety white plastic lawn chairs. It was dusk, and loud discussions were happening around a large campfire.

As the director of outdoor programming at the Prescott, Joshua was fit and tan, just like most Prescott folks I met. Messy hair hung around his head, with a white line of untanned skin starting above the ears and curving around the forehead where sunglasses or a visor sat in a semi-permanent position. He wore a patterned short-sleeved shirt, longboard shorts, and flip-flops. He seemed more a desert-dusted surfer than program director.

He considered the fire, responding to Lucas. "Here's what I want to know: *Who are you?*" He paused and then said, pointedly, *"And why are you here?"*

For a second I thought this was directed at me, having just walked in with Lucas. I'm sure I looked rough.

But he continued. "They are connected questions, and they are not meant in a surface way. There's an *and.*" He paused for effect. "If I had to go further, I would ask: *What are the experiences that inform that view?* That's my question."

Lucas smiled. "Beautiful, man." he said. Joshua had hit upon Lucas's very question. "*Who are you?* is really the ultimate question."

There it was again. *Who am I?* I asked myself. *I don't know*, I responded, still lost on the hike, my brain still trying figure out what had happened.

Mother or Father?

Do you read the newspaper or magazines? Nope.
Which do you like better, my pants or my shoes? Nope.
Coke or Pepsi? Nope.
Do you give up?
Nope.

While in town, I stayed with friends of Lucas and Shara. Lucas had introduced my project to everyone in the house. They seemed intrigued by the idea.

One night, while everyone else was out, I chatted with one of the inhabitants, Jonah, on an off-white pleather L-shaped couch in a dingy, off-white kitchen, on an off-white couch.

"So," he started off, "you're like The Question Guy, huh?" I enjoyed being identified by the project first, and I liked being "The Question Guy." It had a ring to it. Plus it made things more smooth; we could just jump in.

And jumping in was exactly what Jonah wanted to do. He asked a litany of questions, with one interesting commonality: every query consisted of a binary. It wasn't until the fourth or fifth question that I started laughing. Playfully, he continued to generate questions even after I started laughing too hard to say, "Nope."

"*Mother or Father?*"

For some reason this hit me reflexively; my parents weren't an either/or proposition. But I stopped laughing for a minute. My mother's voice, *Go, you might meet someone!* impelled me forward on the project, but our relationship was not simple. Jonah's question reminded me that my father had talked about meeting up in Dallas, where he would be in a couple weeks for a conference. He would have opinions on the journey.

Jonah noticed my sudden change, taking it as a comment on his string of questions. He asked, more seriously, "Will you give me some examples of questions other people have asked?"

Lost in thought, I said, "Yeah, sorry, I got distracted there. But here's some bad news: I can't talk about all the different questions until you give me yours. It's my policy." I gave him an exaggerated wink, to bring back the levity. I did want to hear more of his three-word questions. After hearing so many Deep Thoughts, it was refreshing to have someone ask only questions that could be reduced to Yes or No.

"OK, no more bullshit, here it is. Here's the real deal: *What is your favorite book you've ever read?*" Like Barb back in Oakland, I couldn't tell if he had been thinking of his question all along and was just messing with me, or if clarity had struck that very instant.

Jonah knew Lucas well; he'd been out to The Land many times. For fun, I asked, "What do you think Lucas asked?"

He smiled. "Was it something really serious?"

"It took him a couple days to come to it."

"I think he asked…" Jonah looked at the ceiling and then back at me. "I know *exactly* what Lucas asked," he said, smiling and nodding. "He asked the biggest, deepest question he could come up with, one that might take your entire fucking life to answer: *Who are you?*"

Jonah pointed knowingly at me as we both laughed heartily, "I mean, am I right, or am I right?" A pressure cap had busted off, and we laughed harder than we had before. We both loved Lucas for his character and his devotion to The Land and his indomitable spirit. He lived a life we both wished we could live, too. But there was camaraderie in recognizing we didn't.

Are you willing to die?

The next day, Lucas and Shara and I returned to The Land. Shara's family visited Prescott for a few hours, and her half-brothers, Brent and Kevin, wanted to see what it was like on The Land, so they hopped in her car while her mother and stepfather had lunch in town.

We talked and joked through a tour of The Land. Brent, in particular, enjoyed the primitiveness of it all. Fifteen to his brother's twelve, Brent seemed always in motion; he threw almost every loose rock he came across. I asked him The Question as we hiked, and then later, as we cooked corn over an open fire, Brent responded. *"Is there something more to life than just living in cities?"* He sat, poking at the fire with the most recent stick he had found, his bleach-blond hair blowing in the gentle breeze. He looked over at Lucas. *"Should we be living in other ways?"*

Ironically, as Brent answered The Question, we were far from any cities. In fact, we were so far from any city we were completely off the grid. The cooking fire Brent stirred was built on a hand-carved farm more than an hour's drive northwest of Prescott, itself a city only numbering in the low tens of thousands. And far to the west, from where I'd come, there was Barstow.

Brent's question was not unique for my time in Arizona. Arizonans built questions of straw and mud, strong, strange structures from Early Man. Later, when I asked Brent's younger brother, Kevin, he responded right on the spot. He was only twelve years of age, but still he looked me dead in the eye like a Clint Eastwood cowboy: *"Are you willing to die?"*

After my encounter with the bull, reconnecting with Lucas and the great tug to stay on The Land, I realized I wasn't willing to die. Not here. There was more to see.

After Brent and Kevin returned home, Lucas, Shara, and I spent our last afternoon together. They packed to head out to Joshua Tree, where they would spend time with another group of friends for an annual gathering of climbers and desert crazies that culminated on Halloween. "We'd love to have you join us," Lucas offered, but we both knew this was my time to leave, as well.

I loved The Land, but I wasn't ready to stay. Lucas's purity was not my own. Shame emanated from my tender knee. I arrived thinking I could match the freedom and independence of The Land. It was a life-style so noble, and yet I found myself looking over at my little red car, patiently parked and waiting.

We drove out the unpaved winding red road together in daylight. Shara and Lucas pulled onto the highway, heading west. I pulled off in the opposite direction—east, off to hear more questions, to meet more of America.

Do you believe you have a double out there in the universe?

I drove.

I decided to take a minor sightseeing detour to visit Sedona and stay the night. Outside the city, a mysterious movement stirred a massive flock of starlings. In a pink evening sky, the colony of birds writhed and twisted along the side of the road in a long, black ribbon. The ribbon bent and curved, easily half a mile long, floating back on itself like a three-dimensional sculpture. Hundreds of thousands of birds moved in perfect, disorderly synchronicity, so fast and so continuous, there could be no individual choice. I pulled over to watch these birds singing and flying in a deafening chorus of organized chaos, a free verse poem. Were they aware they were creating this?

My mind wandered back to Lucas. *"Who are you?"* A question for defining a path, carving an identity—a structure for the work ahead. My guard came down. The birds, however, said to me something even more profound: there was not just one question. Sometimes there are no questions. There is only action. We can only be who we are.

Looking in the rearview mirror as I drove the straight, unending blacktop across Arizona, I noticed a car right behind me: little, red, bike on top, one driver. I had the surreal feeling that I was watching myself—a shaggy-haired driver my very own likeness. It was as though, for a brief moment, I was able to watch myself as I drove around the country. I rolled down my window and waved excitedly as he passed. He looked befuddled, smiling a tight, confused smile. Hands stayed on the wheel.

Who are you? I played a little game: What if I just passed myself? It would have been the beginning of the journey, that's for sure, back when I was unsure of the project at all. Back before it was a natural part of me. Back before the big beard. He drove so caught up in his own thoughts. Didn't he even notice to smile and wave back?

Was he happy? I enjoyed the rare chance to see my earlier self reflected back to me, and I wondered if I did truly look like this, my father perched on one shoulder, the free-wheeling figure of Brian on the other, me stuck in the middle.

Are you going to eat that?

I arrived in Sedona, looking for a place to make dinner, driving my car up to a gorgeous perch on a huge mesa overlooking the city. That evening I sat sideways in the driver's seat with the door open, one leg out. *A Prairie Home Companion* crackled through the radio speakers. Out the window, the surrounding auburn and rust country stretched for miles. The dinner menu turned into burritos of refried beans, fresh onion, cayenne, and ripe avocados. I had purchased tortillas at a corner store and still had spices from the "extra food" box way back at the Outward Bound base in Minnesota to make it all come together. Though, truly, I wished I had a lemon for the avocados. One big, fat bright yellow lemon. Goddamn if my Mother wasn't a little bit right, again.

I felt good, like a cowboy after a long cattle run. The landscape was invigorating and exhausting. I cooked my food on my own little stove, high above the town. City lights began to twinkle yellow and white as dusk settled in.

Cooking out in the open in a city, especially an unknown city, posed real problems. Most especially in Sedona, where tourists crawl everywhere in hopes of catching the stunning views that appear around even the most inauspicious corners. Property values were astonishing.

The airport lot where I parked was located on top of a butte, accessible by a road that wound upward until it ended in a flat expanse looking out over the city. In the dusk, warm red tones bathed the landscape, and other buttes poked out of the ground, tall strata of Earth's history. I parked, staring ahead for a moment. It must be beautiful to fly into this airport; just sitting, parked, was itself beautiful. It was worth the detour.

I fired up my stove and shielded it with the car door to cook in semi privacy. I wanted to hide my workings from the view of any audience, including the cops. No one likes a stranger cooking food in public. It reeks of helplessness, almost criminality. I crouched. It would be easy to roll by and kick me off the property. I didn't want to take the chance that I'd get hassled, or arrested, still hungry.

As I stirred the bubbling brown beans, my thoughts bubbled up as well. How interesting it was, watching my question unravel. After asking the same question hundreds of times, the artifice disappeared and the challenges and thoughts of the Asker came to the fore.

In the classroom, they say you need to experience every student situation once, sometimes twice, and then there are no surprises. You lost your homework? There are extra copies available. Didn't bring a pencil? Borrow one from a friend.

The same thing happened here: while The Question was new for each person I asked, it remained a constant for me. I had placed myself in a repetitive situation, and I got to watch, to step outside the conventions. I began to notice things I had somehow missed all along; like Malcolm's strategy of asking one question to hear the answer to another, the Question had that same quality. Challenged to "ask everyone," meant that mentally the asker was investigating a rule. Describing something "everyone" knows about is another way of clarifying a truth about people. By asking a question of this truth, the asker hopes to learn more, to listen for something revealing or challenging. The real question underneath my question was, "*What do you believe is true about humanity?*"

The limitation of only one question just made everything more purposeful and interesting.

How did you end up here, doing this, now?

I camped that night and was on the road early the next day. As I hit the open road outside Sedona, I noticed movement in the distance, on the side of the road. As I drew closer, I could make out a bent figure tinkering on a bike, fixing a wheel or chain. The bike was loaded with front and rear bags, a sure sign of a long-distance rider. It was nine in the morning, and I was on my way to shoot photos in a slot canyon, a field trip I looked forward to. But the image of this biker stuck in my mind. I had been in the same situation many times on my own bike ride across the country. I had so recently been at the side of the road myself, needing help, watching cars with three empty seats approach, watching the driver stare blankly at me while whipping past at seventy miles per hour.

Lucas's idealism and certitude that we should be the change we want to see in the world tugged at my wheel as I passed. I did admire that in him, and I wanted that to be me, too. Plus, the memory of the long hours I had recently waited hitchhiking in the rain, thumb out, knee trembling in pain, sealed the deal. I turned around at the next exit and pulled up next to him, leaning across the passenger seat.

"Where ya headed?" I spoke loudly through the open window.

"Just tryin' to get there," he said, pointing toward Flagstaff, twenty nine miles to the north. I was headed south.

"My name's Larry," he said, squinting.

"Hop in," I said.

In dusty cargo shorts and a faded sun hat, Larry slowly shoveled his dusty bags and bike into the back hatch. I stepped out of the car when he stood momentarily clutching his side after tossing in his last bag. "These hips are toast," he said ruefully.

When he finally sat down, he extended a grubby hand to shake. He proffered a warm beer from his handlebar bag, cracked it, offering me the first sip. I declined. It turned out he was a fair distance from where he wanted to be. He would've been there by evening if he rode fast with a tailwind. But I watched, aware of the huge storm cloud on the horizon, heading right this way, coming for him. He sat, oblivious. He offered his beer again. Again, I declined.

"Just want to let you know, I'm a wanted man. I've got the FBI out on me, and I have a felony warrant for selling alcohol, right here. I got out of jail ten days later, and I went down to Durango. I had some property in Durango that I've got to sell. Southern Colorado. I had this plan that went bad, went real south, real quick."

I stared uncomfortably out my windshield listening. Details piled on details, and his monologue started to extend beyond the farm he used to own, to piping methane, to problems with red mud, wrapping up with a brief history of the KKK. He switched topics like a needle hopping grooves on a worn record. I couldn't get a word in edgewise for the next ten minutes.

Quickly I assessed my new companion: he smelled, he was loud, and he was drunk. What seemed to be a long-distance rider on a tour was just some guy who'd ridden too far out of town when he caught a flat. I don't know if he even noticed the approaching storm.

I stopped, reflecting for a moment. I was being judgmental. I heard my father asking me why I'd gone and done a stupid thing like picking this guy up. I returned to Lucas. What would he have done? Yes, this man stank, but too bad, if you're going to help him out, then go the distance: help him. *It's not actually about you,* I heard Lucas say.

Larry paused briefly, pounded his chest a couple times, and then ripped a long burp as a conclusion to his rambling rant. He smiled at his accomplishment and launched right back in, telling me how he had stabbed a crooked heroin dealer in Durango. I cracked my window and let myself smile.

I couldn't tell why he filled me in on his background of crime and violence, which was hard to believe considering his physical condition. He certainly didn't present the figure of violence—just the drunk guy at the end of the bar who keeps yelling "Freebird!" at every jukebox tune, long after it's funny. And he just wouldn't stop talking. Then it dawned on me. Sometimes kids in my classroom would ramble when they were nervous and wanted to avoid talking about what they were truly anxious about, so I tried it out.

"Hey man, are you nervous?" I said it loud, just right in the middle of his rant.

He stopped, maybe in shock, and briefly fell silent. "A bit," he replied, "you just look like you've been living in the woods and you got all your stuff with you and when you rolled down that window I just thought, 'Uh-oh, climbing in this car might be the end of the line for me.' All I needed was a ride for my bike and some help."

I laughed. "Nobody here is going to kill anybody, got it? I'm not here to hurt you, man. I'm a guy who loves bikes, and you looked in trouble." I laughed again at the absurdity. "You thought I might kill you?"

Larry half-shrugged apologetically. Then he nodded. "Well, or beat me up or something."

"Well, ok then, brother. Let's agree to be helpful to each other." That seemed to seal the deal.

"Alright," he agreed.

"Now, here's how you can help me. I'm traveling around the country interviewing people with a single question. I'd like to hear your thoughts."

"Really? Ok, what's the question, man?"

I asked.

He frowned, scanning his thoughts. "I would ask everyone: *What is the worst town that you have ever been to that you could warn me about?* I've been to some rough places where the cops were out to get me, that's for sure." He grimaced again and burped. "There was this one little town

I was in where I'd scored some primo weed, but turns out it was from a cop and it was all a setup and before I knew it, the DEA is tracking me with a satellite chip in my phone and they got a file on me and…" I smiled to myself. This man was a ramblin' man, nervous or not.

Thirty minutes later we pulled into the parking lot at the brewery. And, for a brief moment, Larry became helpful again. He cocked his head when I slowed down, pulling in. "What's that sound?"

"That is my brand-new muffler." I grimaced. "I think they missed a part. I'm taking it in in Flagstaff this afternoon."

"You should skip this town," he said. "In Phoenix, they will be much more efficient. And cheaper. Here there are horrible, shameful people." I wasn't ready for a rambling litany of injustices, so I just said, "Got it. Thanks, Larry."

In the parking lot of the brewery, after we unpacked all his belongings and said goodbye, Larry asked about my lodging that night. I said I was going to Frank Lloyd Wright's studio east of Phoenix, then heading south. "You should probably comb your hair before you get there," Larry laughed. "Don't want to freak him out. Well, if you're looking for a place to stay, I got a great one." Larry smudged a grubby fingerprint permanently onto my map to show me where to stay down the road. "Now here is a great campsite," he said, twisting his index finger emphatically. A man-made lake south of Taliesin West and due east of Phoenix. It's closer than Tucson, and they'll have just as many of those Tombstone Pizza cactuses for you to take pictures of," he said. "Sure I can't buy you a beer?"

"Nope." I smiled, He was unique company, but boy did he smell, and truly, I wanted to move on. "I'm going to keep rolling. But have a cold one for me!" He would, I knew, cold or not.

I made it to the campground by early evening and swam in the concrete-lined lake adjacent to the parking lot. It wasn't perfect, but like Larry said, it was cheap and a great place to take photos of the saguaros.

If you were an outlaw in the Wild West, would you be a one-gun shooter or a two-gun shooter?

A battered cowboy hat sat wedged between the dash and the windshield. It had survived months of abuse, everything from Burning Man dance parties to soaking rains. I had, more than once, slept in the thing. And now, after all that, yellow cornstalk dust floated off the brim. It was falling apart.

September. Four months on the road. I found myself in the southwest corner of America outside El Paso, far from everything. The entire map, the weight of the whole country, sat above this lonely region. Here I sat in the middle of nowhere, tucked away in what felt like a forgotten corner of the world. I couldn't easily get to a place where I knew anyone. Not one person.

What's your favorite memory?

Later that day, I pulled into a campground and hot springs tucked far off the interstate in New Mexico. I paid, set up my tent, and walked over to the building at the center of camp. I sat down at one of the brown picnic tables, waiting to see if anyone would walk in. The pale yellow walls echoed the weak light squeezed out of a bare bulb. I had been excited about walking into a clubhouse in the evening and seeing families playing board games, someone heading into town—did I need anything? Alas, I was joined only by a couple dozen poorly written romance novels and a worn *Sorry!* board game.

I had chosen to stop at Faywood, a campground centered on natural hot springs in the middle of southeastern New Mexico. For twenty bucks, I got to camp and bask in the warm springs as long as I could stand. In the two days I spent there, I soaked for more than ten hours in them. The whole area sat almost deserted, and the pools were so nice that I pledged to keep this experience in mind whenever things went wrong. I would remember the time I woke up cold—freezing cold— and I could step out of my tent, naked, and slip into this enveloping warm spring. But pretty much every time things have gotten tough since then, I've forgotten that.

But sometimes I do remember.

If you could have a day with no plans, completely open, what would you do?

Renovations were underway, and I could tell that soon this campground would be an expensive spa. All the facilities, such as the big adobe painted reservation area, were under construction. Clearly they would soon be charging much more than camping rates.

The seasons were changing. I'd switched to my winter sleeping bag a few nights before. It had frosted the previous night. The next morning I wrote "ice" in my car window with my fingernail.

I decided to stay at Faywood two days longer than planned, crouching in the ever-flowing hot water, sleeping in my tent, reading, writing, thinking. I needed to be in Texas by a certain date, but until then my time was open. Though I kept silent, loud conversations were going on continually in my head. Stay in the warm water, my knee reminded me, stretch.

I looked forward to the next day of warm soaking. My hike at The Land affected me more deeply than I understood at the time. Then it was just rain-soaked disappointment; here at the empty hot springs, head back and watching the sky change, I could step back, survey the scene. Analyze from the interior.

What is it all about, Alfie?

(Dennis Dragon, co-founder of The Surf Punks)

As I sat in the warm pools, elbows propped up on the edge, I leafed through my blue notebook. Pages and pages of questions; questions filling almost every line. As I turned each page, remembering the asker, I laughed at some of the funniest:

Is it warm in here, or it just me?

Would you mind wearing this mask?

Will the Vikings ever win the Super Bowl?

May I ask you another question after my first question?

How can I have satisfying conversations with my wife?

If you could only ask one question, but you realized afterward that it was the wrong question, what would you do?

As I continued reading, I found myself ruminating on all the questions and the nature of the project itself. When I started the journey, I thought I'd be consumed by challenging questions relating to our human experience, like, *How do we eradicate torture? What is the nature of addiction? Why are we, as a culture, so debilitated by body issues? Why do our schools fail to educate so many of our students?* These are the issues of our day and age. But no one asked these questions. No one.

I noticed that other than off-the-cuff humorous questions, the inquiry people sought maintained a peculiar emotional distance. No one asked me: *Why do we fear the other? How do I know that you won't abandon me?* Or even, *What is fear?*

The biggest category of questions people asked seemed to seek an understanding of the collective experience through an individual lens. Of course, we all want to know: *Are you seeing this, too? How do you understand the world through these undependable eyes?*

Americans asked about the nature of love and happiness and who we are.

What makes you laugh?

Are you content with your soul?

Are you happy?

What is it that makes you feel most alive?

What is one thing that you love in your life?

What are you passionate about?

Where does your deep gladness meet the world's deep need?

What gives you life?

What do you feel called to do?

How are you doing?

Who are you?

What's your worst fear?

As I ruminated, my thoughts turned inward as well. I was lonely. "The reason you don't have a girlfriend," my father had kindly explained twenty years earlier, as I expressed confusion about my early, still-dateless life, "is that you don't have anything to offer."

He was being pragmatic and, he felt, fatherly. I sat in the largest hot spring, thinking over the past. He offered an explanation—one that made sense. How else to figure out this mystery? But at the time, it had hit me like a shot. In my young teenaged psyche it ruptured abdomen, major exit wound. Really, I don't have anything to offer? Yes, it made a lot of sense to both of us, but not for the same reasons.

And it applied today. When I looked at my life through his lens, I could see the logic: beater car, zero investments, no health insurance, no job, and no plan. I looked at all of this with a creative I'll-figure-it-out smile, but I wasn't immune to my father's—and society's—overarching script for folks like me.

This script had done right by my father. At thirty-five, he had a house, a wife, two kids. A rising position as a surgeon.

We were different people, me and my father—I would've made a terrible, terrible surgeon for one—but, like me, there's no way he had a handle on the Big Questions. Nobody does. I just wished we could connect enough so I could learn how he asked the universe, *Where does it start and where does it end? Why are we here? What does it all mean?*

Later I stood at the edge of the largest natural pool, alone, skipping stones. I slung my arm back and watched as the flattest, grayest rock bounced across the top of the water, leaving a rippling trail as its wake. The ripples grew in rings from the center as the stone bounced again. And again, rings beginning to bounce into one another. Eventually, it lost its velocity and slid beneath the surface, finding its flip-flop way to the bottom. I watched as the rings continued to spread out in thin, barely perceptible ripples, until they too disappeared.

CHAPTER 9

TEXAS

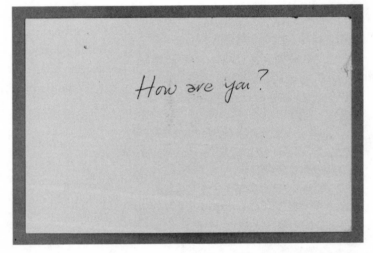

How are you? - Al Franken
(Comedian, actor, writer. Currently United States Senator, Minnesota)

T he next day, I crossed the state line into Texas. Though my thoughts were already ruminating on the conference in Austin six hundred miles ahead, there were a couple of detours in my path.

The first stop was El Paso, a border town teeming with life. Coming in from the west, traveling some of the emptiest roadways of the entire journey, the bustle of El Paso was refreshing. I found a campground north of the city, set up, and then drove downtown to walk around and explore. As the morning became afternoon the temperature rose steadily, and I found myself looking for shade as I strolled. I happened to be at the entrance to the El Paso Museum of Art when the heat became oppressive and I decided it was time to find something indoors.

On my way in the door, I noticed a flier advertising that evening was to be the monthly after-hours party for young professionals. Ten dollars for a potato bar, two drinks, and some conversation. With a big beard and wild eyes, I looked more the part of a walk-on pirate than "young professional." Dinner and couple beers for ten bucks was too good to pass up, plus I was craving some interaction with others. I picked up a ticket.

That evening at dusk I returned to the museum parking lot. I sat in my car, running fingers through my hair. I didn't have a comb, but I had showered at the campground and I had used soap. I secretly hoped the light fragrance of Irish Spring would linger and maybe, just maybe, provide cover as cologne.

When my hair didn't conform to the loose raking, I raked with more gusto, starting to get frustrated. I had removed myself from society and mostly didn't care whether I was "attractive." I enjoyed my beard and mussed hair. But I'd seen many folks walk in from weeks in the wilderness and concluded that I was maybe setting myself up for some kind of embarrassment.

And then I felt ashamed of myself, thinking back to Lucas and The Land and the ideal that by being who you are, you will authentically meet the person who loves you.

But c'mon, seriously? If I ran into someone interesting and attractive at an art gallery, what were the odds they would be attracted to hair going in all directions and worn-out Dickies? Was I being true to myself at the expense of attracting someone else? Lucas's self-assuredness taunted me, but my father wouldn't have approved. "You have nothing to offer someone," played again in my ears. And in a way, he was right. "Would you like to come back to my tent for a drink?" That's not an invitation.

That's a punch line.

There were dance performances and wings with artwork I hadn't explored earlier, and I floated from gallery to gallery soaking in the southwestern colors and forms. With the sparse attendance, I didn't bump into anyone and nothing out of the ordinary happened. I assembled a potato from the bar, grabbed a beer, and tried to plop down on a barely-padded modernist bench. I was going to chalk the evening up to an uneventful single-shoulder-shrug, when a photographer walked up. "Hello!" he began cheerfully. He was young, and he had a big camera with an even bigger lens. A press pass dangled from a bright green lanyard.

"Are you enjoying the evening?"

"Sure," I said, suddenly unsure. I set down my beer.

He continued, "So, I grabbed a shot of you back there, looking over the balcony at the dance performance. Can I interview you real quick for the *Gold Nugget*?" I was processing his question when I realized I had responded as, well, me, and not as The Question Guy. The solo hike and the subsequent days spent alone in the southwest left me in a curious frame of mind. The tables had turned, and not having the shield of the project to protect me, I felt strangely vulnerable.

"So, where are you coming from?" he asked.

"Well…I'm coming from Boston." All the questions I'd been ruminating on, swirling around me, dropped away, and I sat like I was in the glare of a spotlight. I didn't want to talk about Boston. And I certainly didn't want to talk about Harvard.

Harvard. It seemed like an ancient, distant land. Since then, I had let myself get so wild. He would want to talk about that.

"So, Boston, huh? Wow. That's a long way to come for a potato bar and a dance performance."

"Yeah, I'm actually on a road trip." It was strange that I fumbled, just trying to give him the two cents he sought from a Man on the Street for the college paper.

"A road trip! Where are you headed?" He said with enthusiasm, though he looked at me quizzically.

"Texas. Boston to Minnesota to California to Texas, actually." Clearly I had another story I didn't want to tell. And the details I fed this guy were ridiculous. I'm from Boston. I'm going to Texas via California. Was I picking up a shipment of drugs, or human cargo? The awareness of my discomfort just made it all that more strange. My consciousness floated outside me, and stood watching the interaction. *Why are you being so awkward?*

"Nice camera," I said, redirecting the conversation. "That's certainly a fast lens for the length."

"It's the university's, but thanks." He continued to look at me, sizing me up like Kojak must have. "So, are you a photographer?"

"Uh, no, not really," I lied.

"Yeah," he said, clearly suspicious. "Really, you don't take photos? You seem like the kind of guy who would."

"Uh, yeah, I kind of like to, but not as a job or anything."

"Well…OK then." Though confused, he had a piece to write, and this wasn't the story he sought.

I sat, silent.

"Am I bothering you?" he asked, flashing a brief, anxious grin.

"No, hey, I'm sorry," I said, "I've been in my car and on my own for a while and I'm not communicating well. I'm not your best interview right now."

"Gotcha," he said. "Will you just say and spell your name into this recorder so I can credit you in the photo?" He held out a small black machine, almost the exact make of my own.

"Well, I'm going to keep milling about," he said when I finished, gracefully dismissing himself.

It would be the first of two interviews that I sat for the entire trip, both uncomfortable. The second would come at the end of my journey, but during each, the discomfort was palpable.

As he walked away, I thought over all the people I had interviewed. No one seemed to be in discomfort when they were speaking with me, but I hoped I hadn't made anyone uncomfortable. I was also struck by how complex we are as people; sometimes extroverted, sometimes introverted.

This was a distinct change from the other me, the guy who started out the trip wondering if it would coalesce into something. Here I sat, uncomfortable talking about myself, such a change from all the talking and thinking about questions from those around me.

A second irony became clear: the further I moved from regular, casual contact with people, the less comfortable I became being with them. I hadn't asked anyone but a hitchhiker The Question for more than a week. No one noticed me moving through the background, quietly asking questions to myself.

Do you think you could handle living alone on the moon?

This change to the solitary did not bode well for what would be next, standing at a podium, presenting a paper at a conference. Butterflies fluttered at the thought; I was scared. These lonely miles only reminded me how far I had traveled from the life I'd been living of classes in state-of-the-art lecture halls, discussing the fine-point distinctions of post-structuralist educational theory. And I lived consumed by questions, unready to stand before a room full of people and deliver answers. The ivory tower I drove away from stood like a monolith in front of me. And I knew I would arrive thinking different thoughts than all those around me, professors who had just gotten off a plane, grad students finishing up theses. I feared failure.

Stuffed ears, dry skin, disequilibrium, headaches, nausea, and loneliness. Signs that may or may not accompany weightlessness.

How far are you willing to go?

My second stop before the conference took me on a four-hour detour south, a route paralleling the border to Redford, hugging the western edge of Big Bend National Park. An Outward Bound base ran courses out of there, and some friends were leaving on expeditions with students in two days. I would have just enough time to catch them before they left.

A small collection of weathered, paint-peeling wooden buildings made the whole of the base at Redford. Expedition gear was housed in one outbuilding, instructors in the others. I planned to have dinner and help with any details needed for packing.

Stopping at a grocery store on my way to Redford, I picked up ingredients for lasagna. I looked forward to seeing people I knew, folks I hadn't seen since Minnesota.

We said hellos when I arrived, and I threw some items in the spare room I'd been offered and set to work cooking.

Now, somewhere on the Internet I'd read that you could just put uncooked lasagna noodles in the pan, layer the rest of the ingredients, and Voilà! The juice from the tomatoes would hydrate and cook the noodles at the same time as the other ingredients. It sounded like magic so I tried it out, arranging the tomato sauce, cheese and vegetables in the pan. I twisted the knob on the timer, set the old yellow oven on "Stun," and sat down at a cheap little table in the dining room to enjoy the company of the instructors, Wayne and Rosemary. We talked about the expedition they had planned and about my question project, and we caught up on life. Wayne seemed slightly aloof, slightly annoyed, which I chalked up to nerves from the upcoming course he was to lead. Regardless, I felt as if I had come out of my own wilderness, connecting with them. Forty-five minutes later, I opened the oven door to a large puff of smoke.

"Looks like you didn't hydrate that thing enough," Wayne winced, pointing at the smoking remains of dinner. I apologized as best I could, and we picked at the partially cooked center. Not even beer could make the crisp, blackened noodles taste better.

The next morning I came out to the hard-pack dirt loading area to help. Wayne and the Logistics Coordinator, Sharon, were already there loading gear into a truck. We finished, then waited for Rosemary to meet us with a transport van, but it was taking a while. While we stood around, I casually asked Wayne The Question. Instead of offering his thoughts, he turned.

"Does this crap ever stop with you?" his said, his voice cracking. Here in the dry heat, his answer slithered and reared. At first I thought it might be a joke, but his voice burned with a note of real anger. I hadn't seen him in months, and Wayne's tone knocked me off guard. He had heard about my trip way back at the base camp in Minnesota, earlier in the summer. I thought he would be game. Maybe he was mad about the lasagna?

But out here, in the hot Texas sun, it was clear it wasn't the food. Sharon sat on the open back gate of a nearby truck, watching this interaction and starting to giggle. They must have talked, because somehow she already knew Wayne was mad. She seemed ready for a show.

I wasn't sure where things were going, so I just tried to keep it about The Question. "What would you ask everyone you met, Wayne?"

He did not pause. "Dude, I don't care about that crap. What is *your* question? I mean, the question you are asking everyone is the question you are asking everyone? That is circular. It doesn't make any sense." His face tightened as if to spit.

At that moment, after so much alone time, I almost tumbled back down the rabbit hole of self-doubt. But I'd been on the road talking with people for long enough that if I could just keep him talking, maybe I could figure out what had riled him up. Plus, like Mike said at the beginning of all this back in Kalamazoo: *You might get punched!* I held my ground, but I was confused. "Wayne," I said calmly, "I'm just asking a question, trying to figure out what is something that you want to know from everyone."

Wayne continued, provoked. "OK, so you are traveling around the country asking the one question you want to ask everyone *by asking everyone the one question you are asking them.*" He looked at me pointedly, eyes bulging. "You're just going around in circles!"

Ruffled by his anger, I pressed on. "Yeah. But, Wayne, everyone asks something different. Right here, right now, it is *you* who are answering the question."

Wayne looked at me, "But here's my suspicion: you don't actually have an answer for yourself."

The sun beat hot, I entered the fray. "I know! That's exactly what I'm looking for. That is what this whole journey is, man. It's true: *I don't have a question!*" I had never heard myself say this out loud.

But Wayne wasn't through. "You're just driving around picking other people's brains. You're like a human lint roller for truth."

I nodded, agreeing. "Yeah, but that doesn't make me an asshole, man. I want to hear what people say, what they are thinking about. What are people looking for from other people? That is why I'm asking this question. And yes, my own reasons go deep: I don't have strong beliefs in any spiritual system. I'm kind of taking a pulse to see what other people believe. That doesn't mean I'm cheating. I want to know people's questions because I want to *find* my question. What I'm really hoping for is some kind of answer."

Wayne squared off. "Here's my answer: Quit bugging everyone and go and get your own goddamned question!"

Still sitting on the truck gate, Sharon laughed again. With that, the tension snapped, as though cut with scissors. Wayne realized that being aggressive was ridiculous. His face was still red, but he smiled.

I was glad things weren't escalating anymore, but I felt kind of deflated. "Yeah," I said, more quietly. "I want to know what people want to know about. It is not really circular."

Wayne wiped his forehead and crinkled his brow.

"Yes, it is strange." I continued. "But that is why I'm asking this question at all. I'm looking for my own truth." Now Wayne paused, considering. He stuck out his hand, softening.

"Here, take this on your project then: *Will you be my friend?*"

I looked him in the eye. We shook. A big shift was occurring under my feet. It was becoming clear, finally, who I was and what I was looking for. I had given voice to one of the things I'd been searching for, unknowingly, this entire journey.

"You already are my friend, Wayne."

"This is what you need to ask on your journey."

Wayne offered me a clue, one that had appeared at Burning Man, one that would unlock my developing anxiety for the impending conference. I needed to recognize that my journey was both external and internal and that maybe my search for the perfect question was misguided. Maybe what I sought was hiding in plain sight. Maybe the question I asked others was truly my own single question.

I left Redford with a head full of ideas, my path a little clearer, but only just.

What is infinity?

I made it half the eight hours to the Conference, cooking dinner and setting up my tent just as the cool grays of twilight began to descend. I slept with the blue rain fly off the tent that night, only a semitransparent gauze between me and vast constellations of bright stars. I lay on my back, staring at the purple-black above me, thinking about Wayne's challenge. I did want to know my own singular question.

There were so many stars out, and a question from earlier in the trip traveled through my mind, *What is infinity?* This wasn't my own question, but I found myself thinking about it: if we could answer this, we could move forward in understanding our universe.

But then I began to laugh. It sounded like a great question, and of course I was curious about infinity. Infinity was "a really big number," "something that never ends," or "more than a googolplex." I began laughing even harder. All of humanity has already been ruminating on this question, and we never get any farther than the front lawn of our already-known thoughts. We've been thinking about, *What is love?* and, *What is infinity?* and, *Do you know if you're on the right path?* for all recorded history, and still no one had any clue. We weren't any closer to understanding these ideas than when we started, just like me with my blue notebook crammed full of questions. They were amazing and wonderful and revealing, but none of them were mine. I realized, right there, lying on my back, that the questions I was cataloging were interesting, but when I asked, it wasn't answers I sought, but to hear how people engaged the mystery and the absurdity of their lives, of the human condition. The Question, I realized was my way of tapping into others' experiences. My conversation with Wayne made me realize I had found my question: It was the question I was already asking.

What is the relationship between subjectivity and the context in which you are placed?

Rural west Texas is almost a character itself in the movie *Giant* starring James Dean. Its dusty panoramic scenes formed the only picture of Texas I'd ever known, a geography of wide open land dotted with oil derricks, everything everywhere flat, brown, and dry. A thick band of sweat on the rim of a worn cowboy hat, the only evidence of water. A farmhand leaning on a beat-up, light blue Ford truck, skin sunburned and leathery. And that's exactly the vision I drove across, yet, as I made my way into the central region of the state, shrubs and trees began to appear, huddling in small clumps, offering each other small plots of shade. Unlike the Southwest from which I came, the landscape here ran green over rolling hills. A two-lane highway curved up and around winding its way east, cutting a ribbon across a landscape more verdant than anything I'd seen for months, a landscape from which water must spring.

I had traveled deep into Texas Hill Country before even realizing it. A small pond appeared off to my right, the first swimmable standing water I'd seen in weeks. It tapered into a stream, and further down the road it opened back up into a small lake at the entrance to the con-ference grounds. I was in awe of the water. I parked and walked in. "Welcome!" The front desk signage beckoned, "Would you like to rent a boat during your stay?"

What are you doing here?

I checked in, found my simple, rustic cabin with bunk beds, and then walked over to the lunch area. I was officially here. I wandered out of the room and down to the outdoor lunch area, bought a sandwich, and sat down at the closest table. A visiting professor sitting across from me introducing himself his small family.

Though titled *Curriculum and Pedagogy*, the eighth annual confer-ence wasn't organized around common, well-worn topics in education; here everyone shared an interest in nurturing the development of iden-tity above any mandated learning targets or state-administered tests. There were no tables with colorful swag from major textbook companies.

The professor's two children ran around the table, pulling hair and poking each other. His wife pulled a half-smile at my introduction, dis-tracted by the activity of her kids. We talked about their long family drive and methods for keeping their two young children occupied. I introduced the concept of my journey, and how I had happened to leave Boston to arrive in Texas via California. I asked them The Question. She responded first.

"I'm an attorney," she said, "and my first question would be, 'Why would you want to do that?" she asked, with a pained expression that I couldn't read as serious or joking. I had a history of being intimidated by lawyers, often feeling as if I'd confronted an impenetrable wall of logic. Where I was verbose, they were terse. And always right. And this revealed my bias: something in me didn't always believe that attorneys employ the best logic, just the most consistent. And from where she'd started, this conversation appeared to be no different. And to think, with my own studies of language and logic in philosophy, law school wouldn't have been a stretch for possible academic paths.

"Hey, I'm not trying to challenge you here," I said, intentionally staying calm. "I'm just curious, and this is my one question." I said it out loud: this is my question. It fit.

"OK, well, let's be clear asking and answering questions is my job. And, for the record, it's a bad move for an attorney to ask any questions they don't already know the answers to."

We sat a little awkwardly for a few minutes in which I feigned more than the usual interest in the sandwich in front of me. But I was struck immediately by the tactics she revealed, something I had never actually known about law; start with knowing something, turn it into a question, and lob it back at the asker. This was *much* more effective than the way I'd spent my entire life arguing. I usually asked questions to figure something out, and if I wanted to make a point with a question I'd resort to irony or sarcasm. I made a mental note to remember to use this attack strategy on my next journey around the United States. But were we actually arguing?

As we chatted about other things, she seemed to realize I was not, in fact, challenging her. She realized her courtroom-style intimidation. She also knew that regular conversations don't hinge on the idea of a settlement or a plea deal. Her kids continued to play underfoot, and she relaxed a little, looking across the table and smiled tiredly. A kid squirmed into her lap, and she began petting his head. "OK," she said, softening, "I would ask, *How are you doing?*"

My experience with this attorney did not stand alone. Most of the participants at this conference continually exercised their ability to be smarter than those around them. She did soften when given the time, but I wasn't prepared to engage the defensive or confrontational right out of the gate. This behavior felt so contrary to the interactions I was used to. I would ask my question and then remain silent, my goal to be invisible in the thoughts of the speaker. This was different. Wayne must have called ahead.

When is the last time you challenged the status quo?

Across the green-grass lawns of the conference, these intellectually gifted professors and educators shook hands and smiled genuinely, reuniting after a year of teaching and lecturing. Though I traveled here to present my paper, I remained an outsider. Worse, I'd almost completely forgotten the research I'd put into the thing in the months since I left. It felt like a different eon, though it had only been four and a half months since I'd graduated. I had let the wildness and the road consume me.

The scholars at the conference were enmeshed in the ideas of critical theory, considered how power was construed through learning, and how, by understanding both learning and power, we can influence change. I love the intellectual process of examining the unseen structures that compose our reality and our identity, examining the role of power behind motivation. In this kind of work, ideas become gymnastics of word and thought, syntax and symbol.

If Michel Foucault hadn't researched and written *Madness and Civilization*, we would still see madness in isolation, like a scratch or cut, as something you have or don't have and not as treatable or influenced by society. Break out of the idea that students need to sit in rows, facing forward, silent while the teacher lectures, and new ways of thinking evolve and deep questions are raised; *What is the purpose of school?*

I spent a semester at graduate school observing and coteaching in a South Boston High School class, helmed by a phenomenal teacher piloting a truly student-centered learning unit. The goal was this: students recognized a social injustice in their immediate community and were tasked with raising awareness and educating the community on that topic. There were installations on gun violence reported on and photographed by the local newspaper, teach-ins at local schools regarding sexually transmitted diseases. Plays were written, and all kinds of important works done out in the community. Throughout the planning, creating, and implementing, the teacher connected the students' learning needs, crafting persuasive arguments to sway community leaders, as well as reflecting on larger theories of how we all exist together. The students themselves examined the underlying framework of racism and how they could be agents in dismantling that dynamic.

I took this unit and this teacher and wove the narrative of his work in a tough South Boston school within a tapestry of ideas in poststructural sociology. It's this kind of education that we need, not the cookie-cutter crap seen in so many schools, with both teachers and students disenfranchised.

I had never expected this paper would be accepted, or that I'd be presenting an academic paper anywhere on Earth, and yet here I was, somewhat unprepared, to do exactly that. Earlier in the spring, in the classroom, I had set a goal for myself of working on a project worthy of sharing with the rest of the world. The work I'd put in with research and the paper I'd written made me proud, but I remained conflicted by the forum. In some ways, I recognized the importance of presenting ideas in an open intellectual setting, skill-sharing practitioner to practitioner. There was real value in that kind of exchange, and from that perspective, papers should be presented and notes taken and conversations had.

In other ways, I knew this presentation contributed directly to the removed and insular academic environment I abhorred; while some were going to take new ideas back to their instructional lives, many would head right back to offices. Right back to the journals, forever analyzing, forever living in theory. This is the well-armed side against critical theory. I worried that my presentation was not, in some ways, a helpful act for the betterment of education.

How do you know that what you're doing is what you're supposed to be doing?

On Day One I found myself sitting in a presentation room, listening intently to a forum on how the very ideas on which curriculum has been based has been reconceptualized. The presenter was engaging, the material relevant, but my thoughts were drawn out the window to a family in the grass. A small child stood, blowing soap bubbles. The bubbles floated, multicolored, wobbling around in thin air. Not defined by a rigid framework, the surface tension alone held their shape, colorless air the center. The forces of the world—wind, air density, and heat—all helped form the constantly changing shape as it floated away. Its short life ended by a light touch—a branch, the fibers of a shirt. Whatever it encountered made it pop, a silent wet circle on a steel door. The child, laughing, blew another.

The presenter clicked forward to the next slide. The bright colors of this new slide jogged me back to her topic. I saw these ideas, like soap bubbles, in their multicolored complexity and their important, but tenuous, influence on the world. There were so many surfaces against which these ideas would pop. I just hoped that there would always be another educator who would laugh and blow another.

What do you do for a living?

By the end of the first afternoon, I found myself skipping the last panel of lectures and instead heading to the game room to shoot pool. I brimmed full with ideas, and I needed space to process them. The ideas flying around the conference about self and identity attempted to encourage openness, but they had a background in theorists that I didn't know, from books I hadn't read. The conversations from questions at The Land felt elemental: *Why are you drawn to this place? Are you ready to die? Do we have to live like this?* This conference posed more specific questions, and always in the abstract. I needed the clink of solid material. Eight ball, corner pocket. I snuck out to the game room.

The musical guests for the conference happened to be there, too. They were already using the pool table, and they invited me to join in. They were two: Jerry, a punk rock accordionist, and Aaron, the guitarist/singer. We talked for a bit, and Jerry stood closest, so I asked him The Question.

"Normally I ask people what they do for a living or what they consider their vocation." Jerry had parted his red hair neatly down the center in a hipster pageboy. "But you know, the freaky side of me wants to find out everybody's craziest sexual exploits, to find out what's *not* socially acceptable."

After this, Jerry paused, rethinking his question. "Hmm, I don't know. I like hearing people's stories about the world. I'd like to hear everybody's take on what is the meaning of happiness, like, *What would it take to make you happy?*

"Well, I never ask that directly. Usually I'll try a question like: *What have you been listening to lately?* Then they can go through the list of albums they've listened to over the last week or so. It's interesting how that works."

I picked up his thread. "I know sometimes people ask, *What do you collect?* to discover who a person is, where they derive happiness. It's easier to get people talking about the things they like. Similarly, *What have you been listening to lately?* could lead well into, *What do you like?* without saying those words."

"That's true." He smiled and added, "A good question leads you where you want to go without being direct."

Something clicked there, and my thoughts started to connect. It reminded me of the analysis I'd done for my presentation. Yes, this idea is what made good teaching, and the teacher I had observed, work so well; he got his students to ask honest questions about race inequality in their community, then he asked how they could best respond through social justice actions in that very community. He then supported them in those efforts, ensuring projects included context and rigor.

Aaron, the guitarist, bent across the green of the table, lined up his pool cue. I waited until he shot and then asked him The Question. The balls clinked and clacked. He looked down at the table, assessing his next shot.

"So, I can have everyone answer a question. Sounds pretty general." He rolled his cue stick between his hands, frowning. Then he seemed to relent. "OK, I'll play along. It's got to be the same question for everyone, right?" He shot. Balls clinked around the table again. "I don't know, man. I'm not moved by what people want to know. I guess I tend to think I have them figured out anyway, or that I understand why they do things better than they do themselves." He paused. "That sounds arrogant, right? But I don't care, you know?" He shot again, this time haphazardly. The red ball rolled lazily across the green table.

I decided to push him a little. "Ok, look at it this way: What's a theory you could check by asking everybody? There's a collective unconscious that you could reveal or understand better by asking a question," I said, trying to keep things moving. "What would you ask?"

"Right, but I'm not confident that the people I'm speaking to will be able to get around their fears or insecurities enough to describe something that is actually truthful. So, I ask something like, *What's your favorite thing to do?* or *What do you do for fun here?*"

He seemed evasive. I wished I knew why. We finished our game and plopped down in the overstuffed chairs of the game room.

"Alright man, I'm going to go for it. Here's a question I *really* like." He smiled suddenly, mischievous. I wasn't sure why he'd changed, why he was suddenly interested in answering, but my intuition told me this question was the one I wanted to hear the most. "OK," he said. "*If you were to take someone's hand and somehow fasten them in a way that they were unable to resist, and submerge their hand—just the hand—*" His voice become animated as he fastened down an imaginary arm, "*in a vat of boiling oil, and you kept their hand in there for six hours...*" His eyes went manic. "*Do you think that would kill them?*"

His thoughts tumbled out of him. Like Axel the roadie in Santa Barbara, it was clear that he held onto this question; it was His Question, and it was serious. I didn't know what to make of it. I scrunched up my brow.

"Say what?"

He looked at me. "A hand being submerged in the vat of oil."

"That's the question?"

What the hell was he talking about? I thought to myself, but I played along anyway. "Why would it kill them?"

"Well, there have been lots of different theories around that. You could bleed to death, another theory is that..."

That didn't compute: *There have been a lot of different theories?*

"How hot is the oil? Is this like fryer oil?"

"Yeah, their hand would fry up like a French fry." He made a sizzling sound to show he meant business. "Some people say you would bleed to death. Others say the heat would spread up the body and kill you."

I was intrigued. "The rest of your body is not subjected to the heat, though, right?"

"Right, but whatever part of you is close to the oil is subjected to those temperatures."

I couldn't help myself, "Where the hell did you come up with this question?"

Aaron laughed easily. "I don't know. I just came up with it. Some people think you would bleed to death because your hand would just fall off. And some people think the heat would cauterize the wound." Now it was my turn to be incredulous; this was fascinating.

I weighed in. "I think you would die. Not necessarily immediately, but it would be so traumatic to the skin and muscle that there is bound to be an infection in the underlying tissue or some secondary effect at the border of the burned and unburned flesh."

Aaron beamed at my response. "You're wrong, but I like your style," he said. "Most folks don't really even put any mental energy into it. You should have seen this girl's reaction to it at a bar, she acted like I was a freak psychopath or something. I'm so bored of that 'you're crazy' reaction. I was like, 'Yeah, I know it's crazy … *but, really, what do you think?*'"

"Have you ever asked a…doctor?"

Aaron looked at me, shaking his head. "Nope. No, I haven't, but I should. I'm going to."

"That's a path to pursue."

He looked out the window. "Personally, I think that you'd live."

Jerry walked back in from the vending machine room, throwing a handful of peanuts into his mouth.

"So, did Jerry answer your question?" I asked.

"What question?" Jerry asked, chewing.

"I just asked him the hand-submerged-in-the-vat-of-oil question."

"Oh, that," he said, with a sigh, clearly having heard it all before. "You'd totally die."

What do you worry about?

That night I tossed and turned, my mind running in preparation for my presentation. "Why don't I sleep well before I present?" I asked myself as I rolled around. I'd done this a thousand times, whether the night before the first day of school or the moment students arrived at the Outward Bound base. I let the anxiety consume me. Yet always the minute the bell rang to start class, I found myself relaxing; talking to people is my skill set. But my shoulders were tense, and I stayed nervous until the moment I began.

The next morning I woke up, showered, and stood in my assigned room long before my presentation time. I stacked and restacked papers I'd be passing around. I double-checked the projector and ran through the PowerPoint slides I'd composed back in April for the seventh time. I smiled at my own nervousness; I spent time reviewing my paper and I knew intimately what the presentation would cover: I had written it. I lived with the high school students as they lived through it themselves. As seats filled, I took one last breath and began.

How have you changed over your lifetime? How have you stayed the same?

"Hello," I said nervously. Other presenters were seated around me, intent. "I'm here to talk about how an experiential social justice curriculum in a South Boston high school offered a critical exercise in identity and served to bring real change to the lives of the students and the surrounding community." The academics looked at me expectantly, but I had to get something off my chest.

"I'm excited to talk about the research I've done on the power of this unique curriculum, but I have to be honest, my head is in a different place. You see, I've spent the last few months on the road, circumnavigating the US to arrive here. I'm on a journey interviewing people with one single question." I set down my prepared notes; a light had come on. "The power of question-asking has come alive for me in unique ways, and through this process I have come to see what role question-asking plays in our development of curriculum of the self. This teacher in Boston, he arrived at school each morning with one idea: I want to help these kids navigate their world better and be empowered to be agents for positive change in their own lives and their communities." What I had prepared did not deal explicitly with questions, but it felt right and I just kept going with it.

"So how do you design a curriculum that does that? Answering that question is what I saw him do every single day. If something wasn't working, he'd ask again: How do I design a curriculum that helps these students in front of me become agents of change? He even asked his students a variation: How do *you* become an agent of positive social change?" The table in front of me sat in rapt attention. The teacher I had been before grad school took over. I was comfortable, in control, calm. And as I spoke about the amazing work of these students and their teacher, The Question resonated throughout, becoming the framework through which I discussed my entire paper.

I mixed questions into my conclusion. "Questions are Socratic, experiential, democratic, deconstructive, and these forms of inquiry were utilized in South Boston earlier that spring." I was speaking extemporaneously, but these thoughts about questions were very natural. They didn't impede the analysis, because questioning was so ingrained in my consciousness. It was, I realized for the first time, part of me.

Applause at the end made me smile. I'd done it! I gathered my notes at the table and answered questions.

What kind of crap is that?

That evening, I walked down a grassy slope to dinner on the final night of the conference, the outdoor banquet hall standing in the distance. It stood alone, separate from the trees and grass that formed its natural surroundings. Rough-hewn beams held a simple roof, and the dinner area glowed with warm light. Tables were draped with white cloth, white flowers, and soft votive candles. This open-air arrangement was welcoming, but elevated, and seemed to impart a different message.

Instead of tables in the grass, we were set above the surroundings. We were better than the surroundings. Knowledge above nature.

I was caught between two options of where to sit: there was the Old People's table, or the Young, Interesting People's table. I opted for the latter, figuring it would be a fun group to ask the Question.

The conversation at the Young, Interesting People's table floated convivial and easy, but I noticed a lot of theorists were being name-dropped. An undercurrent of peacocks in competition. The subtle message of the surroundings was not lost on this group.

Three men and two women sat at my table. The women happened to be sitting across from me, one ten years older than the other. Everyone was nicely dressed; one of the women wore a loose-ruffled white blouse, the other a smart black skirt. The men had open-collared shirts with the squared or overly rounded eyeglass frames of architects.

As we talked, I found that both women and most of the men were Canadian. In the warm laughter at the end of a joke, I said, "Can I ask you all a question? I'm doing a project where I ask one question, and I'd like to hear your thoughts." Everyone nodded as I asked, and then the table fell silent for a moment. I felt very confident from my experience presenting earlier, and I leaned back in my chair as I asked, interested in the conversation sure to ensue.

The older woman tilted her chin, her long brown hair falling over her ear. She replied immediately. "First, what you're saying is not possible."

I couldn't tell if she had missed something; it seemed a strange way to respond. She kept going.

"Your project's got to be more *Alice in Wonderland,* wherein you open a door that reveals the soil and a depth. You see if the person you are asking is willing to move in. You then go to that depth where they are comfortable and you keep asking questions until you can unpack them, so you get their view of reality or an alternative reality or whatever it is."

I looked at her, confused. "The challenge is exactly that, though. The challenge is asking one single question," I said, trying to figure out where they were coming from.

"Your project cannot be *one question*; it must be a process of questions! One question is not going to find sufficient depth. You must ask many questions. You need to find the doorway you can enter, and you have to move in."

The other woman leaned in, eyes gleaming like a Cheshire cat.

"You have to have a *conversation* with this person you are questioning. You cannot simply have *one* question and *one* answer..."

The older woman jumped back in, "Exactly. You begin that process with a conversation. One question is not a conversation."

I sat dazed, disoriented as if I'd entered a stream of thought midstream, missed the beginning of an important lesson. I leaned forward to listen more closely.

"You think this is all about one question, but it's not. The real challenge is entering a play wherein one's singular question will *arise*." She folded her arms, and now she leaned back in her chair, her throne, and smiled.

Everyone at the table, even the trio of once-jovial men sat silent, nodding. I looked around thinking someone might chip in a question, but everyone around the table seemed to be considering the same strange logic that eluded me. The two women remained aloof, as though they had taught me an important lesson. The over-intellectualization I disdained was happening right here, squashing a perfectly enjoyable conversation. I stuck my finger out for a waiter. I needed a beer. Or ten.

The minute the staff came and removed my plate, I walked off the raised white platform and into the half-lit trees in the perimeter, in search of Aaron and Jerry.

Do you have any tattoos?

I had finished presenting, my biggest responsibility, but the conference wasn't over. The next day I saw more talks and heard about more research projects, and that evening I decided to go into Austin rather than hang around the conference grounds. Proud of myself for presenting, I decided that this was the perfect time to get a new tattoo, something I'd been thinking about for a while. The hot day mellowed into a nice, warm evening, and as I left the conference grounds, the sun dipped low, cleft by the horizon. I drove toward the big downtown, looking forward to my first trip into the city of Austin. It was exciting to think of new ink, and I itched to meet some new people, to be around some different energy.

A pattern of stars in '70s starburst colors on the inside of my elbow was my design of choice, to commemorate the journey with positive energy.

How have you modified your body to match your identity?

Earlier in the week, I had looked up the "Best Tattoo Studio in Austin" and called the shop at the top of the list. That night I drove in, found the shop, and described my design idea. They sat me in an old dental chair, buzzing needle stinging the soft underside of my elbow with bright colors. I asked The Question as the artist, Bob, worked on my arm. Bob thought as he worked, sharing his reflections between painful lines on my arm. I could only hear what he said when he paused to wipe away the blood and dip his needle into the inkpot.

"Well, let's see. If you ask people what their favorite albums are, they are just going to give you a list." He went back to studying my elbow and causing great pain to it. "So you've got to think of something that everyone can answer, or at least contribute to. I like to change things for the better, so how about: *What are you doing to fix the world?*" He squinted, assessing his work. The buzzing and the pain resumed.

A moment later, Bob stopped, wiped, and shared his next thought. "I've got it: *What's the single most important thing you can do to encourage the world?* Something along those lines, so that their question would answer what they think is wrong, without being lame about it. And we'd get something fucking productive out of it."

The buzzing returned.

A few minutes later, he paused, the bright orange star complete. He leaned in, gently dipping the needle into a purple-fuchsia ink pot for the next star, "So, what are you doing this question thing for?"

"Well, it started out for fun," I said. "but doing a big solo project around America means you spend a lot of time analyzing yourself. And the travel has been interesting." I listed all the states I'd traveled and where I still planned to go.

"That's cool you went to all them places," he said, pausing again to wipe my arm. "I went a bunch of places, too, when I was younger. But being alone, that shit's tough. I remember one time I pulled up to a cliff to watch the sunset and I looked at it and it was awesome and shit. But I stood there and went, 'Yup, there's another sunset.' And I left. I stopped having fun doing that kind of thing until I met my wife. Now I got someone to share it with." Another pause, and this time he looked down into my eyes.

"How can you handle being alone for so long?"

I scowled in mock disappointed: I wasn't alone. I was here, I said, talking with him.

With the tattoo completed, Bob sat me up, handing me a mirror. While I looked over the fresh new ink, he yelled out The Question to another artist over a dividing wall. After a pause, the voice responded, laughing.

"Will you give me a buck?"

When do you feel most alone?

I drove back to my cabin at the conference, lost in thought. So much of my interior world came alive on the journey, but externally, things changed. It seemed I always asked, "Do you mind if I join you?" Almost always the group entreated me to join in, it's true. But then I would find myself in the same old situation once again. Chatting. I love it, but the bite-sized pieces of conversation never seem to feed what is needed for real friendship. I was being generous with Bob the Tattoo Artist; more often than I wanted to admit, traveling alone meant being alone.

And maybe because I didn't have anyone to bounce the ideas of the conference off, I could only mull it over in my own brain. These academics were grappling with identity; they were thinking about how to dismantle misdirected power. They recognized the importance of identity in a curriculum and strove for reforms that gave learners understanding rather than facts. They did real and honest good; far more than the concerned opinion pieces and strident voices on the radio were doing. It just felt like a club.

As I drove toward the conference grounds that night, I thought over the questions these academics asked.

What is the relationship between subjectivity and the context in which you are placed?

How do you see things unfolding, as a process?

What road led you here?

What are the ways in which systems of binary discernment—up/down, good/evil, man/woman, etc.—impact your life, and how do you deal with it personally?

Can you have pride without ego?

If you only had one day left to live, what would you do?

Do you feel alone right now?

What do we have to do to make peace a reality?

Their questions were centered from their own lens, which wasn't surprising, but I was surprised that only rarely did people enlarge their scope and ask a question from a larger viewpoint. Which led me to the realization that there was another kind of questioning that never seemed to arise throughout the journey. I asked questions of people from many demographics, age, race, gender. And not a single person asked a question about war, the rise of Arab autonomy, or global warming. There wasn't a question out there about anyone or anything in a foreign country.

I found this troubling. Much later, I would bring it up to a friend with a background in psychology. She said this happens because we worry first about the things we can't control in our local environment. I wondered, while she talked: *Is that why not a single American asked about our impact or responsibility in world events?*

Is the Earth round?

The phone rang in my car, startling me from my thoughts. My father was on the other end of the line.

"Hello there!" he said brightly. "I'm in Dallas, and I wrote in my schedule book that you would be in Texas now, too. Meet me here?"

One more day remained of my conference, and the drive clocked in at four and a half hours each way, but I said yes.

The next morning, my alarm rang into the still-dark morning. I quickly showered and hopped in my car. As I left the grounds and drove north to Dallas, I realized my father had a part in leading me to the place where I sat, hands on the steering wheel, thousands of miles traveled. Though I loved him, in some sense I felt my journey was my own because I drove *away* from his stated and unstated expectations. In our last conversation before I left Kalamazoo, he had asked about my future. My future at the time involved packing and looking over maps, The Question, and traveling. School was done with a capital D for me—hopefully—forever, and I felt successful having just earned a Master's degree.

I don't remember what I said, but I'm sure I cobbled something together about teacher coaching or finding my place in on-the-ground school reform, but it didn't matter what I said. He started nodding halfway through my description and interrupted before I got to the end. "That might be a good start, but have you considered starting your PhD?"

I was a little uncomfortable then, driving out of my way, right to him, three-quarters of the way through my journey away from academia. And the conversation I dreaded most was about what I planned to do after I returned home. The question he most yearned to ask.

We met up at his hotel and then took a little drive to Gilley's, one of the most famous bars in America. Bar tops snaked throughout the cavernous space, lined with barstools made of actual saddles. A mechanical bull in a large foam-filled ring sat off to one side. We arrived at dinnertime, not bar time, so the place sat empty and we had our choice of tables. We sat down at a small two-seater with a single votive candle on the wood top. Cowboy memorabilia dotted the walls.

We ordered, and I asked about the ophthalmology conference my father attended. We chatted about some new surgical procedures that were coming down the pike and what kind of swag the drug companies gave away at their booths.

"How are things on your side of the fence?" he ventured.

"Pretty good," I said, nodding my head, trying to ascertain what territory, exactly, he was inquiring into. He asked about my mother and my time in Santa Barbara. Beautiful place, I told him, always sunny, that fig tree was a treat.

"And the conference?" he asked.

"It's been very interesting," I said. "I presented a paper," I continued, hesitantly, hoping he might remember the topic, fearful he wouldn't.

"Oh?" he said, cocking his head. He didn't remember.

"Yeah, I spent a semester doing field work in an amazing school in South Boston, and I wrote an analysis paper on it. It went really well."

I wanted to talk about it, to describe how I ended up being more confused by the conference than enlightened, but I found myself holding back. This, I knew, entered the terrain known as Baffling. From past experience, there was a fifty-fifty chance he would be interested in my confusion. It would all be easiest if I just described the things he knew well—that this conference happened like all conferences happened, like the one he had attended: sit through all-day sessions, come back to the hotel room, look over promotional materials, have dinner, veg out to *The Tonight Show*, fall asleep, wake up, and do it all again. On the third day, head to the airport. Home on Sunday night, done. I knew the chord he wanted to strike was related to this: We were each in Texas, each at a conference. This is what professional men do. "Yeah, the conference is going really well," I said, leaving it at that.

I also realized he was not going to ask about The Question project. I decided to fill him in.

"Hey, I'm still asking that question I asked people back in Kalamazoo," I said quietly.

"Which one?" he asked, the corners of his mouth turning down as he scanned his memories.

"It's this: *If you could ask everyone you met just one question, what would you ask?* I've interviewed hundreds of people so far. It's been a really interesting project."

Silence. My father furrowed his brow for a second, then smiled. *"Knock, Knock?"*

The server came to the table for our drink order. He winked at me and then turned to the waitress, "I'll take a Corona." Then back to me, "Can I buy you a beer?"

It was a kind offer, and I took him up on it, but my heart was more than a little broken. I didn't know if it was disapproval or apathy or some other dynamic that disconnected him from my journey. I know I had burned him by failing out of fifth grade and then college, but I had done well, too. But even the doing well didn't seem to be enough. He wanted me to pursue my PhD, to become the Director of somewhere or other, to bump against the stars and be all I could possibly be. It was a loving impulse, and in that moment I felt compassion for him; he wanted a successful son, one he could understand.

But he wasn't listening, leaving me unsure of how to communicate. My thoughts flipped, and I started to get angry: How could he not know what I was doing? Wasn't he curious what I had been doing since I left his house five months ago? All the insight I had gained, all the changes I was going through, seemed to evaporate in thin air. I tried to wear a previous version of me, but it didn't fit.

We spent the rest of dinner watching the mechanical bull riders get thrown and walked around the huge space of the bar expressing wonder.

"Wanna ride the bull?" he asked playfully as we looped back to our seats.

"Nah," I said, frowning, "not really interested in getting thrown tonight. Looks painful."

We finished up. We weren't going to talk about the project. I drove him back to the hotel, gave him a hug, and said goodbye.

Where do your emotions lie?

As I drove back south, I tried not to worry too much about my father's interest, or lack thereof. But I couldn't help it. I found myself thinking back to an exchange earlier on the trip, when I painted my car in the driveway.

It was my second day back in Kalamazoo after the family party. I stood on a large rectangular concrete pad, a parking area next to the driveway at my father's house. I had left Cambridge, but now I was leaving home, Kalamazoo. I wanted to carry Brian's creative spirit with me on the journey. An idea popped into my head.

I carried some spray-paint up from the basement and spent time cutting star-shaped stencils out of cardboard. Perfect stencil material. I walked by my father, who sat on a barstool at the kitchen island reading a newspaper. I got to my car outside and realized I had forgotten paint tape, so I went all the way back downstairs. I walked by my father again. I needed newspapers from the recycling, so I walked by again, this time with a white cloth painting mask on.

Briefly, he set the paper down. "So, what's going on here?"

"I'm going to paint my car."

"Oh." He looked at me absently, cocked his head a little, pulling the paper back up. "That's nice."

I don't think he believed me, but on that perfect blue day doing a little work on the car made me happy. I knew little to nothing about the insides—only just enough to get regular oil changes and checkups. But the outside, that was my domain.

I'd found a tint of red that matched the current paint job almost perfectly, and applying it, I found it was hard to tell that three separate cars had smashed themselves into its body.

And now, an array of colored paints in hand, I vowed to restore and infuse it with new, independent spirit for the Question journey. I decided to paint stars on my car where it had been hit. Stars to celebrate indomitability, to revel in curiosity, and to hide the bumps.

I wanted to be meticulous. I wanted it to look good. I finished the last set of stars that afternoon as my father pulled in later, home from work. He coasted up next to my car in the street, looking out of the passenger window. He didn't smile or frown, just arched a quizzical eyebrow. He didn't want to talk about the new, many colors of my car. A drive-by look. *"Why did you do that?"*

Baffled.

Do you believe in God? Why?

Northeast of Austin, exit signs appeared few and far between, a stark reminder of the true size of the state, small Texas communities separated by many miles.

As I drove out of Texas and across the border into the new landscape of the Deep South, I called my oldest childhood friend, Stu. The sun began to set as he answered, gorgeous purple and orange plumes shooting out across the horizon. I called Stu to look for more clarity on my father, to ground me, to ameliorate the anger. He had known me all my life, and I needed a sympathetic perspective. He listened kindly, sharing his struggles with his own father. A conversation we'd had many times.

Stu asked about the project, and I realized I hadn't asked him The Question. He thought for a moment and then said, "I would ask everyone a two-part question: *Do you believe in God?* to start it off, and then I would ask: *Why?"*

This addendum made me chuckle. Stu had a long-standing disbelief in a god that would opt for sleight-of-hand tricks like turning water into wine, but would not allow his chosen people to live harm-free and disease-free for eternity. And the tag, *Why?* was just an invitation to a fight. Stu would retort with some salvo on this theme: Rinky-dink miracles from a charlatan son. An all-powerful, easily angered father who seems to miss the point of his job duties entirely.

I laughed with Stu about his question, but when we hung up, new thoughts jumbled into my consciousness. I thought about what gods do and how they act, and I started in on my father and his influence on my life. My father occupied an important role in my subconscious. And of course he did, he was around from Day One, raising me. He, in fact, created Day One. His concerns about my life instantly became my own concerns about my life; his offhand comments contained real heft. More than any other validation, it was his I sought. And I was more disappointed by his apathy than any other.

Are you willing to try again?

In the middle of the hot afternoon, anything not road, rock, or sky is quickly apparent while driving the long stretches between towns, so coming upon a lone man carrying a red gas can, miles from anywhere, caught my eye. He was heading in the opposite direction, back to where I'd come from, walking with shoulders hunched, defeated. He knew it was hot, but he didn't know what I did: he was very far from any gas station.

I shielded the sun from my eyes and kept driving, but a couple minutes later a black speck appeared, growing. The car. He'd made it pretty far. I sped by in a blur, but noticed there had been a passenger in the seat. With Wayne's insistent question to reach out in friendship still on my mind, I made a decision.

Slowing down at the next access, I pulled a U-turn to backtrack. I eased to a stop a couple dozen yards in front of the gas can, watched as he jogged up to the side of the car and leaned in the open window.

"Hi." He smiled wearily. "I'm Tony." In twelve seconds, he gave me the whole story: his girlfriend needed to get to her probation officer in Austin, a solid hour away, by five. Leaving his girlfriend to sit sweating in the car, pregnant, was no easy decision. He hopped in at my offer, smiling.

We watched the horizon for a while, trading small talk, when I told him about the project and asked him The Question. Tony sat looking out the windshield. He didn't turn toward me to respond, just spoke directly to the large window. "Oh, that's easy. I'd ask, *What will it be like when I'm you?*"

Normally, when people shoot out an answer, without pausing, they say something silly. But this was different. His answer confused me, though he was very sincere. Maybe it came to his mind quickly because it also made no sense whatsoever. "What will it be like when I'm you?" *What the hell does that even mean?*

"I'm sorry," I finally said, breaking the silence, "but what the hell does that even mean?"

Tony laughed a quick laugh. "Essentially, it means just what I said— what will it be like when I'm you? You see," he went on, "I've invented a solution."

"A solution to, uh, what?" I asked.

"To everything," Tony replied. "It doesn't have a name or anything. All it requires is total belief in one idea: When you die, you are reincarnated. But it's not in order. Like if you die in 2056, you're not born in 2057. Instead, you are reincarnated as someone you met in the life you just had. So one day you'll be your grandfather, your father, your best friend. But it doesn't stop there, you'll be the thief breaking into your apartment, a bank president, or a recent immigrant. One day we'll be riding in this car again, but I'll be you, and you'll be me. And at other times neither one of us will be in this car. It will be two entirely different people."

"So, you really believe this?" I asked, trying to gauge his seriousness. I couldn't help it; I laughed.

Tony laughed, too, but he quickly returned. "That's what it takes, man. But seriously, think about it. How different would our world be if everyone knew they'd be everyone else eventually? What if we understood deep down that everyone would be on every side of every issue? Every murderer would know what it was like to be the victim, and every business deal, would be you trading against yourself. It would be the Golden Rule, but it wouldn't be hypothetical. We would admire the people who could create the most positivity in the world. Of course, it wouldn't make the world a perfect place. But, for a while at least, a belief like this might make us all be just a little bit better to each other."

We drove on. Tony played a rhythm on the gas can with his fingers. Clearly he had been thinking about this a lot. I kept a foot on the accelerator, considering the idea. I liked it. Reincarnated through time as each other.

We stopped at the gas station, and while he pumped gas into his red can and then paid, I wondered, "How do we know that this theory isn't happening already?" For some reason, I didn't ask, and we drove the way back mostly in silence. Finally, as we neared his car, I did something I had rarely done. I asked him his question. "So, tell me. What do I have to look forward to? What will it be like when I'm you?"

Tony looked at me with a cockeyed grin. "It'll be fun enough, but, dude, you will almost never make a good decision." He smirked. "Seriously. Mistake, mistake, mistake. And when I'm you?"

"Oh, you'll stumble along at first, but things really pick up in Act II. Still lots of confusion, but also lots of great adventures. You'll get to laugh a lot. And you might not understand this now, but you're going to find your one single question to ask of the world." That brought a smile. It felt like I had made a friend.

I pulled over to the shoulder even with his car, but in the opposite direction. Tony hopped out and bounded across the empty highway. He turned back as he pulled the handle and yelled, "Thank you!" I waited until he gave me a thumbs-up and began pouring gas before I put on my blinker and merged back onto the blacktop, speeding away.

CHAPTER 10

THE SOUTH

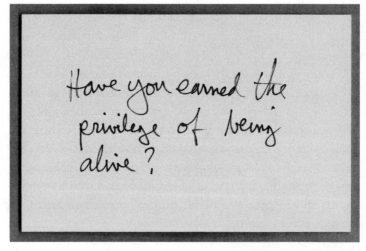

Have you earned the privilege of being alive?
- Frank Oz (Puppeteer (Miss Piggy, Fozzy Bear, Yoda, etc.),
filmmaker, and actor)

And when I return again, you'll have a great, long story to tell.

          —Robert Johnson

I drove out of Texas toward Mississippi with a goal in mind. I wanted to stand at the fabled crossroads, the birthplace of American blues, where guitarist Robert Johnson supposedly made a deal with the devil.

A starless, low-hanging foggy night greeted me as I crossed the state line into Mississippi, my phone going dead in the middle of a call. I held it away from my ear to check: no service. The velocity of the car seemed to slow as it rolled through the dense fog. Humid air hung close. I turned on the radio and tuned in the first station that buzzed and crackled to life. Strange, ethereal music came through speakers, early tribal blues, the fife and drums of Othar Turner. Only an hour or so from Hazlehurst, the birthplace of Robert Johnson, my mind raced with thoughts of devils, of ghosts. The calendar read October 30, the day before Halloween.

I found a cheap motel just outside the city limits and spent the evening reading up on Robert Johnson and poring over maps, trying to locate the mythical crossroads.

Where are my cigarettes?

Two highways crossed on the outskirts of town, and two major streets crossed downtown Hazlehurst. There were two possibilities.

I drove first to where the two county highways, 28 and 51, crossed. I stepped out to survey the area. Cars whooshed by, and a large truck carrying chickens almost ran me off the road. This was too big and too busy to be the spot where such a historic deal had gone down.

The other possible intersection in town seemed only slightly more promising. On the various corners sat a Piggly Wiggly grocery store, Federated Car Loan, and a National Trust Bank. I struggled to imagine Robert Johnson on his knees in this location when the devil, having closed a deal at Federated Car Loan, stepped out to greet him. I drove on.

In the center of town, at what seemed to me the final possibility, a small marble memorial to Robert Johnson stood on the grassy median. There were a number of streets that gathered here, at the center of the small downtown. I got out to look, walked over to the marble memorial, and waited. Nothing happened.

Why was I drawn to Robert Johnson? Because of his status as the quintessential American bluesman; with hellhounds on his trail, found dead at twenty-seven. Only two recording sessions exist as evidence of his entire career. And yet, every single song he recorded in those sessions has been covered many, many times, covered by every band that ever turned into anything at all. His influence on modern music, on everyone from Chuck Berry to the Red Hot Chili Peppers, cannot be overstated. Arguably, Robert Johnson was the most influential blues artist on Earth. Scratch that—one of the most influential musicians of any period. The anticipation of meeting the devil didn't excite me, but the atmospherics of the legend kept egging me on, the same way you'd look out the window flying through the Bermuda Triangle. Robert Johnson embodied what Brian sought, one foot in the world of the living, one foot on the other side.

Convinced the marble monument did not represent the crossroads either, I got back in my car and drove through town past the restaurants and bars all pushed together and into the rundown neighborhoods of Hazlehurst. I decided to do a little more exploring.

To play the club circuit, you wouldn't go downtown. The clubs, many still standing, are huddled in thin trees, rundown and dilapidated, on the outskirts of town. I passed several them that were shuttered, out of business and long abandoned. Even so, tradition watched warily as I drove past sagging doors and darkened dance floors once covered in sawdust and wet with gin.

Are you wandering, or are you just lost?

The conference had shaken me up with its crazy questions and intellec-
tualizing and all the pointing at and shoving of The Question itself. I
headed on my way home, ready for answers. I thought standing at the
crossroads would at least give me a chance with the devil. *Might not be
the answer I want to hear,* I laughed to myself.

I drove away from Hazlehurst, realizing I wasn't supposed to find
the crossroads. And that provided its own gift: There is no fountain of
youth, money doesn't grow on trees, and there is no devil waiting at an
intersection to cure all your—mortal—problems. Robert Johnson just
played his heart out, never knowing with certainty what would grow
from his efforts, whether fame and influence, or just poisoned whiskey
from a jealous husband. We cannot know.

As I drove around Hazlehurst without any clear direction, I arrived
at a new confidence in The Question. In both cases it did what it was
supposed to do—making connections, listening to others. I was inhabiting the project itself. It didn't matter how clever or insightful people
were, or if I found the perfect question, just as it wasn't essential whether
I found the actual crossroads where Robert Johnson stood, or not. Just
listening to others, laughing, reflecting, and applying their thoughts
to my own life, this is what it was all about. It made its own kind of
sense on those back roads; it's the music that counts, not the myth we
build around it.

Have you ever been to Nashville?

It struck me, while I put on a long-sleeved shirt, that this was the first
day of the trip that I didn't sweat. Until this, over eleven thousand miles,
I had perspired across every inch. Here the highway wound north, lined
on both sides with pines and poplars. These were trees I recognized.
Here plants grew green, and bugs crawled over nutrient-rich soil, not
dust, not cacti. Long, low clouds made the scene overcast.

I had lunch in the car at a rest stop and headed north to Memphis. I
called a recent classmate, Kadie, who happened to be living in Louisville,

to see if her offer still stood and that I'd have a place to stay when I arrived. Continuing through Nashville, I exited Highway 40, turning north onto I-65. The day was warm, but as I continued north, a shiver ran through me, a sudden cold settling in.

What's your favorite kind of music?

As I came over a rise outside of Bowling Green, I saw tall buildings poking through a distant sea of green trees. In that moment, it looked to me exactly like downtown Kalamazoo from the vantage of a popular teenage hangout. We'd dangle our legs over a large wall on the side of a steep hill, a dramatic overlook with Kalamazoo's largest buildings reaching to extend beyond the branches and leaves of surrounding forest.

It was, for that moment, Kalamazoo, the city of five months earlier—the fall weather so suddenly like the spring and the geography almost identical, if only in contrast to the dusty, dry heat of Texas, or the lush, verdant warmth of the South.

A displaced familiarity to these buildings made me feel in some way like I was returning to my own city life. It reminded me that I would be living a different life soon, the one I had left. It made me think of Brent's question back in Arizona: *"Do we have to live this way?"*

At the time, he was entranced with The Land and with the hard-scrabble happiness of Lucas and Shara. It struck me then that maybe the question Brent posed was directed at himself. Poking his stick at the embers of a dying fire with eyes glazed in reflection, he seemed to know the answer already. Making good on his answer stood as the true challenge. I think his question—the root of it at least—might have been a different question entirely. Something like, *"How do you live the way you truly believe?"*

As I drove onto Louisville, I put on an album by Bonnie "Prince" Billy, the stage name for the folk troubadour Will Oldham. I'd been listening to his music since the mid-'90s, and each album reflected a shift in style, but each one pulled me in the same emotional direction. He had an amazing, fragile voice: tight harmonies infused with real confidence, the pine-top scent of old America permeating every warbling note.

I'd listened to hours and hours of his albums on the journey, and I hoped to meet him while in Louisville. His most recent album at the time featured his head in profile, and I remember the first time I saw it. We were the exact same age, practically to the month, and it struck me how—with a long, full beard, hair thinning to wisps at the top—his album cover photo was very much a picture of my own profile.

After meeting up with my father in Dallas, I noticed myself drawing up to Robert Johnson and Will Oldham as surrogates that were more my spiritual kin. They lived on the road in a way my father never would, in a way I was only just beginning to appreciate.

I turned up the stereo and sang each song with Will, belting the lyrics at the windshield as I headed north to Louisville. I wanted to find him and shake his hand, to ask him about his life on the road, how he made sense of it all.

What's your favorite holiday?

It was Halloween, and as dark settled in, so too did thick, white snowflakes begin to appear on the windshield. It intensified, snow blowing in alabaster snakes across both lanes. My friend Kadie, a former classmate from Boston, had extended an offer of lodging. She had moved to Louisville on a whim; her aunt and uncle lived there, and they offered a stab at a new life. "I think I'm ready to try Boston again," she had said on the phone. It wasn't working out so well.

As the wind beat harder and whipped the snow into a frenzy, I turned the heat up and continued, in shorts and a thin jacket, doing seventy-five in falling snow. I had ascended too quickly.

Thirty minutes later, stopping for gas became a necessity. My hands went numb as I held the pump handle, wondering if I had sent back gloves and a hat. I jumped up and down to stay warm. *Hello from way down South,* my clothes screamed, *it's nice and warm there!* Other patrons tucked their heads against the wind and snow.

One man stopped, looking at me as if he wanted to say something cutting or funny, but he decided it wasn't worth it and continued quickly to his car. In only a couple short hours, a snowstorm enveloped the freeway. It was hard to believe how quickly things had changed.

I popped the trunk and dug through my backpack for a layer of thicker clothes. I pulled out a sweater from the trunk, and, blinded by the wool as I pulled it over my head, I felt my arm shoot through a hole in the armpit rather than down the sleeve. My face still hidden, I made the sound of an elephant. In this cold, what else could I do but laugh?

Who is your favorite main character in a story?

Exiting off the freeway toward Louisville, I made a quick left off the ramp and a right, and suddenly there I was, pulling up in front of Kadie's house. I hadn't realized she lived so close to the freeway and didn't have any time to process what I was getting into. It had been a few months since we'd talked, but I liked her. I just hoped to not make things awkward. I threw on yet another coat and knocked on the door, blowing into my hands as I waited.

The large, brown door swung wide and Kadie practically leaped out to give me a big hug. As she ushered me inside, I noticed how the frames of her bright red cat-eye glasses highlighted her soft features and warm brown eyes. She caught me looking at her and smiled brightly.

"I'll just grab my bag," I said as I turned away, embarrassed. I stepped back quickly, heading down the steps to my car.

When I entered the house, I dropped my bag in the guest room. Kadie showed me around, pointing out each room and then introducing me to her aunt and uncle. We all shook hands, and then Kadie and I strolled out for dinner. At the first corner, she gave an exaggerated, "Brr," sliding her arm right into the bend of mine. It had been weeks since I had seen a friend, and I liked Kadie. Sarcastic and smart, she wasn't afraid to disagree. She'd crinkle her brow and say, "Hmm, I don't think so," if you claimed something based on sagging logic. Her refreshing honesty was topped with a great sense of humor.

"You're going to make fun of me later because I don't know how to ride a bike, but I'm going to make fun of you right now because your spray-painted bike helmet looks stupid," she'd said when I first met her, as I stepped off my bike on the way to class. We'd become fast friends.

With the warmth of her arm and just the feeling of being in good company, out of the blue I asked, "Can I take you to dinner?"

"You most certainly may, Kind Sir," she said, walking briskly in the cold. Only a few blocks in, we stopped at the big glass window of a nice Japanese restaurant. She lingered, so, feeling magnanimous with chivalry, I said, "We're here!"

We ate tender sushi and drank warm sake and caught up on all the gossip about our classmates since we'd parted in the spring. When we finished, I didn't even look at the bill, though I knew it depleted all the money I had tried to save by making all meals on my camp stove. I set my credit card in the black bill and flipped it closed, looking at Kadie, smiling.

On our way back, we grabbed a horror movie rental in a half-hearted attempt to make the night Halloween-y. We watched it, laughing through all the scary parts. A perfect evening.

The movie ended, and we remained on the couch, Kadie half curled up. I sat with my legs extended on a coffee table. She smiled at me. "So, what's this road trip all about?"

"Well," I paused, considering my next words very carefully. So much had happened.

At my furrowed brow, Kadie began to laugh. "Uh-oh, here comes the long, boring part of the conversation where you talk about all the crap you learned about yourself and yada yada."

My finger hung paused in midair to begin speaking, but I set it down, nodding in appreciation of her assessment. I smiled back weakly, worrying that my thoughts would be too pedestrian. She was a writer and knew much about the world of interior journeys. Plus, I felt a little delirious in her company. I didn't want the night to end.

"I'm just kidding," she said, hitting my shoulder. "I really want to know."

"Well," I began, "I won't bore you with the details, but yeah, I'm on this journey, and, yes, it's fun and, yes, I've met interesting people. But now, after months and months of travel, I'll be back home in a few days, and I'm a little scared that it's coming to an end."

"Ok, so you obviously have some questions on your mind." She smiled kindly. She was smiling a lot, I noticed.

"Questions! Yes, the whole trip is centered on one single question." I described the trip and The Question and a range of the responses. "These questions people have asked on my trip are difficult, and I'm trying to find my way through them," I said.

"Maybe they're difficult, maybe they're not," she said, smiling. "Try me."

I turned from the couch to look directly at her. "For example, *What do you believe? If you could pursue any course in life, what would you do with yourself? Who are you?*"

I flipped my hands palm up and shrugged my shoulders. "I'm trying to figure out the story here."

Kadie imitated my seriousness, flipping her hands up comically and shrugging her shoulders.

She put her hands down, pulling her knees to her chest. "Deep. Got it. So, let's see." She paused in thought. "What this journey means is exactly that. Those questions. When I write, I think about an experience as a whole story. And these questions people ask, they're your starting and ending point. But think about it: in every story, there must be a protagonist, and there has to be a thread." She released her legs and looked out the window before looking back at me. "You are the protagonist. Your story is the journey, traveling around the country, talking to all these people. Then there is the inner journey. You've come to this point, you're asking people their questions, but you must have come to questions yourself?"

I had. Kadie didn't know of the long hours I'd spent trying to find my own question, trying to figure out what I wanted to know. The discovery I'd made through Wayne back at Outward Bound in Texas. The intellectuals at the conference had confused me. There was much I did not know.

"You need to find a way to work in these people's answers to the questions you are looking for." She paused. "You need to stay in the moment with what shocks or astonishes you, or what throws you up against a wall. You are going around looking for answers to questions that don't yet exist."

"Yeah, for real, Kadie. It's like I'm on a *spiritual* journey."

She smiled through a sigh. "OK, if you want to call it some bullshit spiritual journey, whatever. Just keep in mind, you are the protagonist."

I laughed. "Even if I don't want to be?"

"Yes," she said, "even if you have no idea what you're doing."

Like most truths on the journey, what Kadie revealed came when I wasn't even listening deeply: that my story was about the importance of questions themselves, and finding my one true question was integral to that. It would take a few days before I began to understand what she meant. But in the moment, I tried to listen for meaning, but kept missing her cues. Like at the end of the night, when she turned to me.

"Do you want to know my question?" she asked, teasingly.

"Of course," I said. "Bring it on."

"I want to know this: *What is it you're not saying right now?*"

She looked me straight in the eye. I looked away.

We talked and laughed a while longer, but the clock had already moved into the wee hours. It was time to turn in. Kadie showed me the guest room and offered me linens. She offered sheets and blankets and a duvet, and then she plopped down next to me, offering a list of sleeping articles that seemed to go on and on. I didn't know what to say. I kept saying, "No, thank you," politely, but she kept offering, listing much more than bedding. She wrapped up her offers by leaning in and asking, "Would you like some ice cream or bedtime cookies?"

I smiled but declined. "No, but I want to thank you for your analysis of my journey."

She left me to sleep. I climbed into bed alone and lay there, feeling a visceral emptiness. I sighed heavily. Just two days ago, excitement had fueled my days of driving, and meeting up with Kadie seemed so full of possibility. We had a great evening, and then I thanked her for her *analysis of my journey?* I sounded like a pocket-protected NASA engineer. I wanted to kiss her, not commend her analysis. I cursed silently.

A few minutes later, as I fell off to sleep, there came a light knock on the door, the blackness broken by gray open-door light. "Hey," she said, quietly closing the door, walking across the room and kneeling at the side of my bed, "I just wanted to say…"

Blouse brushed arm.

Warm lips found mouth.

Everything made sense.

Fade to black.

CHAPTER 11

HOMEWARD

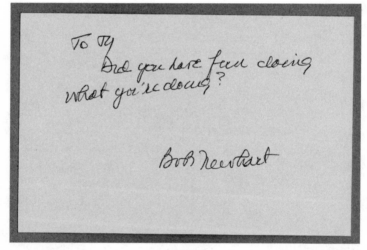

Did you have fun doing what you're doing?
- Bob Newhart (Stand-up comedian and actor)

I woke up the next morning, sun streaming through the window. I practically bounded down the stairs to find Kadie in the kitchen already sipping coffee. "Well good morning to you, Sunshine!" she said with sarcasm, though it came out playful. That I might be welcome on those shores was a wonderful feeling. Whatever feelings had been submerged from my months of solitude were healing through a single evening. I was returning, maybe to real life on terra firma.

We went out to brunch and ate wonderful French toast, discussing what was next for us both. Kadie was going to continue to give Louisville a good old "college try," but I offered that she might return to Boston. "We could try dating," I said, coolly, trying to be low-key. But then I lost it.

"I like you!" I blurted like an eight-year-old.

"And I like you." she said, smiling back. My heart almost burst.

I drove away from Louisville around noon, excited for when our paths would cross again.

As I drove, I thought about Kadie and her reflections, realizing it was not important whether I was doing this project "right." It may have been a simple question journey or even a Bullshit Spiritual Journey—it wasn't the terms that defined the trip. What I realized then was that the journey was never going to end. I began to see what I'd thrown myself into back in Cambridge. While my relentless questioning served the purpose of deep self-reflection, Kadie's warmth and emotional reassurance made me whole. Shortly after I left, she would begin dating her future husband, which was how the chips fall. She found true love, and she helped me see possibility and recognize how deeply I had connected with The Question.

The Question would be around always to help me to learn what other people were seeking from the world. I held out hope that I might have found my own question, but it wasn't solid, still another light in a night sky filled with others' questions. Kadie inspired me to continue, discovering questions I had never considered through others' curiosities. I wanted to call Will Oldham, Robert Johnson, Lucas. I wished I could explain it all to my father in a language he might understand.

Here I was, an astronaut reentering orbit, returning to Earth. And it was here, just before impact, that the protective shield of my helmet came off, and for the first time I felt a breeze on my face, something true space travelers never get to experience.

I left Louisville, the journey two days away from its end. In some ways, I was just beginning to feel like I had gotten The Question sorted out. When I asked people, I knew when they were going to get confused, and I knew how to respond when they were unsure or confrontational. I knew what I wanted to hear from them. Not what they were going to say, but what I was looking for with The Question. It was interesting to be ending an experience right when I began to feel knowledgeable about the process. Maybe that was best.

I continued to drive through flurries across Pennsylvania. At this point, none of the trees had any leaves, late fall having given way to the cusp of winter in early November. I turned the heater knob in denial as I drove in shorts and a short-sleeved shirt. *What are you* not *saying?* Kadie's question rumbled around in my brain.

Somewhere in rural Pennsylvania, I stopped for lunch. To get to Upstate New York on time, I had to rush. I drove through a local fast-food joint for a burrito and some fried Tater Tots.

I had my change out at the drive-in window, and as the cashier flipped open the little window, a loud buzzer went off behind him, drawing my eye over to the fryer. As a gawky teenager clumsily pulled up the fry basket, a horrible thought crossed my mind: *What if he slipped and his hand fell into that fryer oil?*

It would burn, but could he die from those injuries? Aaron's question sat in patent absurdity over the whole situation. What if he stayed like that for *six hours?*

I was going home, back to everything, back to nothing. I was ready. I only had one more stop to make.

Where's your safe place?

While staying at my mom's in Santa Barbara, California, I had received an offer for lodging from a filmmaker and documentarian, a friend of a friend. She found the project intriguing and offered me a place to stay for the last couple days of my journey. *If you would like to share your story with me,* her message said, *I'm all ears, I would love to document this.* She too had studied education through the same program, and in only a couple of quick e-mails, we'd hit it off. I didn't know how to encapsulate the journey for a documentarian, but it seemed like a cool offer, and I was willing to try.

So, I traveled to Upstate New York to sit as an interviewee, as my last stop on the journey. She offered her yard as a place to set up my tent and decompress. I don't know how she knew I sought refuge at the end of my journey, but she was kind to give me space to reflect; I didn't want to be completely alone for the last couple days, but I didn't want to be surrounded by people I knew barraging me with questions I couldn't answer. Susan's place sat very close to the road that would take me home to Boston, and it felt right.

Over dinner after my arrival, Susan questioned me, interested in the journey, trying to get a bead on the whole project. "Give me a sense of what you've been through," she asked me as we ate.

We finished and cleaned up and I sat at the far end of the table as she set up her camera, the lens unblinking, a red electronic light indicating recording was in progress. And then, like the interview with the college newspaper, my mind went blank. "So," she said, lobbing me a softball, "tell me about your travels." I had thought this would be would be easy, fun even, but there at the end of it all, I froze.

I looked down, thinking back to the second night of the journey, sitting on a porch in Kalamazoo with two of my closest friends and wondering if it would ever get off the ground. I worried then that I should have planned the whole thing out more. And yet, if I'd planned things out more, I might never have bumped into Alex the roadie, or Tim the hitchhiker. I wouldn't be so confused about Happiness or how to Inhabit the Confusion. My mind raced, filled with all the interesting people I'd met and the questions, the questions, the questions. I locked up, facing the lens. "Uh, yeah, it was weird sometimes, but mostly good."

I've never seen the tape, but I know, sitting there, my thoughts reeling, I spoke hesitatingly. Reentry would be more difficult than I'd thought.

I don't know how long I sat in that chair answering questions, but it felt like an eternity. Susan was kind enough to stop the interview when it was clear it wasn't going to work out, and we decided instead to catch a late-night movie. Though the theater sat less than thirty miles away, we ended up getting lost and driving a total of one hundred and seventeen miles in a big circle trying to find the theater. When we finally figured out where we were, we were only twenty minutes away from the movie. And only two hours after it had begun.

I found it much more comfortable to slip back into interviewer mode. She answered The Question as we drove: *Why are we, as a species, so destructive to ourselves and our environment?*

It resonated with me immediately; yes, why are we so careless and neglectful? I was listening to a book on tape where the author spoke about the very same human condition, how we show neglect, almost disdain, in the care of the planet's other animals. At the same time, we spend much time deliberating about our own environments, constructing amazing, beautiful buildings in massive, sprawling cities of concrete and glass. *Do we have to live this way?*

The second night, and the final night of my entire journey, Susan was forthright. "You don't really want to be interviewed, huh?" I had to agree. When talking with Kadie, the meanings of the project were clear, but so was my role as a questioner. Here I felt I was supposed to be authoritative, and it just didn't fit. The process of questioning was itself a question.

We tried again for the movie, and this time we knew the way. We had dinner in the mall food court. Susan had a piece of broccoli on the end of her fork, which she wagged at me. "Tell me again why you did all this?"

So many thoughts floated through my head: how I went on a journey of a whim and ended up immersed in the pursuit of my own question and how, finally, I'd found it. But in the bright lights of the food court it all felt too strange to be real. I kept my response to a simple truth, one I could actually answer: The questions.

We walked down to the theater in plenty of time and found good seats in the middle of the row. Then, just as the trailers started, the screen went blank and the back exit doors were thrown open. A teenaged usher in a dirty black tuxedo stepped onto the stage, put his hands to the side of his mouth, and said in a very loud voice, "There is a fire in the mall! We need to evacuate everyone from this theater. Your ticket will be refunded. Please make your way out of the side doors calmly and quickly. Thank you."

After leaving the theater, we sat in the car, trying to figure out what to do next. Susan turned to me, "Do you ever go to strip clubs?"

"Nope, never."

"Do you want to check one out, just for fun?"

I shrugged, and we drove to a place called Night Visions or something with a title that hammers home a double entendre, parked, and walked in. Pop hip-hop pounded and neon lights left the room half lit. The dressing room door behind the catwalk was left open, making the whole backstage its own distracting show. One woman shoved her purse into one cubby of a wall of gym lockers while another sat straddling the gym locker bench, smoking a cigarette.

And that's how I spent the last night of my journey: in rural Upstate New York at a strip club. We didn't stay long and we didn't have any lap dances. This reentry was going very strangely indeed.

But my last days with this interesting stranger were welcome; she allowed me to be lost in my own world, wrapped up in my own thoughts. All the questions, all the people, all the miles, ran on a tape loop through my head. She was kind to inquire, but it when it was clear I was still in the upper atmosphere, she backed off. I wasn't a good interview, and while I felt bad about not being able to be "on" for her work, I was overcome with feelings. I could only apologize.

The next morning I got up early. We opted to get a quick bite at a place she liked in town and then go our separate ways. Her mother was coming for lunch, and I wanted to make it to Boston by dinner. It was a simple parting and unremarkable at the time, but Susan's question would to be the last I would hear for the entire journey.

CHAPTER 12

HOME

GREETINGS TY,
A) WILL THE PATH YOU ARE
TRAVELING TAKE YOU WHERE
YOU WANT TO GO?
REGARDS, STEVE CHMELAR.
THANK YOU FOR YOUR KIND WORDS! - Steve

Will the path you are traveling take you where you want to go?
- Steve Chmelar (Inventor of the foam #1 finger)

"The two most important days in your life are the day you were born, and the day you find out why."

—Anonymous

As I began my drive home, the pieces of the journey I couldn't give voice to with Susan were beginning to coalesce. I had become aware that my question for the world was the one I had been asking all along, but here I began to see why it fit so well. It started for me at the beginning.

My birth came at a time of great change and questioning. It happened like this: Tipsy dinner party guests in polyester huddled around a small black-and-white television, eyes pulling a shuttle across the screen, down. A speck, white as Jesus, splashed into the ocean.

In the hushed silence with injury, death, and immolation on everyone's mind, the room waited, still, for movement. Finally, a hatch was thrown open and square-jawed men waved to America, the hushed silence broken by cheers and toasts. "Take, that Russia!" someone yelled. "Let's do that again!" from someone else in the back. Money poured into a space program. America flung another pod at the moon. My parents discreetly squeezed hands and moved to the bedroom. Take off! I was conceived.

After the moon landing came the Concorde's initial warm-windowed flights, its elegant frame pulling above the horizon until it curved. White-hot jets outrunning the very spin of the Earth, offering unique flight and unique loneliness. It didn't help that at the time of my birth, widening fissures also popped bolts in the marital contract; the marriages of my parents and so many of their friends began a slow decline of love loss. I was conceived thus: tinged with deep future sadness, thrust into a curious generation at the crux of travel.

And so it was that I, like others in my generation, was raised with the challenge to break free of the confines of the atmosphere. But unlike generations before us, the goal wasn't to develop the world we knew or to inherit a vision for the future; instead, we just wanted to pull free of the fabric of gravity itself, to float, free and weightless.

My generation was the first to fear we would not do as well as our parents, and our recklessness had its own brand of flight. More than the intellectualized art-making of abstract expressionism or free jazz, standing defiantly alone in an unknown world, we were brought into the world with the desire to jump off the front of the stage and heave the actual human body into weightlessness. Hopefully the crowd would surf us back to the edge. Evel Knievel showed us how, gunning it towards a line of busses, a long hospital stay on the other side. Skateboarding went from sidewalk surfing to highest-air competitions, dirt bikes from racing to soaring. Homemade launch ramps were built in garages and dragged into streets. Up we went.

But our goal was not refined, extended, controlled flight. We did not seek the lyrical yaw, pitch, and roll of true flying. The point was, for even just a millisecond, to be alone and helpless, to float free in the world, untethered. It was about committing to vulnerability; about, in its own crude way, being in the moment, twisting, turning, breaking free—no more gravity, no more surface, only atmosphere. We weren't dreaming of being stuntmen; we were explorers in the uncharted heavy gravity of near Earth.

It was this background of defying gravity that impelled me toward my own adventure on the road; I was not built to have thunderous certainty, or granite-like resolve. I was born to question everything, to launch myself out into the world, even with the knowledge that the questions would not hold; they would shimmer temporarily and I would come crashing back to Earth. Questions were what I was made of. They were all I had. And Just One Question was what I was supposed to ask the world.

What decision have you made in life that you are most confident about?

In the homestretch to my destination, a few hours drive across Massachusetts, signs popped up for Montreal to the north and Buffalo to the south, beckoning. My thoughts strayed from Cambridge, the intended destination: I could take one of those exits. I didn't have to go home. It didn't have to end. I could turn the wheel and brave the excitement of a new direction. There were still 330 million or more questions I hadn't heard in America. And then, with enough velocity, I could jump the oceans. There were seven billion questions beyond that.

I looked in the rearview mirror. My beard was big. I was tired of living out of my car, tired of relying on other people, not knowing what was next, having all my belongings packed away inside bags and boxes, and all the unpredictability of living on the road.

Driving across Massachusetts, my mind ran to visions of kids playing in sprinklers, families getting ready for dinner, and couples watching TV. Others rushing home from work, shopping, fighting, and laughing. As I rolled down the freeway home, it all just felt different. It felt as if I'd done the whole thing backwards.

What makes us human?

I wish this insight had occurred earlier in life, and I wish I could have offered it to my father. Instead, I was thrown back to the memory of an important moment after graduating from college. It was May 1998. The evening air was warm and welcoming. After stuffing ourselves on grilled corn and pasta in browned butter, my father invited me for an evening walk. He clicked the leash on Sebastian—his old white Scottish terrier—and we strolled down the driveway, discussing my future. College had been slow going, but now a newly minted adult, the road lay before me. Marinating in a stew of confusion about my life's direction, I questioned everything then, too.

That weekend, things between my father and me went well; he mentored and offered thoughtful guidance. And I organized and plotted, attempting life-changing Big Decisions.

Unbeknownst to my father, the best idea so far had occurred to me while I sat on the worn leather seat of an eastbound Amtrak heading to Kalamazoo.

He turned to me as we walked, then paused under the first streetlight. He smiled.

"It seems as though coming back to figure things out is really helping."

"Yeah, that's right, dad. And I've made some real progress. I wrote out a list of the jobs that I most want to do to narrow it all down. You will be pleased to know"—I paused for effect— "that I have come up with my chosen profession."

"That's great, Ty." His shoulders relaxed, and he slowed his pace. This was the kind of news he'd been anticipating for years. "What are you thinking about?"

I hopped up onto the curb to present my new idea. "Well, I love writing, right?" He nodded. I continued, "And I want to do things with my hands." He nodded again. Writing was admirable.

"OK," I went on, emboldened. "Dad, I am going to manufacture manual typewriters." I held my breath on that last word, excited to just say it aloud. He looked at me blankly, then cocked his head, as though to hear better.

"Manual typewriters?"

I pressed on, ignoring the short list of sensible, well-paying jobs I'd brainstormed that sat, waiting, on paper neatly folded in my other breast pocket of my flannel shirt. "I know there are tons of people who still love to type, me included, and I have a great idea on how to paint the typewriters with flames on the sides and..." I loved manual typewriters. I owned four, all garage sale finds.

I was surprised when he did not jump up on the curb beside me and smother me in a bear hug.

"What are you talking about?"

"Dad, this is what I'm most passionate about." In that moment, it was true.

His face turned dark; his reckless, untamed, failure of a son was reemerging. He began breathing heavily. For some reason, I continued.

"I'm certainly no engineer, I'd have to learn that kind of thing. But imagine this: The Kalamazoo Typewriter Company!" I spread my arms across the sky, unfurling an imaginary banner. The sky hung dark and close with clouds.

"That is crazy! You don't know how to manufacture...*anything*." The good-natured repartee we had built up all day Saturday lay broken at my feet. He wanted me to be a teacher, a line item farther down on my other list. His face turned pink, and then he started yelling. "You have *no money*..." He yanked Sebastian's leash to move him along. "*and no business experience*..." Sebastian looked up at me, perplexed.

"That is an *awful idea*!" Half a dozen yards away and walking quickly, he tugged the leash one last time. The dog yelped.

I didn't try to defend myself. I just stood there, stunned. I wanted to share the excitement of finding life's purpose, but I had done it all wrong. He was right: I didn't know anything about building anything.

If I could go back in time, I would release myself from the baggage of my father's prescriptive ideas and recognize them for what they were: messages of hope and possibility. He wanted me to find success with a sensible idea, not failure in unrefined goals. But my questioning meant my goals would never be assembled beforehand. If I could go back to that night, I would forgive my father. I didn't mean to present him with a plan that sounded so crazy, or for any of my plans that seemed unrealizable. I would also forgive my younger self for not recognizing the way my father intended his message. He cared about me, even if he couldn't see me driving home from six months on the road, 12,000 miles and hundreds of questions and a success, understanding deeply some new aspect of America and myself.

Was this unrecognized gulf the truth of all sons to their fathers? I didn't know then that my father would live for little more than a year after my return. And that, in the end, he would never really know about the project.

What's the most beautiful thing you've ever seen?

In the last few miles of my journey, the setting sun burned orange with a power I'd never seen before. I stuck my arm out the window, pointing my camera backwards to try and capture it. The last photo shows a setting sun gently sliding over the horizon, filling the sky with orange and magenta flares as it disappears.

I tilted the lens up, allowing the camera to pan off the horizon cutting diagonally across the sky and out into the young twinkling stars. I drove home, captivated by the stars appearing in the last vestiges of light. Click.

If you could know the end, would you?

I wish I could say there was a unique or unusual feeling that struck me the very moment I pulled back into the driveway of the co-op I had left six months earlier, but there wasn't. There was just my housemate Jen. She stood at the back of her car in the driveway, unloading groceries to make a house dinner. "Ty!" she yelled. "You're back!"

The question epiphany didn't come until a couple years later, sitting on the couch with my buddy Stu and recounting the trip with him.

I told him about the two hitchhikers, one paranoid that I was a violent killer and the other whose question I was still trying to wrap my head around. I ended the story laughing at both experiences, but Stu only nodded at this ending, silent.

"C'mon, you didn't think that was funny?" I asked, still chuckling to myself.

"Kind of," Stu replied, face blank. "But there's something powerful there. You know the idea that all the molecules of the Earth are still around and just being recycled, that we're breathing the same air as Caesar and Einstein?"

"Yeah," I said, furrowing my brow.

Brian popped onto one of my shoulders and laughed; this was going to be good.

My father popped onto my other shoulder, wincing in advance of cliché. As Stu continued, they both disappeared in a puff of smoke.

"Well, that's what is so profound. You drove around the country thinking you were looking for differences between people through their questions, but you found out that we're all trying to understand what it's like to be cut from the same cloth. It's about you and me, it's about you and your father and Brain and everyone. Instead of us all seeing those around us as The Other, your question asks: *What makes us all the same?*" Stu tapped the table to make his point. "It's questions that open everything up for us. What if we recognized all this for what it is?"

I swear a bell rang in the distance. I sat, listening.

"I want to tell you how it feels to be you," Stu said, a slow, knowing smile crossing his face, "and will you tell me what it's like to be me?"

ABOUT THE AUTHOR

Ty Sassaman was born in Kalamazoo, Michigan. He currently owns a home with a woodstove in the Longfellow neighborhood of South Minneapolis, Minnesota. He received a dual BA in English and Philosophy from Western Michigan University and a master's degree in education from Harvard.

A finalist for the Loft Literary Prize, his writing and photographs have appeared in *The Sun* magazine, the *Georgia Review*, *Booth* (online), the *Dudley Review*, on the *TEDx* stage, and in carefully corked bottles thrown into both the Atlantic Ocean and the Mississippi River.

Photograph by Ty Sassaman

APPENDIX

The project is ongoing, but here is a list of the questions thus far:

1. What do you think is the role of the courts in our democracy?
2. If you could have one substance shoot out of your navel on command, what would it be?
3. What are you most afraid of?
4. Should you ever trust someone who doesn't like dogs?
5. Are we going to kiss later?
6. What song moved you to dance the hardest you've ever danced?
7. What's your *real* phone number?
8. What do you collect?
9. What do musicians think about when they write music?
10. What should we do about guns?
11. What's the highlight of your life?
12. Do you know how to water ski?
13. What's your favorite memory from childhood?
14. I'm interested in this area that you live in. What's unique about your area?
15. What is your favorite food?
16. Is the world round?
17. You have a free day, nothing planned, what would you do?
18. What's the most beautiful thing you've ever seen?
19. If you had to choose between two superpowers, would you choose Invisibility or Flight?
20. Is a chicken wing light meat or dark meat?
21. Where are you originally from? Why did you move there?

22. What do you regret the most in your life? (What work have you done to change that?)
23. Why is money so important to you?
24. If you could punch anyone in the face (celebrity, politician, etc.) who would it be?
25. Who are three people that you would like to have dinner with?
26. If you could ask everyone you met one question what would it be?
27. What's the most valuable lesson you've learned and what's the story around that?
28. What's your favorite mistake?
29. Do you think you are on your right path in life? (Have you been able to find your right path?)
30. What are you thinking?
31. What do you want to be when you grow up? (What happened to that dream?)
32. How's it goin'?
33. What is the biggest mistake your parents made?
34. Do you believe that children *are* the future?
35. What is your favorite sandwich?
36. If you could make any movie, what movie would you make?
37. What helps you get to sleep at night?
38. If you could go back in time and poop on someone's floor, who would it be?
39. How do you defend the hypocrisy of your life?
40. What the fuck is your problem?
41. If you were an animal, what animal would you be?
42. If you could write a book, what book would you write?
43. What is your first memory?
44. Do you want any of my extra shit? Do you have any extra shit that I might want?
45. What makes you most happy?
46. How's your penis?
47. What is your ultimate goal for happiness?
48. Will you accept me?

49. Do you have a Corvette?
50. What's your favorite memory so far?
51. Do you feel alone right now?
52. What is it that you do that makes you dynamic?
53. What's your passion?
54. Did you have a good education in life that prepared you or helped you be all that you could be?
55. What would you do with your time right now to create the change that you want to see in the future?
56. If you had a couple of cats and unlimited access to small outfits, what would you do with them?
57. Is happiness something that you realize looking back on it, or is it something you experience in the moment? What is it that brings you happiness in life? Is it a simple thing? What is happiness for you?
58. What question would you ask everyone if you could ask them a question?
59. What really makes you happy in life?
60. What makes you tick?
61. What in life would make you happy? (Are you doing things on a daily basis to achieve happiness?)
62. Suppose that you were not a slave, suppose that all the limitations, all the controls, all the fears, drawbacks, and impossibilities that you believe constrain your choices in your life, were like a Vietnam vet's phantom limb; he feels tingles that aren't there just like your chains that no longer exist. There was a time when we bent before kings and emperors, now we kneel only to the truth. So suppose that this is not a supposition and this is true, what are you going to do about it? If you could do anything, what would it be?
63. What criteria do use to differentiate between right and wrong?
64. Who are you?
65. What contributes to your quality of life?
66. Can you beat me in Ms. Pac-Man, motherfucker?

67. If you had it in you to write one book, what would that book be about?
68. Did you not forget to bring your hang glider?
69. What is your favorite breakfast food? Why?
70. Do you think that you are fat?
71. What is one thing that you love?
72. When did you get laid last time?
73. Can you recommend one place that I should visit or see?
74. Where are you from?
75. What's your angle?
76. What is your name?
77. What question did you choose to ask everyone? (I just want to follow you around but not do all the work.)
78. What's your purpose?
79. Where are you coming from?
80. What do you really think of me?
81. Do you appreciate life?
82. When was the first time you had sex?
83. What kind of drugs did you do before you were twenty?
84. Did you laugh a lot as a child?
85. What is infinity?
86. How do you fuck shit up?
87. Do you believe?
88. Are you content with your soul?
89. Why are you so lame?
90. Can I have a moment to think?
91. Do you want to live forever?
92. How many people do you think that the person next to you has slept with?
93. If you died and were born again as one of your friends, which friend would it be, and why?
94. What's your favorite restraint?
95. Do you want to smell my armpits?
96. Do you want to see me pee off a goalpost?
97. Are we ready to go home?

98. Why do we need to ask questions?

99. What makes you laugh?

100. Are you happy?

101. What are the ways in which systems of binary discernment (up/down, good/evil, man/woman, etc.) impact your life, and how do you deal with it personally?

102. If you could be any animal, what would you be and why?

103. Do you feel like there is a black hole out there that sucks everyone and everything in?

104. Do you have any questions?

105. What about Evan?

106. What's your sexual fantasy?

107. Do you want to go on a bike ride with me to the beach with my dog?

108. What's your e-mail password?

109. Are you going to eat that?

110. Do you like bread? Because I like bread.

111. Will you get me another spoon please?

112. What's the capital of North Dakota?

113. What do you want someone to ask you?

114. What's your life story up until this point?

115. Do you love animals?

116. What is truly important to you?

117. What is it that makes you feel most alive?

118. What makes you feel wild? And what is wild? (A lot of people associate "wild" with a particular time or experience.)

119. What is The Land to you?

120. How do others view you? Is that an accurate assessment? And if not, how do you view yourself as a person?

121. What is your essence? Describe yourself as something that we all know culturally (mountain lions, hawks, half-eaten pint of Ben and Jerry's on your wool sweater sleeve, etc.).

122. What motivates you to keep living?

123. What makes you *so cool?* (I wanted to try get something that makes people feel good. It doesn't have to be said that way; it can be, "What makes *you* so cool?" if you want to.)
124. What is one thing that you love in your life?
125. Who are you, and why are you here? What are the experiences that inform that view?
126. What would you do about overpopulation?
127. Is there something more to life than living in cities? Should we be doing something else?
128. Are you willing to die?
129. What are your favorite books?
130. Do you think permaculture is sustainable in the long term?
131. What is the truth that you believe in?
132. Where are you going?
133. What are you doing here?
134. What is the worst town that you've ever been to that you could tell me to avoid?
135. What are you passionate about?
136. If you were an outlaw in the Wild West, would you be a one-gun shooter or a two-gun shooter?
137. What's the coolest bar (in this area)?
138. Great ape, lion, grizzly bear: which would win in a fight?
139. If you were to take someone's hand and somehow fasten them so that they couldn't resist and submerge just their hand in boiling hot oil, basically deep frying their hand, for six hours, do you think that would kill them?
140. What do you do for a living?
141. What is your craziest sexual fantasy?
142. How are you doing?
143. What moves you?
144. What road led you here?
145. What are you wearing?
146. Who farted?
147. What do you legitimately think of me?
148. How do you see the world unfolding (as a process)?

149. Where does your deep gladness meet the world's deep need?
150. What gives you life?
151. What do you feel called to do?
152. What is the relationship between subjectivity and the context in which you are placed? How does the background behind you construct your subjectivity?
153. Knock, knock?
154. What is one the single most important thing you can do to encourage/fix/contribute to the world?
155. Can I have a dollar?
156. What are you *not* saying right now?
157. Why are we as a species, so destructive to ourselves and our environment?
158. What was before the big bang?
159. Name three of the most important issues in the United States (not personal, but public policy issues) and how would you like to see them resolved?
160. Are you happy?
161. What's your earliest memory?
162. Does this hat make me look fat?
163. Tell me the difference between yourself and me?
164. What decision have you made in life that you are most confident about?
165. What drives or propels you?
166. Do you believe in God? Why?
167. Which do you like better, *Revolver* or *Rubber Soul*?
168. What do you value most in life?
169. What kind of toothpaste do you use?
170. Are you happy?
171. Are you single?
172. Do you know that there are people in the world who love you?
173. Can I borrow five bucks?
174. If I was a worse man, I would ask you for your PIN #.
175. If I was a better man, I would ask you how I could be of service.
176. What makes you happy?

177. Do you believe that Jesus Christ died for your sins?
178. If you could choose only one memory to take with you to the afterlife, what would it be?
179. What do you need to do to be happy?
180. Is it all worth it?
181. If you could have dinner with three people in the history of the world, either dead or alive, who would it be?
182. Do you think you will die satisfied?
183. What advice would the now you give to yourself ten years ago?
184. Have you wet your bed as an adult (meaning 30+ years of age)?

185. Do you really feel that in your profession you're doing something that Peteers?

186. How did you end up here, now, doing this (whatever you are in the midst of at this time)—going back as far as possible/necessary?
187. What makes life worth living?
188. What do you want but are afraid to admit to yourself that you want?
189. Where and how deep is your love?
190. Do you pick your bellybutton and subsequently sniff your finger?
191. What are you *really* afraid of?
192. Are you a boy or a girl?
193. What did I just say?
194. How do you define god?
195. If you didn't have to work for a living, what would you be doing?
196. Have you ever been in a relationship that went past the three-year mark and if so, how did you deal with the problems that came up?
197. Do you see the goodness in other people?
198. One question I would ask anyone that they would answer honestly?
199. What's the first thing that you remember?

200. What's your most valuable life lesson so far?

201. How can I ask questions of other people questions in a survey to be cool like you?

202. What stories do you keep alive?

203. Who are you?

204. What's the most sexually perverse thing you have ever done (or thought about doing)?

205. Do you believe in something enough to die for it?

206. What about your upbringing makes you decide what life you are going to live?

207. What's your most favorite thing to do in the world?

208. Or what is your most favorite thing that you have done?

209. What games did you play as a child?

210. Did you see me in *A Few Good Men*?

211. Why?

212. What was the worst part of your life?

213. Who has made you want to be a better person; who has made you change?

214. Do you really mean anything you ever say?

215. Where do you see yourself in ten years?

216. What's something that would make the world better?

217. What do you value most in life?

218. Are you right- or left-handed?

219. How did you end up doing what you are doing, job/lifestyle-wise?

220. Bears fan?

221. What does peace mean?

222. What is your purpose here on earth?

223. Why is it that every time you are drunk I owe you $20?

224. What is the best college? (And why?)

225. If you could do your life over, what is the one thing that you would do differently?

226. What dream, wish, or hope is it that keeps you looking forward, motivating you through times in your life that otherwise seem bleak?

227. What is the one thing about your life that, according to you, has defined you the most?

228. How many siblings do you have, and where are you in the mix?

229. How old were you when you lost your virginity?

230. What's the first thing you do in the morning?

231. Do you like to watch the sun rise or set?

232. Will you smell my finger?

233. Do you have a penis or a vagina?

234. What makes you feel socially awkward?

235. Beatles or the Stones?

236. Why is this question important for me to ask?

237. Where did you grow up?

238. Were you on a team or a member of a club in high school?

239. Would you rather be blind or really ugly?

240. Hokey Pokey or Limbo?

241. What do you live for?

242. Are you struggling to pay your bills?

243. If you didn't have your current job, what would your top choice be? If you had to make a career change, what would it be?

244. Why is he still in the Sudan?

245. If you had a lot of money, a billion dollars, say, what would you do with it?

246. Are we late?

247. If aliens came down and told you that you could only drink one type of beer (i.e., lager) for the rest of your life, what would you choose?

248. Can you say, across the board, that everybody grows from challenge?

249. Did you have a good education in life that prepared you or helped you be all that you could be? What do you think contributed to that? Is the system responsible for that? Or is it the lack of a good system that is responsible for that?

250. How long do you think it will take to evolve to the next level from where you are now?

251. Are you going to finish that?

252. If you had to choose one memory to keep and remember for the rest of your life (and beyond), which memory would you choose?

253. Do you every feel like you are emotionally and mentally crippled by the conditions of the postmodern world, and that even the small glimpses of beauty that move you are somehow terribly painful?

254. If you could ask everyone you met one question, what would you ask?

255. What is one thing that you can do tomorrow to make this world a better place?

256. Can I trust you? [Looking straight into eyes]

257. If you could introduce everyone to one artist or musician, who would it be?

258. What is your worst nightmare?

259. If you could pick two people from history to have a conversation with, who would it be?

260. Do you believe that there is one god, only one god?

261. I'm running to be the first ever Hegemon of the new world government that will unite all of the peoples of the world and bring peace to humanity. Will you vote for me?

262. If you could go one place on earth, where would you go? And why?

263. What's your greatest travel adventure?

264. Is George Washington rolling over in his grave?

265. For you, what is the meaning of life?

266. If I could ask everyone I meet one question, it would be: What question they would ask if they could ask every second person they meet the question they asked one person before that. (Have you gotten many of these?)

267. If you could change one thing in your life, what would it be?

268. What does family mean to you?

269. Tell me about your earliest memory.

270. What kind of person do you want to be?

271. How did you get here, where you are in life?

272. What's working for you today?
273. What connection helped you today?
274. What is one tangible thing you can accomplish in the near future that will change your life for the better?
275. Where do you go in your head to get in a state of attunement with the universe?
276. Which bulk food bin would you live in?
277. Who is your celebrity crush?
278. How did you get through the very hardest thing you've had to deal with in your life? What made you believe it was worth it?
279. What motivates you?
280. When you were in your early twenties, what is one thing that you wish you would've known?
281. What dessert are you having?
282. What is your most unhappy memory of your parents?
283. What do you hate?
284. Do you think the American experiment is still working?
285. What one place on this earth do you want to visit, and why?
286. What's an obsession for you that you're reluctant to tell others?
287. If you could jump into the setting of any book (or any story) and live there, what book would it be?
288. What's the best accidentally dirty thing that you've ever said?
289. Do you find this question interesting?
290. What is your point in this world?
291. What do you do that is meaningful?
292. There is a division between people who don't want to be ignorant about *anything* and those that don't care. Which side are you on?
293. What kind of underwear are you wearing?
294. Describe a moment when you were most happy?
295. What is your power animal?
296. How could you ask everyone you met one question?
297. Aren't you glad you met me?

298. If anything, what do you believe is the most important characteristic you have in common with every person who has ever lived?
299. What's your e-mail address?
300. Who loves you?
301. What's your name?
302. What single event in your life has had the biggest impact on you?
303. If you could be really good at something, what would it be?
304. If you had a choice between a Nobel Prize and an Olympic medal, which would you choose?
305. What is the experience of this place for you?
306. What's the most interesting thing you've ever done?
307. What's the most important lesson you've ever learned that you would want to share with others?
308. If you have a spork and no knife, would you be tempted to use it like a knife?
309. What are your feelings about tomato juice?
310. If you could fill a swimming pool with anything, what would you fill it with?
311. What's your favorite self-help remedy?
312. If you could walk a mile in anyone's shoes, who would it be?
313. How do you realize the common good?
314. What kind of underwear are you wearing?
315. What's the sexiest piece of music you've ever heard?
316. If we don't question our beliefs, how will we ever learn?
317. Where are you going?
318. Do you believe we went to the moon, and are you ready to go back?
319. What's the best thing you've ever done in life?
320. What floats your boat?
321. Is there relief from suffering?
322. Can you appreciate Dumb and Dumber?
323. When all is said and done, will you have said more then you have done?
324. What's your name?

325. What would you like to dip your churro in?
326. Are you still sleeping?
327. Has life met your expectations?
328. What's the one thing that you *need* sexually?
329. How much would you pay me to jump off this thing?
330. Why is it the simplest questions (What is love? Who is god?) are the hardest to answer?
331. How often do you scoop your cat's litter box? If you don't own a cat, why not?
332. What's the story to your life?
333. How would you describe yourself, and how would your friends describe you?
334. What's your credo statement?
335. What would you tell your five-year-old self?
336. When you saw me for the first time, what did you think?
337. Have you lived your life to the fullest?
338. What's your biggest insecurity?
339. What's the most interesting thing you've ever done?
340. How have you learned to love?
341. What's one thing you regret?
342. How do you decipher between truth and lie?
343. When's the last time you had a boner?
344. Will you describe the color blue to me?
345. Will you sit down next to me?
346. Do you believe that space is infinite or finite?
347. Why do you continue to live and work?
348. Why did George Clooney leave *ER*?
349. What's the strangest place you've ever woken up?
350. What's your name?
351. What is true happiness?
352. Can I get you a drink?
353. Where are you from?
354. What's your favorite color?
355. Do you like the smell of your own farts?
356. What's your favorite word?

357. What's your vision of your death?
358. What else did God fuck up?
359. Do you want gravy with that?
360. How's your day?
361. Why are you passionate?
362. Have you ever shit yourself running?
363. Do you believe in love at first sight?
364. Want to know who stalks you on Twitter?
365. What makes you feel drawn to people, both as friends and romantically?
366. Are you with the person you love?
367. Can you tell me where a restroom is?
368. What fulfills you most in your life today?
369. What's your story?
370. Am I meeting the true you?
371. What's your favorite food?
372. Do you think I'm pretty?
373. What question do you want to answer?
374. Are you happy?
375. What question can I ask you that will make you say, "Peanut butter"?
376. If you had to cover everything in your house in one and exactly only one color, what color would you choose?
377. Who's fired up?
378. What's your favorite album, book, and film?
379. What is your name?
380. Have you seen my...? (keys, purse, son, daughter)
381. What's your favorite kind of cake?
382. What do you daydream about most often?
383. What is your current struggle?
384. Would you take Christ to be your savior?
385. Are you awake?
386. Do you want to give me a million dollars?
387. What's one piece of advice you've learned from, and how it was helpful in your life?

388. If you could change anything about yourself, what would it be?
389. What's the wisest thing a child ever said to you?
390. What have you always wanted to do that you never have done?
391. 'Sup?
392. What is one thing you would like me to know about you?
393. Do these pants make my butt look fat?
394. If you had a mustache, would you wash it with shampoo or face wash?
395. Do you want to go to heaven?
396. What is this life? (Often it is kind of rhetorical, but the world does baffle me constantly.)
397. What movie do you think everyone in the world should watch?
398. If you could have only one possession, what would it be?
399. How are you seeing the world in which you live?
400. If you could choose to die, how would you die?
401. Do you like my pants?
402. Do you know Jesus?
403. What is your favorite book you have ever read?
404. If someone from another planet asked you what your purpose on this planet was, how would you respond?
405. How could I make your life more happy?
406. What would you put in a box?
407. Do you believe in God?
408. What makes you happiest?
409. What is the most vivid nighttime dream you have ever had?
410. What is one thing you regret in your life?
411. Why?
412. What is your biggest insecurity?
413. Will you be my friend?
414. Who was that guy that said that one thing again?
415. How many sex partners have you had?
416. Will you make out with me in the bathroom tonight?
417. What did you want to be when you were a child?
418. How do you eat your corn?
419. Would you want to be a cowboy or a pirate?

420. Where is your moral compass when most of the world lives in an immoral society?
421. What are you doing here?
422. What's your life story?
423. Do you read the newspaper?
424. What makes you feel alive?
425. What would you do if there were no consequences?
426. What is your greatest regret?
427. What do you think about all the time?
428. What is a simple pleasure that means more to you than it would to others?
429. What is your favorite cookie?
430. How would you define and describe joy in your life?
431. What's your favorite soccer team?
432. If you only had one outfit for a week, what would you wear?
433. What is true love?
434. Have you read *Mrs. Dalloway*?
435. What would solve the world's problems?
436. What are you here for?
437. What is your deal?
438. What is your passion?
439. What is your favorite snack?
440. When was the last time something magical or awesome happened to you?
441. If you had only one day to live, what would you do?
442. What do you collect?
443. What would it take for Americans to turn away from consumer culture?
444. What is your vision for the world?
445. What's your story?
446. If you could, would you want to know the day that you were going to die?
447. Do you want to participate in a free radon test?
448. Is this a representation of your shoddy craftsmanship?
449. What's your answer to the question asked to everyone?

450. What age do you have to be to pee your pants again?
451. Why are there some creatures hatched and others born live?
452. What's your favorite memory?
453. What should you be doing and why aren't you doing that?
454. What is your favorite band that no one else has heard of?
455. I would ask people what is the most interesting thing about them.
456. If you were going to die in one month, what would you do?
457. If you were going to start a company, what would it be?
458. When are you happiest?
459. What's the greatest lesson you've learned?
460. What do people thank you for most often?
461. What person in your childhood (age five to twelve) was your favorite?
462. What would you like to be your final immortal statement?
463. What role does music play in your life?
464. What was your favorite meal?
465. How much better would life be if a liar's pants actually did catch on fire?!
466. What do you think it would take for people everywhere to get along with each other, which would naturally result in a better world of peace?
467. In your home, what is dust, and where does it come from?
468. If there was a zombie apocalypse, what would you do?
469. What is good?
470. Are you in the matrix?
471. Why not?
472. Are you happy?
473. What's the wildest idea you've ever had?
474. What's up?
475. What is your major malfunction?
476. What's the answer?
477. Do you like to party? (This one is best when you get into a NYC taxi.)
478. If you could be a tree, what kind of tree would you be?
479. Where's the bathroom?

480. Where's my money, bitch!
481. Door number one, or door number two?
482. May I ask you a question?
483. What the fuck?
484. How's your day?
485. How would you honestly describe yourself?
486. Have you ever smelled the sweetness of wet green grass in Oklahoma?
487. How come everybody gets sick?
488. If you were going to die today, what would you change?
489. Who are you? Who do you think you are?
490. What are you most thankful for?
491. Are you happy?
492. What makes you happy?
493. Is your life fun?
494. Coke or Pepsi?
495. What's the best experience you've ever had?
496. How does it taste?
497. What is the meaning of life?
498. Does this look infected to you?
499. Who the fuck do you think you are, anyway?
500. Would you be willing to shoot me in the face if I ever asked you anything meaningful?
501. Fuck you? (with a question-y tone)
502. What is your tombstone going to say?
503. Will you rent my apartment?
504. What is the best advice you could give if you could only give one piece of advice?
505. I would ask everyone to reveal a secret.
506. What's the hardest thing you've ever had to do but was worth it for a relationship?
507. Where is your bliss?
508. Tell me who you are. Who are you?
509. Do you ski?
510. What do you think is the meaning of life?

511. What makes you *you*?
512. What's the last thing you think of at night?
513. What are you afraid of?
514. What's the one thing that you do for yourself that helps you relax?
515. What's your purpose?
516. What gives you hope?
517. Would you rather live in a society on the rise or in decline?
518. What is your favorite dinosaur?
519. What do you wish you would have accomplished in your life?
520. What is the one thing in your life that you hold above all others? What would you die for? What is beyond you, bigger than you?
521. What is your truth?
522. What is the best thing that ever happened to you?
523. What's for dinner?
524. When's the last time you challenged the status quo?
525. If you were queen or king, what would you change?
526. What makes you happy? (I don't really care about the answer, but it immediately makes them think of something positive for them, it's not an answer for me.)
527. Where do you go when you die (your eternal destiny)?
528. What would you say to god to show you deserve to get into/ be let into heaven?
529. What do you treasure and why do you treasure it?
530. What's a better appetizer than a sandwich?
531. Do you believe that the sandwich is the perfect food?
532. Can I have a quarter?
533. Can you have pride without ego?
534. What's your favorite musical note? What color is it?
535. What do you believe in?
536. Do you believe in past lives?
537. How good are your cookies?
538. How deep is your love?
539. Can you prance the polka? Is that possible?
540. What do you put in your oatmeal?

541. When is the last time you threw up?
542. Is that a tattoo?
543. Can I have some money?
544. What's your favorite snack to eat when you're bored in class?
545. If you could pick one life event to define your personality, what would it be?
546. Who took my bike?
547. What question would you ask of everyone in your circle that is unanswered (about some shit of yours that got fucked up, some injustice that someone you know could answer)?
548. What is your passion?
549. What's the story or the background of your name?
550. Will you tell me about something you know a lot about?
551. What's something you care about?
552. What's something you'd be proud of on your deathbed?
553. If you could have a tattoo of anything, what would it be?
554. If you could do anything right now, even if it wasn't humanly possible, what would you do?
555. If you could say only one word for the rest of your life, what would it be?
556. What brings you peace?
557. What drives your passion?
558. If you could be a kindred spirit with anyone from history, who would it be?
559. What do you really need?
560. If you could go back and relive (not redo) a five-minute span at any point in your life—having the chance to see, hear, smell, touch—gather the information one more time, but this time with the knowledge you want to preserve it—what would that five minutes of time be?
561. What are your most valuable life lessons learned?
562. What case would you make for yourself before god to be let into heaven?
563. If you could change who you are, who would you be?
564. Will the elephants survive?

565. Regular or Goofy?
566. Is there hope for humanity?
567. What is your greatest struggle?
568. Are you satisfied with your life?
569. What is *the* purpose in life?
570. How do you find peace?
571. What are some of your most memorable life experiences?
572. Was it worth it?
573. What are you holding on to that you haven't had the courage to say?
574. Do you like the food?
575. Do you think I'm sexy?
576. What do you live for?
577. What justifies your existence?
578. Where are you going?
579. What are your hands for?
580. Are you who you want to be yet?
581. What's your purpose?
582. Can I have a dollar?
583. What gives you hope?
584. How were you loved, and would you want to be loved differently?
585. Where do you find peace?
586. What do you love most?
587. When's the last time you crapped your pants?
588. What would you do if you knew you could not fail?
589. What question do you want me to ask you?
590. I already ask everyone I meet one question.
591. What do you live for?
592. Got any beer?
593. Just what the hell are Slim-Jims made of, anyway?
594. If all the world is a stage, where the hell's the audience supposed to sit?
595. Do you do like Metallica?
596. Th' HELL'S wrong with you, foo'?!??

597. Will you sleep with me?
598. WHO'S GOT THAT BAD ONE?
599. Are you Jesus? Ok, it's not the rapture yet. Whew!
600. Do you rock?
601. Have you ever felt the pitter-patter of the rains across the hills of Patagonia?
602. Can I ask you a question?
603. Would you mind wearing this mask?
604. What would *you* do for a Klondike bar?
605. Do you babysit?
606. Chicken or ribs?
607. Will you be my friend?
608. Is that my stapler?
609. How much do you like chocolate with peanut butter?
610. Would you dance?
611. How are you going to get home?
612. How would you describe your life in one word?
613. Do you like syrup?
614. Why are you in such a hurry?
615. What completes you?
616. If the outcome could be as you wished, what would be your one do-over?
617. What's your greatest accomplishment in life?
618. Where are you going?
619. Will the Vikings ever win the Super Bowl?
620. Are you happy?
621. What makes you *you*?
622. When was the last time you did something for the first time?
623. Why are women always late to things?
624. Who do you think has more chances of winning this election?
625. In the Philippines, a villager asked me where I was from. I said America. He said "No, what island?" So that is my favorite question, "What island are you from?"
626. How do you make gyros?
627. What is your favorite band/singer?

628. Why do girls go to the bathroom together?
629. Why are you mad, bro?
630. How about that hot waitress?
631. Will you give me $20?
632. What don't you want to know?
633. How do you think you will die?
634. Will you sleep with me?
635. Wanna get high?
636. I love your shirt; where did you get it?
637. Where will you go when you die?
638. When do I get my money, bitch?
639. Why are you such an asshole?
640. What's your problem?
641. What is your favorite activity?
642. Where's the beef?
643. Do you believe in limits?
644. Given the choice, would you rather be incarnated as a huge rock or a small pebble?
645. What will it take for you to be completely open to love?
646. Are you a fan of Ernie or Bert?
647. What keeps you from loving fully?
648. What would your last meal be?
649. What do you have planned for your next big event?
650. Can you do a *Back to the Beach 2*?
651. Can you find a problem in having the confidence that your future household is rock solid?
652. What's your favorite comedy?
653. German shepherd or border collie?
654. What's it all about?
655. What would you do if you could do anything you wanted for the day?
656. Why walk when you can fly?
657. What future event will shape the rest of your life?
658. Did you see this pic of you?

659. What is the one thing that you are better at than everyone you know?

660. At the end of the day, what kind of tired are you?

661. What's your definition of happiness?

662. What is your passion?

663. Why is Hate running our world instead of Love?

664. Is it warm in here?

665. How much time do you think that you have left?

666. Why did you vote for Obama?

667. Would you rather be addicted to drugs or trapped in a cult?

668. What's your favorite app?

669. Who *really* let the dogs out?

670. Who stole the cookies from the cookie jar?

671. What do you think?

672. Do these pants make me look fat?

673. What was the best meal you've ever had?

674. May I ask you another question after my first question?

675. What do you love about yourself?

676. Do you swing?

677. What's your name?

678. What are you trying to do?

679. How do you know what you are doing is what you are supposed to be doing?

680. What makes us human?

681. Why do you love who you love?

682. What do you think of the world?

683. What do you think was invented first, the cup or the knife?

684. Can you describe three people who have inspired you to be who you are?

685. What makes you just sit and look?

686. What do ya want for dinner?

687. Is the universe infinite?

688. What's the plot here?

689. What's the most heartbreakingly sad song you know?

690. So, what's *your* story?

691. Which of your teachers changed you the most?
692. What kind of dog do you have?
693. Is it wrong to throw bacon at a vegetarian?
694. What do people thank you for most often?
695. What's the name of your friend's band again?
696. What does heaven look like?
697. Why is world peace so elusive? Do you think it will be achieved in your lifetime?
698. Are you happy and why?
699. What is your favorite movie?
700. Do you like TV shows like *The Simpsons* and *Family Guy*?
701. Does Wii get you going?
702. What is unconditional love, and how can I love everyone?
703. When is your birthday?
704. Do you feel uncomfortable around people with disabilities?
705. What is your favorite vegetable?
706. What is your most major short-term goal?
707. What is your favorite song?
708. Do you believe in Christ?
709. What are your interests and hobbies?
710. Did you ever teach people like me to believe in god? And why?
711. What's your favorite beach?
712. What does your heart tell you?
713. Where were you born?
714. Do you show favoritism to your friends or coworkers?
715. What do you see yourself doing in ten years?
716. What is the healing dance of your heart?
717. What do you like to do for fun?
718. What do you see yourself doing in five years?
719. What is your favorite decade and memory?
720. What is heaven?
721. What college did you go to, and did you have fun?
722. How do you be so romantic?
723. Now that you are on the cliff of ambition, do you still have goals?
724. Why is the world round?

725. What is your favorite vacation destination?

726. Do you believe in Jesus Christ?

727. Why do you have faith?

728. The Beatles said, "All you need is love." Who said it and wrote it?

729. How many people think that aliens exist?

730. How can I have satisfying conversations with my wife?

731. Why do I feel tired and depressed most mornings?

732. Will the world last another day?

733. Why does this generation have no discipline?

734. If you could have lunch with Jesus and ask just one question, what would it be?

735. What does heaven look like?

736. Where are all the guys for older women? (I'm a cougar.)

737. Where is the spirit in the body?

738. Do you understand the difference between sight and seeing?

739. What aspects of your belief system (BS) are the result of cultural brainwashing?

740. What will bring peace to the world?

741. Where was your favorite dream happening?

742. Do you like my shoes?

743. If you ever find a good answer, one that is pure and beautiful, without a hint of irony, might you be willing to send it to me?

744. If you could only ask one question, but you realized afterward that it was the wrong question, what would you do?